honeymoon marriage™

DISCOVER the SECRETS to ACHIEVING the MARRIAGE of YOUR DREAMS

Darren and Donna McNees

Published by Blue Sail Publishing, Inc., Reno, Nevada.

All scripture quotations are taken from *The Holy Bible, New International Version* Copyright © 1973, 1978, 1984 by International Bible Society.

This publication is designed to provide accurate and authoritative information in regard to the subject matter covered. It is sold with the understanding that the publisher and author are not engaged in rendering legal, financial or professional services. If professional advice or other expert assistance is required, the services of a competent professional person should be sought.

Readers and users of the information contained in this book are strongly cautioned to consult with a physician or other health care professional before utilizing any of the information. The author and publisher make no representations or guarantees that any of the information will produce any particular medical, physical, emotional or other result, and none of the said parities is engaged in the rendering of medical advice.

The author and publisher specifically disclaim any liability, loss or risk, personal or otherwise which is incurred as a consequence directly or indirectly of the use and application of any of the contents of this book.

Printed in the United States of America.

ISBN: 0-9721903-0-9

Library of Congress Control Number: 2002093079

DEDICATION

This book is dedicated in loving memory of my mom,
Mary Ann Rhew. Thanks, mom, for your friendship, your
laughter and sense of humor. Thanks also for teaching me to
accept everyone for who they are. I know you're singing and
dancing in heaven and I can't wait to see you there!

And my big brother, Perry, thanks
for sharing with me your love for art and music,
and for always being there for me when I needed you.

I miss you both.

Donna

This book is also dedicated in loving memory of
my grandma, Eli Juengling, for her unwavering faith and
gratitude for all of God's many blessings in her life.

Darren

CONTENTS

INTRODUCTION: SETTING THE STAGE FOR SUCCESS

Congratulations! By reading this book you are taking an extremely important step toward improving your marriage. You are now part of an elite group of people. It is said that less than 10 percent of Americans will ever read a self-improvement book, and only a fraction of those people will read a book on how to improve their marriage. You have already proven that you are serious and committed to improving your life by investing your time and money in this marriage manual. For this, we commend you.

This book will reveal to you several extremely important secrets that are necessary in order for you to have a Honeymoon Marriage. These secrets will enable you to live a life overflowing with love and happiness. They will dramatically improve the quality of your marriage regardless of its current condition.

Just like a single spark can start a forest fire, a single idea can light your relationship on fire. One amazing idea can change your life forever. The ideas shared in this book will energize your relationship, allow you to experience greater intimacy and bring you true happiness.

You will experience incredible joy, passion, romance and fun in your relationship by applying the principles and ideas outlined in *Honeymoon Marriage*. Its breakthrough concepts are unique because they not only address the dynamics of your relationship, but they also focus on *you* as a whole and amazing person. *Honeymoon Marriage* will change your life forever! You will learn how to have abundance in every area of your life including finances, self-improvement, optimal health, spirituality, self-confidence, passion, romance, intimacy, self-discovery and of course, fun.

All of these things are possible and you can have them, but they won't just fall into your lap. You have to go after them. You have to be the one to make it happen. As you read this book, you are in the driver's seat; you are the one who is in control of whether or not you apply these life-changing truths. By starting to read this book you have already taken that first crucial step. You have already proven to yourself that you want to experience the best that a marriage has to offer. Now the biggest and most important question—Are you willing to do what it takes to have a Honeymoon Marriage, or are you content with living the rest of your life exactly as you are today?

What do you want?

Before anything can improve in your life, you must first figure out what it is that you want. What do you want? It sounds like an easy question, one that you should be able to answer without even thinking about it. At the core we are all very much alike. We all want the same thing. Our gender, race, religion, age, experiences, the choices that we make and our upbringing make us all different, yet we all still want the same thing. Some think it is fame, while others think it is fortune. Some want to be successful in their endeavors, while others want to be popular. Some want to make a difference in the world; others want to have fulfilling relationships. What do you want? Could it be the dream house, a luxury automobile, exotic vacations, a husband who buys you flowers every week or a wife who appreciates you? You may think that what you want is something tangible like most of the examples listed above, but it isn't. Think harder; look deeper inside yourself for the answer. What is it that *everybody* wants?

You, me and everyone else on the planet wants to be happy. Sounds simple but it is true. Deep down everyone wants to be happy, yet most people are not as happy as they could be because they are looking for happiness in all the wrong places. All of the examples listed above are external examples of what many people think will bring them happiness. These things will not bring you happiness in and of themselves. Don't misunderstand us—we don't think that wanting or having any of these things is wrong, but they won't bring you happiness if you are currently unhappy.

Back to our original question, what do you want? More specifically, what do you want to get out of this book? What do you want to learn? What do you hope the end result will be? What kind of a marriage do you want? Are you looking for insight that might help you counsel a friend who is having a rough time in his or her relationship? Do you already have a good marriage but want to make it even better? Or, perhaps you are looking for answers to what seems to be a hopeless situation. These very important questions require thoughtful consideration. Use the spaces below to write down what you want in as much detail as you can. Don't read another word until you feel that you have written down what it is that you truly want (use another sheet of paper if you need to). Take your time. Treat your list as though someone was going to give you everything that you ask for.

1. _____
   _____

2. _____
   _____

3. _____
   _____

4. _____
   _____

5. _____
   _____

Why?
It is not good enough to know what you want. You must also know why you want it. "Why" is where your emotions take a front-row seat. A "want" backed by a strong emotional "why" is a very powerful force. Again, why did you buy this book? *Why* do you want a Honeymoon Marriage? What would your life be like if you had a better marriage? Can you imagine your dream life? What would it be like? Take time and concentrate on this. Imagine how it would feel. Continue this "daydream" until you have a clear picture in your mind of exactly what having a Honeymoon Marriage means to you and how that kind of relationship would make you feel. Don't read any further until you "feel" how great it would be. How badly do you want to feel that way every day? Your answer to this question will dictate how much you get out of this book and how much its truths will improve your marriage. Write your "why" down on the spaces below while it is fresh in your mind.

Why you want the Honeymoon Marriage:

_____

_____

_____

_____

_____

_____

_____

_____

Write down the key ideas that come to you as you read _Honeymoon Marriage_
Ideas will jump out at you as you read through this book. Some of these ideas won't be written on the pages, but will pop into your head as an inspiration. Make sure to write down your thoughts as soon as they come to you. Don't make the mistake of thinking that you will remember them later, because you won't. Even if the thought seems silly, write it down. Have a pad of paper and a pen or pencil handy for this purpose. This book is yours. You don't have to return it to the library, so feel free to highlight or underline any area that stands out to you. When you are finished reading the book, go back and reread the highlighted or underlined sections. You may even want to commit some of them to memory.

The buck stops here
While reading this book, your focus should be on _you_. Have an open mind and a receptive spirit. If you are willing to make positive personal changes, then you are one giant step closer to achieving the Honeymoon Marriage.

> _"For things to change, you must change,_
> _and for things to get better, you must get better."_
> _- Jim Rohn -_

This book should be used as a mirror, not as a club to beat your spouse over the head with. Resist the temptation to point out all of the things that your mate does wrong or all of the things that you would like him or her to start doing. Make sure that _you_ are doing everything first. As the saying goes, "People who live in glass houses shouldn't throw stones."

It is best if husband and wife both read this book—but only if each one wants to. You can share one book or you can each buy your own copy, whatever works best for you. We share most of the books we read, however, some are so good that we each want our own copy to do with as we please. We have two copies of eight different books in our library. Don't buy a copy for your spouse unless he or she asks you to because that may cause your partner to get defensive. Instead read this book from cover to cover and do as it instructs. As you are reading, share the insights you are gaining with your spouse. Your comments, and more importantly the changes your spouse sees in you, should be enough to pique your spouse's curiosity and cause him or her to want to know more.

When you are finished reading the book, set a time aside when you and your partner can be alone. Tell your spouse that you love him or her and that your relationship is very important to you. Tell him or her that you have learned a lot from this book and that it would mean a lot to you if he or she read it as well.

Remember that your focus should be on you and not on your spouse. It is okay if your partner is not receptive to reading this book. Don't press the issue. It would be better for your mate not to read it than to read it under duress. If you apply the principles outlined throughout *Honeymoon Marriage*, your marriage will improve even if your partner never reads one page. Kind of takes the pressure off, doesn't it? All you have to be concerned with is you.

Know where you are and where you are headed

Rate the current health of your marriage on a scale from one to ten, one being that you are about ready to file for divorce, ten being that you couldn't imagine having a better marriage. Write that number here _____. Now write your rating goals for the time periods given below in the "desired results" column.

	Date	Desired Results	Actual Results
One year from now			
Nine months from now			
Six months from now			
Three months from now			

Fill in the date column using today's date as the starting point. When each date arrives, re-rate your marriage and write the results in the "actual results" column. If your actual results are not equal to or greater than your desired results, determine what you can do to make them so. You may find it useful to reread a section or two or possibly the entire book to help keep you moving in the right direction.

We would love to hear how well you are doing. Please feel free to send us your numbers and comments by going to www.honeymoonmarriage.com and clicking on the keyword "marriage rating." There will be a form like the one above that you can fill out and submit to us.

Who is responsible for the current condition of your marriage?
You are. Now hear us out before you get upset and throw this book out the window. If you are being treated poorly by your spouse, it is likely that you are unknowingly giving him or her permission to do so. Your actions may be causing, encouraging, or allowing this kind of behavior to happen.

How you think and feel about yourself will be reflected back on you. How you *act* will determine how your mate *reacts* toward you. Years ago we heard Earl Nightingale say, "It is our attitude toward life that determines life's attitude toward us. Our attitude tells the world what we expect in return." Your answer to the following questions will give you a better perspective on the areas that need attention in your life. Be honest with yourself and write down whatever comes to your mind as you think about each question.

- Are you proud of who you are and what you have become?
- Do you look for what is right about yourself and others, or do you primarily focus on what's wrong?
- Do you have to always be right, or can you live with your differences of opinion?
- Do your feelings get hurt easily?
- Do you get angry easily or often?
- Do you complain a lot?
- Do you avoid problems?
- Do you compare yourself to others?
- Do you like your body?
- Do you feel sexy and desirable?
- Are you vibrant and full of life?
- Are you a self-confident and secure person?
- Do you look for ways to please your spouse?
- Do you think that you have something important to contribute to your marriage?
- Are you always striving for ways to improve yourself?
- Do you think that your ideas are important?
- Do you live in the past?
- Is there something that you haven't forgiven yourself, your spouse or others for?
- Do you feel loved?
- Do you respect yourself?
- Do you believe you deserve to be loved?
- Are you overly critical toward yourself or your spouse?

- Are you comfortable spending time alone?
- Are you happy?
- Do you love yourself?

If many of your answers to the above questions were less than positive, don't lose hope. At least 90 percent of this book is focused on what *you* can do to improve the quality of your marriage as well as the quality of your life. Our goal is that you achieve the Honeymoon Marriage by being the best that you can be. As soon as you improve yourself, you will start to feel better about you. And from there, look out world, here you come.

Expect great things to happen.

"The quality of our expectations
determines the quality of our action."
- Andre' Godin -

Reading this book and thinking that nothing will change in your marriage is a sure-fire way to guarantee that nothing will. You have to believe that things can and will improve and look forward to a brighter tomorrow. Your expectations coupled with just the right amount of diligence, determination, persistence, focus and prayer will cause you to have a very happy marriage. Expect great things to happen and they will!

What is the most important ingredient in the Honeymoon Marriage?

People are always looking for a shortcut in today's instant-gratification, silver-bullet, magic-pill, drive-through society. Have high blood pressure? Don't worry about your diet or exercise, just take a pill. Don't have time to make dinner? No problem, just drive to your favorite fast food joint and order a meal to go. There may be a "most important" ingredient in your favorite dessert recipe—however, if you forget to include one of the "less important" ingredients, it won't turn out as good as it could be. The same thing is true with the Honeymoon Marriage. It isn't just one thing that makes it work, but rather a combination of many very important ingredients—ingredients that must be added at different times and in different amounts depending on the situation at hand.

Our relationships are not machines. If a machine breaks down all one needs to do is fix or replace a part or two and it is off and running like new again. Your marriage, in contrast, is like a complex living organism with many needs. First, you have to identify what those needs are, and then you need to supply those needs on a regular basis. This book will help you to identify what many of those needs are and how you can fulfill them. Our recommendations shouldn't be looked at as being all-inclusive, but rather should be viewed as the beginning of your journey toward marital bliss.

It is possible for you to have an abundant life and a terrific marriage. It is all up to you and you can do it. Let's recap our first steps:

1. Determine what you want.
2. Develop a strong emotional "why."
3. Rate your marriage on a scale from one to ten and set your three, six, nine, and twelve month goals.
4. Discover what you need to change about you.
5. Expect great things to happen.
6. Be patient—Rome wasn't built in a day and neither are good marriages.

One last thought before you begin.
It is important to eliminate all of the excuses. We once heard a very successful multimillionaire say, "You can make excuses or you can make money, but you can't make both." The same is true about having the Honeymoon Marriage. As you read through this book you might come upon topics that make you say, "That won't work for me because . . ." If that is what you believe, then that will be your reality. However, if you believe that you can find a way to make your marriage great, then that will be your reality.

"They can conquer who believe they can."
- Virgil -

If you really want the best that life has to offer, then ask, "How can I make the suggestions and principles in this book work for me given my current circumstances?" Look for ways to make your marriage the best that it can be instead of finding reasons why it can't be the best. No more excuses. No more settling for second best. Now is the time to take charge of your life. Now is the time to live your life by design. Now is the time to apply the secrets that will give you the relationship of your dreams.

SECTION 1

MARRIAGE
THE ULTIMATE
"SOUL MATE"
EXPERIENCE

CHAPTER 1

EXPERIENCE THE BOND THAT CANNOT BE BROKEN

A great marriage is a wonderful thing. Few things on this earth can even compare to it. Unfortunately, the word marriage has lost much of its meaning. Many people enter into marriage too lightly and leave it too easily. In some cases marriage is looked at as a higher level of "going steady." If everything doesn't work out as you had planned, you can always break up and go your separate ways. Even some of our religious leaders take marriage too lightly. At a wedding we attended several years ago we overheard the minister talking about a couple who had recently gotten a divorce. He was the one who had married them, and he said very proudly that he knew that their marriage wouldn't last. He had even guessed as to how long it would last. We couldn't believe our ears. That's like giving the car keys to a thirteen-year-old. You know it's a bad idea, but you do it anyway.

Fortunately, there are spiritual leaders out there with more integrity than that. We have heard of several who have refused to marry couples for very legitimate reasons. Unfortunately, these same couples can shop around until they find a minister, priest, or rabbi who will. If that doesn't work there is always the judge.

Perhaps if more couples looked at marriage as a bond that cannot be broken, they would try harder to make their relationship work. Marriage is not an excuse to throw a big party for friends and family, it is a covenant between husband, wife and God. A marriage is a union that was meant to last a lifetime. It is the integration of two separate lives into one new life.

The soul mate experience

Yesteryear's meaning of the word marriage has been replaced with the phrase "soul mate." Surely a soul mate is forever. This must be a bond that cannot be broken. If only you could find your soul mate, then you could truly be happy, right? So what is a soul mate?

A soul mate is not some mystical relationship that one happens upon by chance. It's not a perfect person who will always do and say the right things at the right time. A soul mate is not someone who can read your mind or feel your pain, nor someone who you coexist with in eternal peace and harmony. A soul mate is someone who will always be there for you in the good times and the bad. A soul mate is your best friend. He or she cares about your thoughts and feelings. He or she always wants you to be happy. A soul mate will encourage and support you, your goals and your dreams, and will put your needs above his or her own. There is such a thing as a soul mate, and that person is called your spouse. A soul mate relationship is developed over time. It takes a conscious, full-time effort to make your marriage as good as it can be. The Honeymoon Marriage is the soul mate experience.

Quitting is not an option

Your view on what a marriage should be will greatly affect how it will be. If you focus on how you would like your marriage to become and believe that this view is possible, then it is. Do you think of marriage as being a safe haven, someplace that you can go to escape the stresses of life, or is your marriage a cause of stress? Do you feel relaxed when spending time with your spouse, or is this time a source of tension? Do you look at your spouse today and think that you will be together for the rest of your life, or do you think that you may end up parting ways? Regardless of how good or bad your relationship is, decide today that quitting is not an option. Divorce is not an option, nor is separation. You have only one choice, and that is to do everything within your power to improve your marriage. Decide today.

The word "decide" holds a very powerful meaning. It is derived from the Latin word *decidere* which means, "to cut off." In other words, when you decide on something, you cut off from all other possibilities. Once you have decided that your marriage is a bond that can never be broken, don't change your mind.

We realize that this next paragraph may be hard to swallow, especially if you have already been through a divorce, but it must be said. We can't change what has already been done in the past. All we can do is learn from the past and make today and our future life the best that it can be.

Never think of divorce as an easy way out. Divorce is never easy and it can even cause more pain than living in a less than perfect relationship (this discussion does not include abusive relationships). This is especially true when there are children involved. Years ago a couple in an unhappy marriage would stay together, "for the sake of the children." Today that is no longer a concern. It's not that people don't love and care about their children, they just don't think that a divorce will be that hard on them. Unfortunately, they are very wrong.

Divorce can and does have a negative impact on children. Even though it may not seem logical to us adults, many children internalize divorce and think that it was somehow their fault. And being shuffled back and forth between parents or not seeing one of the parents for an extended period of time isn't good, especially for small children. Children need stability and consistency in their lives.

Contrary to what appears to be popular belief, children need a mom and a dad both living under the same roof. Some kids of broken homes will grow up bound and determined that their marriage will never end up in divorce. Many others will follow their parental example.

"If you can't be a good example,
then you'll have to be a horrible warning."
- Catherine Aird -

We believe that the grass is oftentimes greener on the other side of the fence, but not when it comes to marriage. The numbers don't lie. If what you need is a different husband or wife to make your marriage one that will last the test of time, then the statistics should confirm that theory. If the grass is greener on the other side of the fence, then the divorce rate of second marriages should be much lower than that of first marriages. If all you needed were a better spouse, wouldn't it be reasonable to assume that the second marriage dropout rate would be around 10 percent? After all, there will be at least that many people who will never be happy no matter what their circumstances. Statistically speaking, however, the grass is very brown on the other side of the fence.

Some studies show that as many as 70 percent of second marriages end in divorce. If you drop your current husband or wife and trade him or her in for a different model, there is a 60 to 70 percent chance that you will go through the pain of divorce all over again. Given those odds, doesn't it make sense to try as hard as you can to make your current marriage work?

If your marriage isn't working, don't assume that things will improve by changing your spouse, because *he or she* may not be the problem.

> *"You can't change a flat tire*
> *by changing the driver."*
> *- Lou Holtz -*

If you haven't already done so, decide today that quitting is not an option. You know the saying, "Winners never quit and quitters never win." You can have a winning marriage by applying the principles discussed throughout this book. We can't promise you an easy road ahead, but the payoff will be well worth the effort.

UNFAILING DEVOTION

Before we can discuss the steps that will enable you to have a Honeymoon Marriage, we must first establish a solid foundation. Without a solid foundation, your relationship will be susceptible to a myriad of internal and external forces, which can ultimately lead to the collapse of your marriage. Your foundation starts with a commitment--a mindset that is so strong and so determined that nothing will get in the way of achieving your goal. Your goal should be to have the most loving, nurturing, romantic, passionate and mutually fulfilling relationship possible. It all starts with your level of devotion.

How committed are you to your relationship and to your spouse? Are you devoted to your mate? Devotion is the state of passionate dedication and loyalty.

Let's break down devotion into its three parts and discuss the importance of each.

Passion
Another word for passionate is enthusiastic. You can tell when someone is passionate about something. You can see it on his face and hear it in his voice. His enthusiasm is contagious and people like to be around him. When people are passionate about something it occupies their thoughts and actions. They are very focused and determined to achieve their goal. Nothing or nobody can stop them.

Some people are more enthusiastic or passionate about an interest, hobby, cause or event than they are about their marriage. These people are living with a roommate and not a soul mate. Their marriage has lost the appeal that it once had and there is no driving desire to get it back.

What do you get excited about? Is it shopping, watching the football game or stock car race or planning your next vacation or surprise birthday party? Is it the new house or car, receiving advancement at work, the new home entertainment system or volunteering at the homeless shelter? Are you excited about spending time with your spouse? Does the thought of being alone with him or her give you something to look forward to?

Until you become passionate about improving your relationship, you will never have the Honeymoon Marriage. So how do you become passionate about your marriage?

- Make having a great marriage one of your highest priorities in life.
- Close your eyes and imagine what it would feel like to have a Honeymoon Marriage.
- Fill in as many reasons as you can why you *must* have a great relationship with your mate.

1. _____

2. _____

3. _____

4. _____

5. _____

6. _____

7. _____

8. _____

9. _____

10. _____

- Know that a Honeymoon Marriage is possible and that you have the ability to improve yourself, hence improving your relationship.
- Tell other people about your goal, but don't let them discourage you.
- Read books and/or listen to tapes on relationships at least thirty minutes every day.
- Each day empty your mind of negative, troubling thoughts and fill it with positive, hopeful ones. We will discuss the power of your thoughts and how you can

control them in the chapter entitled "Expanding your mind--the pursuit of knowledge and wisdom."

"Conditions are created by thoughts far more powerfully than conditions create thoughts."
- Norman Vincent Peale -

Passion will be talked about several times throughout this book. It is one of the key ingredients to success in every area of life. Passion can be a natural outpouring of your personal makeup or it can be learned and developed. You can actually *choose* to become passionate about making your marriage the best that it can be. And as you begin to see small results, your enthusiasm will grow and in turn so will the results.

Dedication

Webster's dictionary defines *dedicate* as, "to become committed to as a goal or way of life." Your commitment to your spouse needs to be a way of life. It also needs to take priority over other commitments in your life. It is very easy to let other things come between you and your spouse. What makes matters worse is the fact that a lot of these things are important. Just keep in mind that nothing on this earth is more important than your relationship with your spouse. Not your job, your parents or even your children. All of these things are important, but they must be placed behind your relationship with your mate. In doing so, all of these other important things in your life will flourish as well.

Make it your goal to have the best marriage possible. We will give you tips as to how you can accomplish that goal throughout this book; however, the first bold step is up to you. Set up a time that you can be alone with your husband or wife without any distractions. Then tell your spouse that you are committed to making your marriage the best that it can be. Do this only if you are ready to take action and make it happen. Don't worry about *how* you will make it happen, just decide that it must happen and that you are ready to do your part.

Loyalty

The word *loyal* is derived from the Latin word *legalis*, which means "legal." It is unwavering allegiance. Loyalty is a character trait that can transcend your self-serving desires, the hard times you face and even your fears. Many people have even given their lives because of their loyalty to "King and Country." A person who was not loyal to his or her country could be arrested for treason.

Loyalty is the glue that binds you to your marriage. In marriage you are bound by a pledge. On your wedding day you pledged your lives to each other. You made a binding promise to always be faithful to each other and to your marriage. When you think of a friend as being loyal, that means a lot. You know that you can always count on your friend and that he or she will never desert you. The loyalty in your marriage should be even stronger than that of a friend.

Your loyalty for your partner needs to be so strong that you would defend, support, encourage, protect and honor him or her in every situation. There is no turning back. You are in this for life. It is up to you to make things work and to never give up no matter what circumstances come your way.

Without devotion, the life-changing truths shared throughout this book will do you little good. Take away the powerful driving emotion of passion and you will give up when you don't see quick results. Without being committed to making the principles outlined in this book a way of life, you will fall right back into your old habits--the habits that got you to where you are today. And your loyalty makes you a rock, a pillar of strength in your relationship.

Passion, commitment, and loyalty--now that's a foundation worth building upon.

CHAPTER 3

HOW TO DEVELOP A MARITAL PARTNERSHIP FILLED WITH RESPECT, TRUST AND APPRECIATION

As a married couple, you are not just two people living in the same house. You are a team of two. Your team has the goal of winning in this game called marriage. Every decision that you make and action that you take will affect how well your team performs. If you learn to work well together, recognizing and utilizing each other's strengths, talents and abilities, then you will reach the goal of achieving the Honeymoon Marriage. If, on the other hand, you try to do it all on your own or don't participate at all, your team will suffer.

The chapters entitled "Discover who you are and who your spouse is" and "Discovering your spouse's desires" will show you how to identify these strengths, talents and abilities. This section will focus on your team attitude.

Independence
There is a strong independent spirit running through America. We are taught that independence is a good solid trait to have. We are told that we should be able to do everything on our own--make our own decisions, call our own shots and live our own life. While this sounds like an admirable trait, an independent person doesn't work well as a team player.

Independent people do not need or rely on others. They don't concern themselves with the opinions of other people. Independent people need no help, and therefore don't seek advice, counsel or guidance. They are oftentimes described as a rock, an island or the Lone Ranger. They need to be in control and want to be the one to make all or most of the decisions. If someone offers to help them or to do something for them, they quickly reject the offer knowing that they can handle it. Not only do they not seek advice, but they don't receive it well either. To independent people, there is no such thing as constructive criticism, only criticism. They oftentimes take constructive criticism as a personal attack rather than as a suggestion. In extreme cases they have the "It's my way or the highway" attitude. Because they are used to doing things and making decisions on their own, they can tend to be somewhat bossy.

Thinking that you can do everything by yourself and that you don't need or want your spouse's help is not the right attitude to have. Independence can drive a wedge between you and your husband or wife. There is nothing wrong with being able to do all or most everything yourself, however, it is not healthy to want or feel that you need to do most things without the help of your spouse. This kind of unhealthy control can make your spouse feel like nothing he or she does is ever good enough. Perhaps you can do a better job in certain areas. If so, you may want to tell your spouse what you are looking for, or learn to appreciate and accept that your spouse has a unique way of doing things, even though it may not be your way.

We all have the basic desire to feel wanted and needed. An independent attitude can leave your spouse feeling empty in this area. That empty feeling can lead to feelings of inadequacy, unimportance or insecurity. From there it can get even worse. If not trained properly, our minds tend to gravitate toward the negative. These negative emotions can cause one to think the following:

- If I am not good enough, maybe my spouse would be happier with someone else. Perhaps he or she is already interested in someone else. Or,
- I would be happier with someone who wants and needs me.

We realize that these examples seem extreme and perhaps irrational, however, our mind doesn't always think rationally when dealing with strong negative emotions.

Dependence

We all like to know that we can depend on others. This kind of dependence is healthy as long as you don't depend on people too often or to do everything for you. If one team member has to carry too much of the load him- or herself, the whole team will suffer.

An unhealthy dependence is when you cease to think for yourself. It is not a case of submitting your will to another, but rather not having a will of your own. An example of unhealthy dependence would be not being able to or being very slow to make up your mind. Common statements could include, "What ever you want is fine with me," "I don't know, you decide" and "What do you think we should do?" All of these statements sound harmless enough. And they are as long as they are not your everyday responses. Our mind is like a muscle. If it is not exercised regularly it becomes weak and unable to do simple tasks. If you have a hard time making up your mind, then you have most likely relied on others to make your decisions for you far too often. A marriage is more alive and productive when two opinions, two thoughts, two desires and two wills come together and form one opinion, one thought, one desire and one will.

Your thoughts, opinions and desires are a very integral part of your happiness and well-being. Don't suppress them or keep them from your spouse. Share them often. They are a part of you and need to be expressed in order to grow. Never shrink as a person and feel that your thoughts, opinions and desires are silly or unimportant. An unhealthy dependency can lead to feelings of inadequacy and even depression. This kind of dependence does not allow you to become the person that you were meant to be. You are a very special person, and what you have to offer your spouse is unique and important. Your spouse needs you, all of you, in order to be fulfilled and truly happy in your marriage. Not only will dependence hold you back, but it will also hold your spouse back as well.

Independent dependence

No one is 100 percent independent or 100 percent dependent. Some people have an unhealthy balance of both. You could be independent in that you make most of the decisions; however, you may be dependent emotionally. Controlling people tend to have an unhealthy dependence. They are insecure in their relationship. If all of your spouse's free time has to be spent with you, then you are emotionally dependent on him or her. This can lead to your spouse feeling trapped or smothered.

The need for a friend

If you are a man, you need male friends. If you are a woman, you need female friends. Not just casual acquaintances, but true friends. Someone that you can share your thoughts and feelings with. This is especially important for men because they tend not to have as many, if any, "close" friends. This oftentimes causes them to want to control their wife's activities or be upset when she spends "too much time" with her friends or family. Men need male friends.

Men feel that they need to be the solid, stable emotional rock in front of their wife and family. They don't always feel comfortable sharing their concerns, feelings and aspirations with their wife. They don't want to look weak and sometimes fear rejection or criticism. These fears are not necessarily justified, but they can exist. Even though most men are not comfortable with the idea of sharing this kind of information with other men, once they do it, they will feel an awesome release. They will realize that they are not alone and that other men are going through the same things that they are. There are some things that men go through that only another man can relate with, and the same holds true with a woman and her female friends.

A man shouldn't feel that he needs to carry the weight of his concerns on his shoulders alone. These pressures will add up and can manifest themselves through anger, impatience, frustration and blame. If you are a woman reading this, encourage your husband to develop male friendships and don't be offended if he doesn't feel like he can share all of his thoughts with you. In time he may feel more comfortable sharing some of his deeper thoughts. That is as long as he doesn't feel threatened, but instead feels accepted. What we are suggesting is a close male friendship, not just going out with the guys for a beer after work every day.

There are many civic and religious organizations that have men's groups that meet on a regular basis. Some of these groups discuss the challenges that men face, and they are a great place to develop friendships that can foster a relationship as described above. Likewise, there are women's groups that meet regularly as well. Make sure that the people in the group that you attend focus on positive, encouraging and uplifting things. It is important that you are able to discuss the challenges that you face in life as long as these discussions are directed toward a resolution and not just an excuse to hold a gripe or gossip session.

Interdependence

Interdependence is reciprocal dependence or mutual reliance. You both feel dependent upon each other and you show it though your actions. The interdependent person asks for help, seeks advice and values the opinion of his or her spouse. In the Honeymoon Marriage all important decisions are made jointly. Both husband and wife feel like equal partners. There is mutual respect, trust and appreciation shown every day. Interdependence is the goal that you should strive for in your relationship.

The power of synergy

Something very powerful happens when a couple works as a closeknit team. This dynamic is called *synergy*. Synergy is derived from the Greek word *synergos*, which means "working together." We have all heard the saying that two heads are better than one. Synergism suggests that two people working together toward a common goal are much more effective than the combined efforts of those two people working separately. Through synergy, one plus one doesn't equal two, it equals three, five or even twenty. The reason is simple.

In a given amount of time, there are only so many ideas that you can come up with in order to solve a problem. After a while the proverbial well runs dry. Your spouse can work on the same problem and come up with a separate list of solutions. Let's say that you came up with fifteen possible solutions and your spouse came up with twenty-three. The total number of possible solutions thought of is thirty-eight. Now let's put the two of you in the same room working on the problem together. Your spouse states his or her first idea, which causes you to think of something that you never would have thought of on your own. This new idea is also something that your spouse would have never thought of. That newly created idea causes you to think of others. By the time you both run out of ideas the list totals sixty-three. Now you can take the list, which you jointly created, and pick the most practical solutions to your problem.

When doing this synergistic activity, it is important that you reserve judgment until the list is completed. No suggestion is a bad one. Never tell your spouse that his or her idea won't work. This will interrupt or stop the creative flow of ideas and cause your spouse to "think" too much instead of saying the first thing that comes to mind. Ideas form the foundation upon which great things are built. Share and ask for each other's ideas and opinions often. Treat your spouse as your most valuable asset because that is what he or she is. Rely on each other and know that together you are strong. Together you can overcome every obstacle. The Honeymoon Marriage does not exist without mutual reliance.

The foundation has been laid

So far we have discussed the following:

- Marriage is a bond that should not be broken.
- The Honeymoon Marriage is the soul mate experience.
- Decide to never quit and that divorce is not an option.
- You need to become passionate about improving your marriage.
- Make your marital relationship your number-one priority.
- Tell your spouse that you are committed to making your marriage the best that it can be.
- Your unwavering allegiance to your spouse and your marriage will enable you to work things out and never give up no matter what.
- Interdependence is the secret to a successful and mutually fulfilling relationship.

Now that a strong marital foundation has been laid, you can build on it by applying the other secrets to achieving the relationship of your dreams. These secrets will revolutionize your marriage. So, if you are ready to live your life filled with passion, romance and happiness, simply continue reading as we take you down the road to the Honeymoon Marriage.

SECTION 2

Passionate
Butterflies

CHAPTER 4

UNLEASH THE ROMANCE AND PASSION IN YOUR RELATIONSHIP

Do you remember the first time that you went on a date with your spouse? If you are like many people, you experienced a little anxiety or nervousness just prior to the big date. Your heart was beating a little faster and you may even have had butterflies in your stomach. Why did you get nervous? Why did the butterflies appear? You got nervous because the date was important to you. You wanted to make sure that nothing went wrong and that the night would be perfect.

You took extra time to ensure a good first impression. Perhaps you bought a new outfit or took extra time picking out one that you looked and felt the best in. You probably looked in the mirror several times before you walked out the door. All of the effort and preparation was worth it. You looked and felt great. Then your nervousness increased somewhat as the meeting time drew closer. And then the moment arrived, the moment when you saw your date at his or her best. Wow, your date looked fantastic, and you become slightly self-conscious and hoped that he or she thought the same of you. The look on your date's face told you that he or she did. Now you were off to what you hoped would be a wonderful evening.

The first destination was your favorite restaurant or perhaps one that came highly recommended. As you walked in you couldn't help but feel good knowing that your date was with you. You felt on top of the world and you liked that feeling. As the evening progressed, your nervousness faded as you engaged each other in conversation. The meal was great and the company was even better.

After dinner maybe you headed toward the beach for a moonlit walk. The sky was clear and the reflection of the full moon was glowing on top of the calm waters. You walked along the beach with the fresh, cool air blowing in your face as you learned more about your date. You decided to sit down and watch the waves roll in for a while. As you sat there listening to the waves fall on the shore, you both became silent, cherishing the moment. You were now experiencing the perfect moment in time. Time seemed to stand still. You felt tranquil and life was great. You could live in that moment forever.

It got late and you knew that you should be heading home. As you spent your final moments together, you wondered if your date felt the same way that you did. After a minute of awkwardness, one of you broke in with, "I had a great time." Perfect, now the pressure was off. The sentiment was quickly returned and one of you suggested that another date was in order. You were both in agreement and even though you hadn't yet parted ways, you could hardly wait until you went out again. You ended the night with a hug or a kiss and went your separate ways.

You were now on cloud nine. You were so excited that you could hardly contain yourself. You lay in bed staring at the ceiling, unable to fall asleep. You had no idea what would happen next, but you knew that you liked the feeling that you had that evening. Each day that went by before your next date seemed like a week. Your date was on your mind the whole week, and you couldn't wait to see him or her again. When the second date night arrived, there came the butterflies again. This time they weren't there because you were nervous, but rather because you were excited.

If only these kinds of feelings could last a lifetime, but that isn't possible after you have been married for years. Or is it?

Donna's butterflies: Sometimes I still get butterflies in my stomach while waiting for Darren to arrive from out of town. I can't wait to see him and for some reason the anticipation and excitement can make me a little nervous. I call this feeling Passionate Butterflies. This may seem odd given the fact that we have been "dating" for almost fifteen years. But to us it makes perfect sense. We are passionate about each other and about our marriage. When we are apart for any length of time, we cannot wait to be together again. Time flies when we are together and it slows down when we are apart.

How can this be? How can we still feel this way about each other after twelve years of marriage? What is the secret? Actually there are many. As you read through this book, you will discover that the Honeymoon Marriage is possible and that you can have one. Applying these secrets to your life and your marriage will bring you true romance and lifelong happiness.

Romance

Many women dream of a romantic life where their prince charming or knight in shining armor sweeps them off their feet, carries them off into the sunset or some such fantasy. Romance is a big seller. Romance novels are big sellers. Daytime television is filled with soap operas that display their version of romance. Movies promise it. Travel agents promote once-in-a-lifetime romantic get-aways. Everyone is looking for it, some find it, but few live it. And it is those few who live a life filled with passion.

Romance doesn't have to be a grand production or a once in a while occurrence. It is possible to live your whole life filled with romance. It can be as small as a touch, whisper, kiss or embrace.

> *Your lover places a hand around the back of your neck. His or her hand hugs your neck gently and pulls you close. You draw closer together until your lover's cheek touches yours. A chill runs up your spine as he or she whispers, "I love you."*

Your spouse's love for you isn't a feeling—it is a fact. A fact that is stronger than anything Hollywood could put together. This fact is not reliant upon a one-time event or the perfect evening. This kind of romance is available every day in the Honeymoon Marriage. True romance can last forever. It can even grow stronger with time.

A couple of days ago we spent some time in two small bookstores. Usually we walk around to see what's new and buy a book or two that interests us. This time we went in to take an inventory of what people were buying. We went through every aisle and read the titles of dozens of books. We noticed which sections had the largest selection of books and which ones had the fewest. We were amazed at what we saw.

The two biggest selections by far were the fiction and the romance sections. Each store had hundreds of romance titles. We then went to the relationship section of the bookstore and found about fifty books on sex and only about six books on how to improve relationships.

That experience made it painfully clear why so many couples are unfulfilled in their relationship. Many people read stories of the fanciful romantic life, but few read about how to achieve such a life. Would you rather read about romance, or would you rather experience it firsthand?

Romance is necessary in order to achieve the Honeymoon Marriage, yet many couples would admit that the romance department of their relationship could use a little help. Help is available, but only to those who earnestly look for it. Improvement in any area of life is a simple five-step process.

1. Realize and admit that you need or want help.
2. Look for help and seek expert advice.
3. Apply what you have learned.
4. Continue the learning process.
5. Never give up until you have reached your goal.

So what exactly is romance?

Romance can be different things for different people. Recently we were with a group of couples, all in their thirties, discussing romance. Several people gave their definitions of what romance was to them. One said that it was getting flowers. Another said that his ideal was a quiet romantic dinner. Some liked candles lit throughout the house. One said that she would love to get love letters or cards from her husband. Another said that he loved dressing very casual and going to the local coffee shop and having great conversation with his wife. One found specially prepared food to be very sensual. Another said getting gifts was romantic. Still another said that she liked going for long walks together. And the list went on.

The women in the group gave 70 percent of the romantic suggestions. Some of the men didn't say anything. As you would guess, women in general desire more romance in their relationship than do men. It isn't that men don't need or want romance, it is just that their needs are slightly different than their wife's.

What was it that these couples really wanted? Was it the flowers, cards, letters, walks, intimate conversation, candles, dinner or gifts? Yes and no. Yes, they do want these things, but the things alone aren't what they really want. What they want is what these things represent. What they want is the *feeling* that they get when they receive these things.

Women and romance

When a woman receives flowers from her husband, it isn't the flowers themselves that melt her heart, it is the meaning behind the flowers. She will get completely different feelings when a dinner guest brings flowers than she will when they come from her lover. Same flowers, different meaning. To most women the gift of flowers from their husband means that he cares about them. It is a physical way to show her how much she means to her husband. The wife feels special because her husband went out of his way to show her how devoted he is to her. This gift is almost like saying, "Will you marry me?" all over again. She feels pampered and loved. She loves the attention. Wow, all this from a grouping of colorful plants? That's right—you see it isn't the gift, it is what that gift represents. The same type of thing holds true for cards, candlelit dinners, love letters, presents and other small yet meaningful signs of affection. But that alone isn't enough. She also needs to hear him tell her that he loves her, that she is beautiful (a woman can never receive too many sincere compliments), and last but not least she needs several hugs throughout the day.

Unfortunately, many men don't know that all of these *things* are much more important than their physical appearance. When a woman gets a baby-sitter, cooks a wonderful meal and sets the table with wineglasses and candles, she is preparing much more than just a dinner. She is setting the stage for a "romantic" evening. One where she will hear and feel all of the wonderful things that she needs from her husband.

Bob, Jackie and the romantic dinner

Bob knows that his wife Jackie is preparing a meal for the two of them, but he has no idea what she has in mind. He has a terrible stress-filled day at the office and gets a project dropped on his desk at 4:30 that needs to be completed by noon the next day. He figures the best way to handle the project is to jump right on it and get as much completed as he can that night. He calls Jackie at 4:45 and tells her that he has to work late and explains his circumstance. He apologizes and tells her that they can try again next week. All is okay in his mind. He rescheduled "dinner" for next week and he can now tackle the project at hand.

Meanwhile, Jackie is at home all alone. She had been preparing that evening in her mind all week. Everything was perfect. The kids are spending the night at Grandma's. This was an evening that she so desperately needed. This was to be a time of bonding together as a couple. Depending upon their relationship and his past track record, there are a couple of ways that she could respond.

In the first scenario, Jackie is crushed! She says to herself, "Doesn't Bob know how much time and energy went into planning this evening? He always puts that job ahead of me and our relationship. He doesn't understand how I feel and how much I needed this night." Then she might ask one of the most damaging questions that a person could ask herself: "Why is this happening? Why does this always happen to me?" That kind of a question opens up a Pandora's Box full of possibilities. These possibilities are not necessarily true; they are just possibilities that our mind comes up when we ask ourselves this question.

Some of the answers could include, "He doesn't care how I feel or how much this evening meant to me. All he cares about is impressing his boss and moving up the corporate ladder. I wish he would pay more attention to me. All I want is for him to be there and to show me how much he loves me. Instead I am all alone. This isn't fair." In a worst-case scenario, she may even think that her husband doesn't love her anymore or that he doesn't find her interesting or desirable. After all, if he did, surely he would be there with her instead of at the office. The more she thinks about it, the more upset she gets. Of course, any other negative scenario can also be played out in her mind. Our imaginations are very powerful. That is why we need to be very careful as to the type of questions we ask ourselves. More will be discussed regarding the power of our minds in the chapter entitled, "Expanding your mind—the pursuit of knowledge and wisdom."

Now consider a second possible scenario. Jackie is still very disappointed, but she knows that Bob didn't ask for this project to be dumped on his lap at the last minute. She knows that they can have their romantic dinner next week. She may even start to feel sorry for her husband knowing that he is under a lot of stress at work, that his boss is a jerk and that he would much rather be at home enjoying a quiet, peaceful dinner. That feeling could grow into compassion and cause her to want to do something really special for her mate when he gets home from his long day at the office. So she asks herself one of the best questions that can be asked in this situation: "What can I do that will still make this night a special one?"

Knowing that he will be very exhausted, she comes up with the perfect plan. She finishes preparing the meal and treats herself to a wonderfully peaceful evening (it has been a while since she has been all by herself with no noise and no distractions). The dinner is fantastic! Everything was prepared to perfection. Then a thought hits her. It has been quite some time since she has had the house all to herself. Why not take a hot bubble bath? She draws the bath while playing her favorite music in the background. As she is lying back soaking it all in, she thinks about her husband again. "If only he could be here with me. Here I am living the good life while he is slaving at work. I want to make this night really special for him." The more she thinks about it, the more loving she feels toward him.

The facts have not changed. The facts are that she was preparing a wonderful dinner experience and that Bob won't be there to enjoy it with her. What happens from that point on has everything to do with the choices Jackie makes as to how to handle and react to these facts. Let's continue Bob and Jackie's story for each of the two above-mentioned scenarios to see how the night turns out.

Scenario one continued

Bob gets home at 9:30. The pressure at work seems to be getting worse, and he ended the workday in an argument with his boss. He is starting to hate the job that he loved just one year ago. He is beat and is looking forward to relaxing with his wife. At least she doesn't yell at him and expect miracles. He opens the door only to find that all the lights are off. He turns on the lights, takes off his coat and shoes and walks right past the dining room, not even noticing that the table is set as though they were expecting royalty for dinner. Everything looked perfect—however, both plates were clean.

He then calls out for his wife. "Jackie, I'm home. Where are you?" He doesn't hear anything so he figures that she went off to bed. He turns the light off and walks through the family room toward the stairs. As he enters the family room, he notices Jackie sitting on the couch in the dark and says, "Hey, what are you doing sitting here in the dark? How was dinner?" She doesn't say a word. He figures that something is wrong and asks, "What's wrong?" "What do you mean what's wrong?" she replies, "Everything is wrong." "What happened? Are you okay?" he asks with a very concerned tone of voice. "You know exactly what happened," she replies.

Bob is confused; it doesn't even dawn on him that she is mad at him. After all, all he did was reschedule their dinner engagement, and that wasn't his idea anyway. So he asks her again, "What's wrong?" "You don't love me," she replies. Bob can't believe his ears. He wasn't putting up with all of the grief at work because he liked it. He was doing it for his family, for the people he loved. So he replies in a neutral voice, "Don't be silly, of course I love you." That did it—all of the negative emotions that Jackie had been building up inside during the last five hours erupted. She started using those relationship-killing words, "You always . . ." and "You never . . ." That was all Bob needed to hear. It wasn't bad enough that he was under pressure at work and getting yelled at during the day by his boss, but now he had to come home and get accused of not loving his wife. He yelled back at her saying, "What do you think I work so hard for, because I like it?" She replied, "Well you must like it better than spending time with me." And the conversation went downhill from there. They ended up going to bed not speaking to each other.

Scenario two continued

Now consider the ending of the second scenario. As in the first scenario, Bob gets home at 9:30. The pressure at work seems to be getting worse, and he ended the workday in an argument with his boss. He is starting to hate the job he loved just one year ago. He is beat and is looking forward to relaxing with his wife. At least she doesn't yell at him and expect miracles. He opens the door takes off his shoes and calls out, "Jackie, I'm home." She yells from upstairs, "I'll be down in a minute." She comes down the stairs and greets Bob with a bright smile and a huge hug. He tells her, "You are a sight for sore eyes. I had the worst day at work." I'm sorry," she says, "Would you like to talk about it?" "No," he replies, "I just want to relax and forget all about it."

Bob is so emotionally spent that he doesn't even notice that Jackie is wearing a bathrobe. She tells him, "Why don't you come upstairs and I'll give you a back rub." "That would be great," he says, as the stress of the day starts to melt away ever so slowly. He lies down on the bed and she starts to rub away even more of his stress. He tells her, "That feels great. You really know how to relax me. I love you, Jackie, you're wonderful. Sorry I had to cancel dinner, I'll make it up to you next week. As a matter of fact, I'll take the whole day off."

Then Jackie does something really special. She showers Bob with appreciation and encouragement. "Bob, I'm sorry that you had to miss dinner too. Not to make you feel bad, but it was fantastic! More than that, I'm sorry that you have to put up with such a bonehead boss. I really appreciate all of the things that you do for the kids and me. You are so awesome and extremely talented. They don't know how lucky they are to have someone like you. You are also a great husband. I love you, Bob." He rolls over and gives her a big kiss and a hug. She then tells him, "There is one thing that I had planned for tonight that we can still do together." She then slips off her robe to reveal the sexy lingerie that she had purchased especially for that evening. And they lived happily ever after.

Both of these scenarios are possible. These kinds of stories are played out every day throughout America. Each example had the same exact circumstances, but a very different conclusion. One scenario will place this couple one step closer to divorce court, and the other will bind them closer together. One leads to bitterness, sorrow, loneliness and pain. The other leads to a life filled with romance, passion, honor, love and happiness. Which scenario will be played out in your life is largely up to you.

Men and romance

Earlier we made the distinction between romantic acts and the feeling that we get from these acts. Women want to be pampered and want their husbands to pay attention to them. These "romantic" acts make them feel special and help them know that their husbands are thinking about them and care deeply for them. They want to know that they are cherished and desired by their husband. A man, on the other hand, doesn't necessarily need these "things" to fulfill his romantic needs. A woman wants a love letter or a card as reassurance that her husband loves her. A man already knows that his wife loves him (not that he could ever grow tired of hearing her tell him that). What a man would need in a letter or card is encouragement and a boost to his ego.

He wants to hear how great he is (not that a woman doesn't) and that he is appreciated for all of the hard work that he does. He wants to know that she believes in him with all of her heart. A man's idea of romance is being treated like a hero by his wife. He wants her to be proud of him. Romance to a man is also more physical, whereas a woman's needs are more emotional. Physical intimacy is one way that a man shows romantic interest toward his wife. If his wife is non-responsive or never initiates sex, that can have the same effect on him as never giving his wife flowers, cards, love letters, compliments or hugs does on her.

Some people think that if they have to tell their spouse what to do, then it isn't romantic. They want the other person to figure it out on his or her own or be spontaneous. Write this next sentence down because it is very important. If you want to have a mutually fulfilling relationship with your mate, then stop expecting him or her to be able to read your mind. *News flash—he or she can't!* That's right, your spouse can't read your mind, so stop thinking that he or she should know what to do, or what to say, or what he or she did to offend you, etc. Don't drop hints or beat around the bush, either.

That doesn't work. We know that this may sound harsh or rub you the wrong way, but we are trying to help you to have the Honeymoon Marriage. To do so, you will need to think differently than you have in the past.

Many arguments start because we assume that our spouse should know what to do, and then when it doesn't happen we get upset.

Tell your spouse exactly what you want, how often you want it, and if possible, tell him or her what it will mean to you and how it will make you feel. Give your mate as much detail as possible. That will help him or her to remember to repeat the things you appreciate in the future. It is especially important for men to know why these "things" are so important because to him, they are just things. He needs to know what they represent and to be told the meaning and feelings behind them. Be patient, you may have to tell your spouse several times before it becomes something that your spouse does on his or her own. The topic of getting what you want out of your relationship will be discussed in greater detail in the chapters entitled, "Discover who you are and who your spouse is," "Experiencing fulfilling communication" and "Discovering your spouse's desires."

So whose job is it to keep the romance alive in the relationship? Is it the woman's responsibility or the man's? The answer is both. It is the woman's responsibility to tell her husband what she wants and needs, and it is his responsibility to give it to her. Likewise, a man needs to tell his wife what he wants and needs, and it is her responsibility to give it to him. A marriage is not a fifty-fifty, "I'll meet you halfway," or "I'll do this if you do that" kind of a relationship. In a marriage you need to give 100 percent of yourself and do everything that you can to keep the relationship healthy and strong. Even though husband and wife are both responsible for every area of their relationship, there are areas where one of you has the *primary* responsibility. The romance department is one of those areas.

The one who carries the primary responsibility for the romance in a relationship is the one who needs it the least. This is the opposite of what most people think, and it is one of the reasons why so many couples struggle in the romance department. The Honeymoon Marriage is all about meeting the other person's needs. By doing so, your needs will also be met. If your spouse is the one who needs the romance in your relationship, then you are responsible to give it. If you are the one who needs the romance, then your partner is the one responsible for fulfilling that need. In most marriages that would mean that the man is the one who is *primarily* responsible for the romance in the relationship. He is the one who needs to find out what his wife needs, how often she needs it, and then give it to her. Women—just be careful not to make it a one-sided thing or you will lose his attention fast.

Passion

Passion is the opposite side of the romance coin, and it is absolutely necessary in keeping a marriage exciting and new. Romance is much easier to sustain throughout the years when passion exists in the relationship. Passion is a strong or driving desire or devotion. The stronger your desire is to please your spouse, the better your relationship will be. The more committed and devoted you are to your partner, the happier your marriage will be.

Passion is one of the key elements necessary to achieve massive success in any area of life. Michael Jordan is passionate about basketball. Mother Teresa was passionate about helping those in need. Arnold Schwarzenegger was passionate about bodybuilding. Oprah Winfrey is passionate about empowering others. Thomas Edison was passionate about inventing things that everyone thought were impossible. Are you passionate about your marriage? Passion is one of the key ingredients to achieving the Honeymoon Marriage.

Earlier we told you about passionate butterflies. How is it possible to keep that level of excitement in a marriage throughout the years? It is possible through a consistent and focused effort. There are many people who are passionate about a particular area of their life regardless of how long they are exposed to it. There are painters that have been painting for most of their lives but still love to paint. Some are even passionate about their work. Painting is one of the ways that they express themselves. They will even get nervous just prior to an exhibit that will display their works. Many of the most popular public speakers get nervous before a presentation. They may have been speaking in front of large crowds for twenty years, yet the butterflies still creep in. Why? They get nervous because they care. If they didn't care about what they were doing, didn't care if they did a good job, or didn't care what kind of an impact they would have on their audience, they wouldn't get nervous. There are people from all walks of life who are passionate about their work. Why then should it sound strange that one would be passionate about his or her marriage?

Passion and romance have their foundation in a healthy and mutually fulfilling relationship. Throughout this book, you will find many practical tips that will enable you to build and keep a strong foundation. But the first steps are up to you. These steps are as follows:

1. Desire to have a Honeymoon Marriage.
2. Believe that the Honeymoon Marriage is possible.
3. Be willing to continually improve yourself and your marriage.
4. Decide on a daily basis that you will have a Honeymoon Marriage.
5. Never give up trying.

Plan on keeping the romance and passion alive in your marriage
Most successful ventures begin with an end result in mind. Knowing what you want the end result to be is of critical importance in making it become a reality. Once you have a clear picture in mind as to your ultimate goal, then you are ready to put together a plan to make it happen.

"Our plans miscarry because they have no aim.
When a man does not know what harbor he is making for,
no wind is the right wind."
- Marcus Annaeus Seneca -

Weddings are planned. A building isn't built without a plan. A successful business starts with a plan. Vacations are planned. Planning in athletics is so prevalent that we have coined a phrase that is used in many areas of life. It is called a "game plan." Does your marriage have a game plan? Do you have a step-by-step plan put together to improve your marriage and keep it strong? Or are you just winging it and hoping that everything will be okay?

If things are not as good as you would like them to be, then it is time to plan for improvement. This book should be looked at as a guide to lead you toward the marriage of your dreams. Your results will vary depending upon your determination, persistence, introspection and the application of these truths. Not all of your answers will be contained in the pages of this book, but while reading and reflecting, you will think of things that have never crossed your mind before. These new ideas will have an impact on your marriage and your overall happiness. As mentioned earlier, have a note pad handy, take notes and highlight the sections that jump out at you.

You have already written down what you want from your marriage and why you want it from the instructions given in the Introduction. You did do that exercise, didn't you? If not, reread the Introduction, take out a note pad and start writing. If all you want is an education, then you may continue reading. However, if you want to see changes in your relationship, then you need to follow all of the instructions given in this book. So stop now and start writing. Take your time and be as specific as you can. The better you know what you are aiming for, the better your chances will be of getting it. Remember to think big. Put your critical mind aside for a while and write down a detailed description of your *ideal* marriage even if you think it is impossible. Forget about what is possible and only focus on what you want.

> *"Aim at the sun, and you may not reach it;*
> *but your arrow will fly far higher*
> *than if aimed at an object on level with yourself."*
> - Joel Hawes -

At first, you may think that some of the suggestions in this book don't apply to you or that they won't work in your relationship. The truth is, you will never know unless you try them. By trying we mean applying, and not just once or twice or for a while, but rather until you see the results you are looking for. One does not become a concert pianist after his or her third practice. Likewise, many of the principles that are taught throughout this book need to be placed into practice for several months in order for you to see optimum results.

The question is not will these principles work in your marriage, but rather will you work these principles into your marriage? We have applied the principles taught in this book and they work. We are living, breathing proof that the Honeymoon Marriage is possible. Our greatest desire is that you will join us and experience for yourself everything that life has to offer you.

The bottom line

Romance is important in your marriage. Doing the "things" that most people consider to be romantic can be fun and they can even cause you to feel closer to your mate. It is important that you spend time alone with each other without the kids. It is important that you do the little things that make your partner feel special. It means a lot to know that someone is thinking about you. It is good to buy the flowers, write love letters, enjoy candlelit dinners and the like. All of these things are good, but they are not the romantic things that you absolutely need in order to have the Honeymoon Marriage.

In our opinion, the truly romantic things are not mentioned above. We would gladly give up all of the romantic ideas mentioned in this chapter in exchange for the things that truly make us happy and draw us closer together as a couple. What we find truly romantic is not what our partner can do for us but rather what we want to do for our partner. These unselfish, caring things are what will set your relationship on fire. The chapter entitled "Small things mean a lot" lists many of the things that we consider to be romantic. Most of these things may not seem romantic on the surface. They will not be the things that Hollywood promotes. These small things will not find their way into the latest romance novel, but they will find their way into your heart and soul.

Romance is being committed to your relationship and to each other. Romance is the "soul mate" experience. It is not a thing that you do or feel as much as it is something that you know. Romance is knowing that you will always be there for your spouse no matter what. Romance is striving to improve your relationship and yourself. Romance is giving the best of YOU to your lover.

The more you practice the principles taught throughout this book, the closer your relationship will become. You will learn that your husband or wife was not put on this planet to complete you, but rather to complement you. As discussed in the last chapter, you will experience the power of synergy with your partner where one plus one equals three, four, or even five. But for now, remember this—when it comes to your marriage one-half plus one-half equals only one-half. If you come into a marriage incomplete (having only half of what you need to be happy), and you marry someone who is incomplete, your union will not make you a complete person.

The bottom line is that your partner doesn't have the ability to complete you or make you happy. Happiness is something that you have to find within yourself first before you will ever be happy with someone else. Once you are happy with you, then and only then can you experience the best that a loving relationship has to offer. *Honeymoon Marriage* will not only give you some practical tips on how to improve your marriage, but it will offer you some guidance toward being the best that you can be as well.

The best gift that you could ever give your spouse is to be the best you that you can be—mentally, physically and spiritually.

CHAPTER 5

DATING YOUR SPOUSE— REKINDLING THE FLAME

Do you remember when you first started dating your spouse? Remember how much you looked forward to that night. It didn't matter where you were going or what you were going to do. You looked forward to each date even more than the last. Just the thought of being with that person put a smile on your face and a skip in your step.

Dating is a very important part of the courting process. You are able to learn about each other and determine if you are compatible enough to continue seeing this person. During the date your focus was almost completely on each other. It was a time of sharing, having fun and becoming better friends. While courting, you were on your best behavior and tried to make sure that everything went well. Your date's needs came before your own. Wherever he or she wanted to go was fine with you. We think that it is safe to say that you went out of your way to please him or her.

As you dated for a longer period of time, you began to learn even more about that person. As your feelings grew deeper, you wanted to spend even more time together. The decisions that you made revolved around the person. In a way, he or she became the center of your universe. You felt great! You were happy and life was grand. You felt very special because your date treated you like you were royalty. You were on top of the world and everything seemed a little brighter. This is how you wanted to feel for the rest of your life so you decided to get married. The date was set and the rings were purchased. You couldn't wait to spend the rest of your life with this person. As the big day drew near, you started to get a little nervous, perhaps fear poked its head in for a moment, but all in all you were excited and looked forward to finally being husband and wife. The wedding day happened in a flash and you were off on your honeymoon. You had a blast! Wow, life can't get any better than this.

We can remember being at a Christmas party and the conversation led to us talking about a recent vacation getaway we had just taken. We no more than got the words out of our mouths when several of the couples one at a time described how great their honeymoon was. All of these couples had been married for over ten years. They spoke about it as a once-in-a-lifetime experience never to be repeated again, as if the honeymoon was the pinnacle of their marriage. We are not just talking about the location or the amount of time spent; we are talking about the experience. We think that secretly many couples wish that they could go back to the way things were when they were dating. At least they want those kinds of feelings back. They want their mate to look at them with the same glow in his or her eyes. They want once again to be the center of their spouse's universe.

Dating is very important even after marriage. This is especially true if you have children. It is critical that you put aside time to be alone with each other, preferably outside of your familiar environment. We knew someone in high school whose parents had a date night every Thursday. They had four children and still made a point to take time to date each other. Needless to say, it was obvious that they liked each other. There was definitely something different about them versus most of the other parents that we knew growing up. The reason they were different than most parents was because they were *doing* something different.

Great marriages don't just happen. It is not luck that causes some to live a life of marital bliss while others are going into divorce court. It is what you *do* that makes a relationship great, not what you wish for. And one of the things that you can do is to date each other. Of course that means no kids, just you and your lover. Some couples have a problem leaving the kids at home with a sitter while they go off on a date. They feel like they are in some way neglecting their children. Many couples see no benefit in being alone with each other because they enjoy being together as a family. For some, their whole life revolves around their children.

The most important person on the planet is your spouse, not your kids or anyone else for that matter. Your kids won't feel the least bit slighted by your strong affection toward each other. As a matter of fact, they will appreciate it. Children need to feel secure and safe in their home environment, and there is no better way to give them that feeling than to be head over heels in love with your spouse. We once heard Greg Buchanan, world-class harpist, say, "If you really want to impress your kids, love your wife."

By dating your spouse you also reduce the risk of having "empty nest syndrome." Empty nest syndrome is the empty feeling one can get when his or her kids leave home. That is a natural feeling and is quite harmless in and of its own. However, there can be a darker side to this empty nest situation. It is not uncommon these days for husband and wife to split up within a few years of their children leaving home. They made it through the "tough" times, raised a family, lived together for twenty-five years and now they are getting a divorce. Why is that? Once the kids are gone, they no longer have anything in common. Their lives were devoted to fulfilling their children's needs and they forgot about each other's needs. They focused on their children's goals instead of their own. Their dreams were not their own as they lived their lives through their children (the importance of dreaming together will be discussed in the chapter entitled "Grow together by dreaming together"). Slowly but surely they started to grow apart, yet they didn't notice it because they had the children as their common bond.

Dating your spouse is not an option, it is a necessity. Your marriage will improve and you will be setting a great example for your children.

You may come up with a dozen reasons why you can't go on dates with your spouse and why it won't make a difference. It worked pretty well the first time you did it, didn't it? Then make it work again. Notice that we didn't say *let* it work again. The success of your marriage is a choice, not some random act of chance or circumstance. Decide to go on a date with your mate, choose to make it fun and choose to make it improve your relationship. You can control the outcome of your life by taking control of the actions that you take to improve your relationship.

> *"Man is not the creature of circumstances.*
> *Circumstances are the creature of man."*
> *- Benjamin Disraeli -*

Decide right now that your dating experience will be an awesome one. Expect the best and you greatly increase your chances of experiencing the best. Don't be too concerned how the first date goes, and don't be surprised if the magic doesn't just pop back into your relationship. Improving your marriage is a process, not a one-time event. Regardless of how the first date turns out, plan for the second date, then the third, etc. Be persistent and be patient. Anything worth while is worth your time and effort. The object of your dating experience is to convince your husband or wife all over again that you are the one that he or she should marry. Put on your best behavior and go out of your way to please him or her.

The amount of money that you spend is not important, however, spend below your means. Great experiences are priceless but they don't have to cost a lot of money. Read the chapter entitled "Small things mean a lot" to get a few suggestions. Try to go somewhere that you normally wouldn't go with each other. New scenery is great for igniting a new spark in your relationship. You don't have to limit your choices to "mature" locations. Go to a park or playground and swing on the swings together. When was the last time that you rode on a seesaw? How about a merry-go-round? Go for a long walk holding hands. Use your imagination. The important thing is that you are spending time together, just the two of you, outside of your familiar surroundings.

To find out what other couples are doing on their date night or to enter your own suggestions, go to www.honeymoonmarriage.com and click on the keyword "date night."

Your marriage is the most important earthly relationship that you can have. It affects every other area of your life as well. Make the time, make the arrangements and save the money. Your marriage is worth it. Everything that you do to improve your relationship with your partner brings you one step closer to the Honeymoon Marriage.

CHAPTER 6

BEDTIME HARMONY—
AN OASIS OF LOVE

Could you use a little more peace and harmony in your life? The way we look at it, peace and harmony are like money. You can never get too much of it, and if you have more than you need, you can always give some of it away. Of course in doing so you will receive even more in return.

Pay close attention to the common thread that is woven throughout this book. This thread is one of the natural laws of the universe. It can mend a broken relationship. It is strong enough to pull you out of the most dire situation. This thread can bind everything together in perfect harmony if used properly. It is able to give you happiness and prosperity. It is the creed of the wise, yet remains invisible or ignored by those who need it the most. This natural unchanging law is known as the *Law of the Harvest*.

This law has been in existence since the beginning of time, however, we oftentimes forget that it still applies to our lives. Very simply it states that whatever you sow you will reap, whatever you plant you will harvest, whatever you give you will get. It is no mystery that when you plant wheat, wheat will grow. No sane person would plant wheat and expect an apple tree to grow. Why is it then that we can argue and fight yet hope to live in peace and harmony? The reason is that we don't fully understand, appreciate and apply the *Law of the Harvest* to our lives. We expect that we can get whatever we desire in life regardless of our actions and the choices that we make.

Most people *want* to be wealthy yet never seem to get ahead. Some *want* to have a more fulfilling career yet are stuck in the rat race. Many *want* to have a great relationship yet fall short of their expectations. We all *want* to be happy and live a fulfilling and prosperous life, yet not everybody does. After a while some of us give up the hope that these things are possible for us to have and stop wanting altogether. We may even think that only the "lucky" people can have any or all of these things or that we are "unlucky" because of the circumstances in our lives. Well, you can wait on "luck" or "some day I'll . . ." if you want to. You can continue to go through life the way you have been and hope that things will get better. Or you can live a life of abundance by adopting the *Law of the Harvest.*

"Give and it will be given to you."
Give whatever it is that you want more of in your life. In order to have more you must give more. That doesn't make sense to us if we forget the *Law of the Harvest.* Have you ever met a grumpy, unfriendly person? Did you want to spend a lot of time with this person and get to know him or her better, or did you want to leave as quickly as possible? No one likes to be around unfriendly people; hence these people do not have many friends. How many friends will you make if you never talk to anyone? In order to have friends you must be friendly.

There is something inside of us that causes us to want to give back whenever someone else gives to us. If someone tells us that we are wrong, we want to tell that person that he or she is wrong (we look at it as proving that we are right). If you yell at someone, he or she will most likely yell back. If someone does a favor for you, you want to return it in kind. If you smile at someone, he or she will smile back at you.

> ***Darren and the difficult coworker:*** Several years ago I was in a situation where I had to work with someone who didn't have the reputation of being a person who was very easy to get a long with. Everyone without exception told me how difficult she was. Some even tried to avoid or work around her. I was told that she had a very negative attitude and that I had better watch my back. Fortunately, I have developed the habit of not listening to the things that people say about other people. She seemed a little standoffish when I first met her, but it didn't take long and we got along just fine. She was just as easy to work with as anyone else that I dealt with in the company. Why is it that I got

along very well with her when most people didn't? Did she all of the sudden change her personality and become a different person? Perhaps she acted differently toward me because I acted differently toward her. When she would try to argue, I told her that she was probably right and that I would look into it further. When she would complain, I would empathize with her. When she was short with me, I tried to be calm and patient. It didn't take long and we got along great. Whenever I would ask her to do something, she would act on it immediately. I gave her what no one else gave and I received what no one else received.

The following experiment is fun and can demonstrate in a small way that the *Law of the Harvest* can work with people. Say hello to the next ten people that you come in contact with and notice that most of them will say hello in return. Say hi to the following ten people and notice that most of them will say hi.

It is amazing how much easier life becomes when you start to give whatever it is that you want in return. In our travels we have noticed and experienced how difficult it can be to deal with the general public. Airport gate agents have to put up with a lot. Business travelers who don't know the *Law of the Harvest* can be a very unkind bunch. They can get very unreasonable when things don't go according to plan. Some treat the gate agents as though they were the ones who caused the bad weather, delayed the arriving flight, made them arrive late for their flight, caused the mechanical difficulties or oversold the flight. We enjoy watching people and get a kick out of watching these irate passengers. They work themselves up over something that they have absolutely no control over, treat people harshly and then expect those people to go out of their way to help them. We haven't witnessed a very high success rate among these types of people.

Show kindness and patience instead and the success rate increases dramatically. We have been rescheduled to different flights and have been moved up to first class without being charged a premium all because we smiled, were very cheerful, complimented the gate agents on how well they handled themselves while dealing with unpleasant travelers, and asked if they could help us solve our problem. On one particular trip, we arrived at the ticket counter at Chicago's O'Hare airport only to discover that our flight was leaving out of Chicago's Midway airport. We very politely explained our predicament to the gentleman behind the counter and asked for his help. He told us that we could fly out of O'Hare and return to Midway. We asked (not demanded) if he could find something that arrived at O'Hare as well since our car was parked there and thanked him for looking. He found a flight that got us in at a much better time than our original flight and didn't even charge us the several-hundred-dollar ticket difference. This is just one small example of how we have received kindness in return for kindness and patience in return for patience. Some would say that we are always lucky, but we prefer to look at it as knowing and following the universal laws. Give the things that you want and your life will never be the same.

> *"How you give love is how you live love."*
> *- Jaci Velasquez-*

Cooperation

When two people come together in a relationship, there are bound to be differences of opinion. These differences can be a great tool in helping us expand and grow. If we keep an open mind, understanding our differences can make us a more well rounded and balanced person. Some of these differences can even lead us in a better direction and cause us to make better decisions. Our differences can have a positive synergistic effect on our lives.

You and your spouse are a team. You are partners in this thing called life. You can either let this partnership help you to live a more fulfilled life or you can treat your spouse like he or she is the competition. Cooperation or competition, which do you think will bring you the most success in your marriage? The answer to that question may seem obvious, but are you practicing cooperation in your marriage? Are you working together to achieve a mutually beneficial outcome? Is your marriage a partnership or just two people living in the same house? Your answer to the following questions will give you some clues:

1. Is your way the right way? Do you have to always (or often) be right?

> *"The greatest of all faults, I should say,*
> *is to be conscious of none."*
> *- Thomas Carlyle -*

2. Do you and your spouse discuss all major purchases prior to buying anything, and have you agreed to what constitutes a major purchase?
3. Are you both in agreement as to what you will and won't spend money on and where you will invest your money?

4. Do you focus on each other's strengths or on each other's weaknesses?
5. Do you notice all of the things that you do better than your spouse, or do you notice the things that you need to improve in your own life?
6. Do you try to change your spouse's mind to your way of thinking or are you willing to change your mind?

> *"I was going to change my shirt,*
> *but I changed my mind instead."*
> *- Winnie the Pooh (A. A. Milne) -*

7. Do you agree as to how your children should be raised including discipline, allowance, curfew, education, religion, dress, friends, chores, etc.?
8. Do you have written plans for your future and discuss them with each other regularly?
9. Do you always look for ways to improve yourself and your marriage?
10. Do you always give your spouse the benefit of the doubt and reserve judgment until you get all of the facts?
11. When your spouse offends or hurts you, do you try to understand what the motive was behind your spouse's action, or do you just get mad at him or her?

It doesn't matter how long you have been married—if you don't treat your relationship like a cooperative partnership, you will never have a Honeymoon Marriage.

Don't fight

Disagreements can be healthy in a relationship. However, there is never room for fighting in the Honeymoon Marriage. We once heard a counselor say that the couple that doesn't fight doesn't have passion in other areas of their marriage either. With all due respect, he was dead wrong. We suspect that he "practices what he preaches" due to the health of his own marriage. One doesn't have to spend a lot of time with the two of them to realize that their marriage needs a lot of work. He is living in a fantasyland thinking that everything is peachy, whereas his wife is very unhappy and unfulfilled in her relationship.

If you want to get a quick read as to the health of any marriage, just ask the woman how she would rate their relationship. Most women know the condition of their marital relationship much more accurately than do their husbands. Some men are even clueless in this regard. That comment is not meant to be a jab at men, it is just that men and women are very different. Men tend to be project oriented whereas women tend to be more relationship oriented. Other men-women differences that can cause friction in a marriage, if not understood, will be discussed in the chapter entitled "Discovering who your spouse is."

"Never yell at each other unless the house is on fire,"
- H. Jackson Brown, Jr. -

Words of wisdom from Darren's Grandma: My Grandma used to tell us, "Kids, never fight. No one wins if you fight." My Grandparents were married for 66 years, until death did they part.

Those are words of wisdom to live by. The reason why fighting can be so damaging is because it involves our emotions. When our emotions get involved, we may say harmful things that we don't mean, things that can never be taken back. Have you ever noticed that two men can get into a heated debate over a certain issue to the point where they are almost ready to punch each other's lights out, and then two hours later they act like nothing ever happened and are best of friends again? Why is that? There are many reasons, but the one that stands out the most in our minds is the fact that they don't take the attack personally. Their friend is attacking their idea, facts or figures; he is not attacking them. They both realize this fact, and everything will work out fine in the end as long as they play by the rules. In other words, their relationship is not at jeopardy as long as they fight fair.

The moment the argument escalates to the point where a personal attack enters into the dispute, the outcome can be very different. A lifelong friendship can very easily dissolve depending upon the severity and sum total of these personal attacks, unless one of them is man enough to apologize. That is why fighting is so damaging in a marital relationship. The fight may start over a trivial matter, but then quickly escalate into an exchange of very harmful words. This is true because of four relationship factors.

First, there is more vulnerability in a marital relationship than in any other kind of relationship. The more intimate the relationship, the more vulnerable we become. Our spouse knows our weaknesses, our passions and our fears. He or she has the ability to hurt us like no other person on the planet can. The acceptance of our partner is very important to us.

The second factor is that oftentimes a critique is not meant as a personal attack, however it is taken as one. We too often translate the statement, "I don't like it when you . . ." to mean, "I don't like *you* when you . . ."

Darren: I may not like it when Donna leaves the portable phone wherever she used it last, but I still like her. I may not accept the behavior, but I still accept and love her.

The third factor harkens back to our childhoods. When we were small, our knowledge and vocabulary was very limited. Not knowing how to properly express ourselves, we resorted to name-calling shortly after an argument started. Even as adults we revert back to this childish behavior. Our adult name-calling takes on a different, even more damaging form. The following are some examples of our more sophisticated name-calling:

- "Are you blind?"
- "When will you ever learn!"
- "I am very disappointed in you." This statement should be phrased, "I am very disappointed in what you did. That is not like you, you can do so much better than that."
- "You jerk!" And several other negative expletives that you are very familiar with.
- "I can't believe you did that again!"
- "You always . . ." or "You never . . ." Be very careful of this one. Odds are pretty good that that statement is not true. The moment you say those words, your mate becomes defensive and will most likely not be open to anything that you have to say from that point on. Those statements may even cause your mate to think of all of the things that *you* always or *you* never. Remember the *Law of the Harvest*. If you continue to sow seeds of "you always" or "you never" into your relationship, then that is what you will reap. Whatever you focus on and hear over and over again becomes a reality. This will be discussed in detail in the chapter entitled "Expanding your mind—the pursuit of knowledge and wisdom."

The fourth factor is that as the argument progresses and our emotions rise to the surface, we pull out the big guns because we want to "win." Wanting to make our point, we pull from every resource available including the past. Stay out of the past! Leave it where it belongs. Bringing up the past in an argument is like pouring gasoline on a fire. Don't go there; instead focus only on the present situation no matter how difficult that may be.

Let's say that you "win" a fight. What have you really won? Have you grown closer to your partner as a result of it? Does your spouse feel like it is easier to be him- or herself when he or she is around you? Regardless of how old you are or how long you have been married, fighting is immature. If you fight a lot, it is time that you grow up and develop your peacekeeping skills. Otherwise you will continue to rob yourself of the kind of joy that an awesome marriage can give. Why would you treat a complete stranger better than your spouse? Why would you be more careful about the words that you use and the things that you say to your boss than the words that you use and the things that you say to your life partner? It just doesn't make sense.

Be the bigger person

We're sure you are familiar with the saying, "It takes two to tango." It takes two to debate, it takes two to argue and it takes two to fight. Perhaps you are married to someone who loves to fight. He or she loves to try and prove that he or she is right and you are wrong. There is no quicker way to take the wind out of such a person's sails than to remain calm and tell him or her that you do not wish to participate.

> *"Nothing gives one person so much advantage*
> *over another as to remain always cool*
> *and unruffled under all circumstances."*
> *- Thomas Jefferson -*

Instead of engaging in an argument, tell your spouse that you would love to hear what he or she has to say, but only if he or she can talk in a calm and civil manner. Tell your spouse that you love him or her but that you do not want to fight. Ask if he or she is willing to continue without yelling. If not, then say you will be in the other room or outside and that your spouse can come and talk to you as soon as he or she has cooled off. If your spouse agrees, then listen without interruption. Effective listening skills will be discussed in the chapter entitled "Experience fulfilling communication."

> *"If you will invest time in listening,*
> *you will save that time in arguments."*
> *- Joyce Meyer -*

Control your anger

You may be familiar with the jewel of wisdom that says never to make a major decision when you are angry. Why is that important? When we are angry, we oftentimes don't think clearly or at least don't think things through. Controlling your temper is not about suppressing feelings. Holding in your emotions or pretending that they don't exist can be just as harmful to your relationship as arguing and fighting all of the time. Suppressed emotions can also lead to serious health issues. You can let out all of your feelings and emotions without raising your voice or yelling. Lashing out at someone in anger at the drop of a hat is a bad habit that can be corrected through self-discipline. The following are some steps that will help you overcome your anger:

1. Realize that you have a problem with anger.
2. Have the desire to want to change.
3. Make a conscious effort to catch yourself every time that your anger gets the best of you.
4. Immediately apologize if your anger was directed toward another person and let him or her know that you are working on controlling your anger. Something very powerful happens when you share your goals with other people. This is true in every area of your life. When we made a goal to be out of debt within twelve months, we told almost everyone we spoke to. Every time we mentioned it, it became more real to us. It was almost as though we had a silent support group that was cheering us on. Not only did we pay off our debt, but we paid it off two months ahead of schedule. Don't worry about what people will think of you. Odds are they already know that you have a hot temper, and you will gain a lot of respect if your friends know that you are working on it.
5. When you catch yourself getting angry, think about what it is that you are angry about. Oftentimes in a relationship we are the victims of misdirected anger. We may snap at our spouse when it is really our boss that we are angry with. Because we haven't dealt with the anger we have toward our boss or whatever else, any little thing can set us off. It is as though we are a land mine just waiting to explode as soon as someone rubs us the wrong way.

Man is measured by the size of
the thing that makes him angry."
- J. Kenfield Morley -

When you discover what it is that you are angry about, determine if it is really worth your mental anguish. Sometimes it is good for us to get angry. Anger is appropriate when it moves us to better ourselves, others and the world around us. But more often than not it does more harm than good.

6. Find an accountability partner other than your spouse whom you trust. It is important that you choose a partner of the same gender for reasons that will be discussed later. Let this person know that you have a problem with anger and that you would like him or her to hold you accountable for your improvement. Meet with your partner once a week to discuss your progress. This suggestion may seem a little extreme, however, only you can determine just how important your marriage is and what you are willing to do to make it better. You can also use your accountability partner to help you in other areas of your life as well.

7. When you get angry, give yourself some time and space to cool down before responding.

Thomas Jefferson said that we should count to ten before reacting when we are angry. Ten seconds may not be enough reflection time to avoid an argument. Would you decide to buy a house or move to a different state after thinking about it for only ten seconds? Of course you wouldn't. But yet we react very quickly toward our partner when he or she has done something that has hurt, saddened, offended or made us angry. We need more time to process that kind of information prior to doing something that may cause the other person to feel the same way that he or she just made us feel.

"When angry, count to ten before you speak;
if very angry, an hundred."
- Thomas Jefferson -

We don't take our potential arguments seriously enough. We are hurt and we want to feel vindicated. And we want it immediately. If you had an important presentation to make in front of a group of your peers, you would spend a lot of time preparing for it. You would want to make sure that everything you said was accurate and taken the right way. We are sure that you would agree that your marital relationship is more important than a presentation, yet when it comes to our feelings we don't always act like it. We are not saying that you have to put together a presentation prior to engaging in a potentially heated dialogue with your spouse. But it is always a good idea to reflect on the situation, determine how your mate might receive your input, and speculate as to how he or she might respond. After taking a few minutes to think about your feelings and what it was that caused them in the first place, you will cool down somewhat and be better equipped to carry on a calm conversation. You may even figure out that you have overacted or misinterpreted your spouse's reason for acting the way he or she did.

Write vs. fight

Writing our thoughts on paper is a powerful way of sorting out the feelings that are racing in our heads. Putting our thoughts to paper is a common practice in the business world; however, we rarely do this in our personal life. We recently ran into a friend of ours whom we hadn't seen in years. After a little catching up, she told us that she was having trouble deciding on her future career path. She was a flight attendant and loved the benefits. She was also thinking about going to cosmetology school. The school she was considering would cost around $10,000 per year. She wasn't sure what to do.

While talking to her the answer was obvious to us. We wanted her to come to her own conclusion so we asked a couple of directed questions. We asked her if she had to pick one career right now on the spot, which would it be, what was her gut feeling? We then asked her which career she thought she would enjoy the most and give her the most satisfaction. Finally, we told her to get out two pieces of blank paper when she got home, write "flight attendant" at the top of one page and "cosmetologist" at the top of the other, and draw a line down the middle of each page. On the left side of each page she was to write down all of the positives of each career and on the right all the negatives. We have done this exercise on several occasions and it has given us a much clearer picture as to which direction to take.

Writing down your feelings is not only a good way to sort out the pros and cons of any given situation, but it also a great way to work through your emotions. Writing about any strong emotion is in itself therapeutic and can help you to release these emotions before they cause you and/or anyone else harm. Once you have your feelings on paper, you can decide if you have a valid reason for feeling the way that you do, if you are overreacting, or discover that you may have misinterpreted the perpetrator's intent.

John Gray in his wonderful book, *Men Are from Mars, Women Are from Venus*, suggests that couples write love letters prior to engaging in a potentially harmful argument. He suggests that the letter be divided into five sections: anger, sadness, fear, regret and love. The idea is to keep writing until you have worked through all of your negative emotions and can get to the love section. The P.S. should be what you would like to have your spouse do. An example would be as follows:

Dear Bill:

I want to always be able to share my feelings with you. Today you really upset me when you watched the second ball game of the day instead of talking with me when I came home from picking up the kids from swimming lessons. I told you that I really needed to talk to you and you blew me off to watch the game. It really hurt me and made me feel like the game was more important to you than I was. This wasn't the first time that you have done this to me and I am concerned that it won't be the last. I know that you need your time to unwind and relax, but I need you too. I am afraid that if we continue like this things will only get worse and we will eventually start to drift apart. I don't want that to happen to us. I want to feel close to you, and I am sorry that I don't feel very close to you right now. I wish that we had a closer relationship. Bill, I really do love you. Our relationship is very special to me and I want to stay that way.

I love you,

Karen

P.S. I would really appreciate it if you would take time away from your interests when I have something important to tell you. Your undivided attention is very important to me. That way I will know how important I am to you and will feel like you will always be there when I need you.

Telling their spouse what they would like for them to do can be difficult for some people, especially women. Women are more prone to thinking that their husbands should already know what it is that they want and should do it without prompting. We don't disagree with this logic, however, that is not the reality of most relationships. One of the ways to get what you want is to ask for it. Other ways will be disclosed in Section 4—"The Quickest Way to Get What You Want."

Forgiveness

Unforgiveness can destroy any relationship, and a marriage is no exception. Unforgiveness will not only destroy a relationship; it can destroy the person who holds on to it. Studies have shown that unforgiveness can even have adverse effects on one's health. Unforgiveness can make you sick, literally. Some of the most awesome advice regarding forgiveness is summed up in just one line. It is a quote found in the Bible that states, "Do not let the sun go down while you are angry." In other words, don't go to bed angry.

Remember the game hot potato that we used to play in grade school? The object was to get rid of the "hot potato" as quickly as possible before someone with his or her back turned yelled "stop" or the music stopped playing. The person left holding the "hot potato" was the loser; he or she was out of the game. The same is true for the person holding unforgiveness in his or her heart. Unforgiveness is something that you want to get rid of as quickly as that hot potato.

Unforgiveness can lead to resentment, anger, bitterness and cynicism. How can you have an awesome relationship with someone that you are bitter toward? Unfortunately, unforgiveness does not get better with the passing of time. As a matter of fact, it often grows more intense as time passes by. One unforgiveness builds on top of another until something gives. That something could be your mind, your health or your relationship. If you want to have a Honeymoon Marriage, you must be willing to forgive freely and often.

In a relationship, there is another very important side to forgiveness. And that is to ask for forgiveness. Depending on one's personality, this can be even harder than forgiving. This is where pride pokes its ugly head into the picture. Why should we ask for forgiveness when we were right and our actions or words were justified? Marriage is not a contest. What difference does it make who is right and who is wrong if an action or words are coming between you and the one you love? The phrase, "love is never having to say you're sorry," must have been coined by a divorce attorney. If you never say that you are sorry, then you will most likely not experience the Honeymoon Marriage.

Do you truly want your marriage to be the relationship of your dreams? Well, you better get used to saying those three magic words. No, not "I love you," the other three magic words—"I am sorry" and "please forgive me." Some people think that asking for forgiveness is a sign of weakness. Nothing could be further from the truth. It takes a very strong person to ask for forgiveness, especially when that person may be right. What can be a better example of strength than a strong marriage? And a strong marriage is impossible without forgiveness.

Success in any area of life requires a lot of work, and marriage is no exception. Be sensitive enough to know when something is bothering your spouse. Ask your spouse what's wrong. Ask if you have done something to offend or hurt him or her. If so, tell your spouse that you are sorry. If you are on the receiving end, accept their forgiveness and forget about it. Forgive and forget. Is that possible? We get concerned when we hear people bring up something that someone did to offend them several years ago. Is it just that they have a good memory? We don't think so. It is more likely that they never forgave that person. Some people even try to use past events as leverage against the other person. Again, a marriage is not a competition. In a marriage, if there is a winner and a loser, you both lose.

Life is not fair, and bad things do happen to good people. Unforgiveness doesn't have to be against your spouse to have a negative impact on your marriage. Things that have happened to you throughout your life can have an impact on your marital relationship. Sally comes home from a rough day at work. She got into a disagreement with her boss again and she is extremely upset. When she comes home that evening, the last thing she wants to talk about is work. Her husband says something that sets her off. She snaps at him before he realizes that he said something wrong. He asks her, "What's your problem?" in a harsh tone of voice and things go downhill from there. Why did she get into an argument with her husband over something trivial? It is because she did not forgive her boss for the way he had treated her that day and she is now taking it out on her unsuspecting husband.

Unforgiveness can also be a catch twenty-two or a trap that you don't want to get out of. Why would you want to hold on to unforgiveness when you know how harmful it can be? You may think that you are punishing the person that you have unforgiveness toward. Deep down you are saying, "You really hurt me and I am going to punish you by never forgiving you for what you have done." If you do that, whom are you really punishing? Is the person who hurt you affected by the feelings that you hold inside? Of course not, that person will go on with his or her life while this unforgiveness eats away at you. By not forgiving someone, you give him or her the power to hurt you over and over again every time that you think about the person or the situation. Do you want that person to have that much control over you? Do you want him or her to control your life, your health, and your marriage? If your answer is no, then forgive the offender because unforgiveness only hurts the person holding it.

We may also feel that forgiving someone makes what he or she did to us okay. Forgiveness is not acceptance. Just because you forgive someone doesn't mean that what the person did was right or that it is okay for him or her to do it again. Maybe the following analogy will help: Let's say that unforgiveness is like a fire. When someone wrongs you, he or she lights a fire inside of you. The fire hurts and unless it is extinguished, it will burn you up inside. Every time you think about what the person did, you add kindling to the fire, making it grow hotter and hurt more. The fire will continue to burn for as long as you keep holding onto it. The person who started the fire isn't getting burned because the fire is only in you. If you don't get the fire under control, it will begin to burn other areas of your life. Forgiveness is the fire extinguisher. Use it to put out the fire.

We can't always control what happens to us, but we can control how we react to those events. We can decide how we will let those events affect the rest of our life. Forgive, let it go, and let the healing begin in your life.

Unforgiveness is so dangerous because we don't realize what kind of an impact it has on our life. Over the years, we may not even realize that we are still holding on to it. But don't be fooled, it is still there and it can rear its ugly head at any time. So how can you fix a problem that you don't even know exists or realize what a major impact it has on your life? Look for the warning signs. The following are a few things to look for:

- If your relationship isn't going as well as you would like it to and you can't figure out why.
- You get angry at the drop of a hat.
- Your feelings get hurt very easily.
- You start to cry over small issues.
- You have problems with intimacy.
- You have ulcers or are on the verge of a nervous breakdown.

Never go to bed angry with your spouse or anyone else for that matter and you will see your marriage improve greatly.

The peaceful retreat
Our cat Smokey has a favorite hiding place under our bed. Any time he is afraid or wants to get away from his big brother, Jasper, he retreats to the bedroom. This is a place where he feels comfortable

and safe. He knows that everything will be all right as soon as he is nestled under the bed.

We need to treat our bedrooms the same way. Our bedroom needs to be a place of love, peace, security and intimacy. The bedroom is the last place you will see before you go to sleep and the first place that you will see when you awake. Never argue in the bedroom, but instead make sure that the time that you spend there is a positive experience.

We have never had and never will have a television in the bedroom. In the bedroom, we are either sleeping or focused on each other. It is difficult enough to find enough quality time alone with each other, and we prefer not to compete with a television set or anything else. We are not against this kind of entertainment; we just prefer that it not be brought into the bedroom.

When was the last time you and your spouse sat up in bed with the lights off at 1:00 in the morning and talked? Remember when you were a kid spending the night at your best friend's house? You were having so much fun that you didn't want to go to sleep. You stayed up with the flashlight on so that your friend's parents wouldn't know that you were still awake. Sometimes we still need those late-night talk sessions. Bedtime is a great time to release some of the things that are still on your mind as long as you play by the rules outlined in Section 3—"How to Help Your Partner Understand You."

Ask your spouse what he or she is thinking and then just lend your ear. We can remember about a year ago, we got to bed at around midnight and then started talking. It didn't take long until we were sitting up in bed talking about some of the recent events that had taken place in our lives. One thing led to the next until we found ourselves talking about our dreams with so much passion that they felt real (you will have a better idea as to how this kind of thing can take place after reading the chapter entitled "Growing together by dreaming together"). We talked until we couldn't stay awake any longer. What an awesome time that was! We had to get up very early that next morning, but for some reason we didn't feel tired the whole day.

Make a habit of going to bed before you get tired. That way you are more open to whatever happens next.

Keep your bedroom a refuge from the cares of day-to-day living. Never fight in your place of sanctuary. Let it be a place where you are reenergized and refreshed. Never let the sun go down on your anger and you will experience bedtime harmony—an oasis of love.

SECTION 3

How to Help Your Partner Understand You

CHAPTER 7

DISCOVER WHO YOU ARE AND WHO YOUR SPOUSE IS

Who are you really?

One of the keys to developing an excellent marital relationship is to discover who you are and who your spouse is. What makes both of you tick? On the surface this may sound like an easy thing to do. But in reality, you have to dig deep in order to discover the answer to this question. This may seem like a silly question, especially if you have been married for a number of years. You may think that you know your spouse perfectly well. After all, how could you not know someone you have spent so much of your time with? Knowing someone's likes, dislikes, mannerisms and temperament, however, is not the same as knowing the deepest desires of his or her heart. That is something that your spouse may not even know him- or herself. That is where you come in. You can help your spouse discover who he or she really is. You can also help your mate discover who he or she would like to become.

"The greatest good you can do for another
is not just to share your riches, but to reveal to him his own."
- Benjamin Disraeli -

Just because your spouse has been doing the same thing for years doesn't mean it is what he or she should be doing or would even like to be doing. Oftentimes we get into a rut or we become comfortable with the status quo. We may lose sight of the dreams that we once had. Once you have discovered the hidden wants and dreams of your spouse, you can help support your mate in becoming the best that he or she can be. Knowing your mate's dreams can help you to encourage and keep him or her on track. Life has much more to offer you and your spouse than what you have currently experienced. Life can even offer you more than you could have possibly dreamed of.

"It's a funny thing about life; if you refuse
to accept anything but the best, you very often get it."
- W. Somerset Maugham -

What are your spouse's goals, dreams and aspirations? This is an ongoing exercise, and it can be done together. Ask each other questions like, "What do you enjoy doing the most? What would you like to be doing? If you had no limitations, what would you do with your time and money? What makes you happy and feel good about yourself?" The answers to these questions are very important as they will help tell you who you are and what you should be doing in life.

Too many people define themselves by their jobs. I am a nurse, I am a plumber, I am an engineer, I am an attorney, I am an electrician, I am a teacher, I am a football player, etc. This may be what you do for a living, but it is not necessarily who you are. You are so much more than your job. Even if you love your job and are passionate about it, you are still more than what you do forty-plus hours per week.

When traveling, one of the first questions the person sitting next to us will ask is, "What do you do for a living?" Just once we would love to hear someone ask, "So what do you do for fun, or what are you passionate about?" If we started defining ourselves by our giftings instead of our jobs, we might stop comparing ourselves to other people.

We sometimes act as though the amount of our income or the position that we hold ranks our level of importance in society. Your importance in this world is not in how much you make, but rather how much you give. Give a lot and you are a lot. The next time someone asks us what we do for a living, we plan to say, "We are encouragers." We bet the conversation from that point on will become a little more interesting. Who knows, we may even be able to encourage that person.

We need to be very careful when we use the words *I am*. When we use those words, our subconscious mind picks up on it and makes it so. Make sure to use only the descriptions of the person that you want to be. This topic will be covered in more detail in the chapter entitled "Expanding your mind—the pursuit of knowledge and wisdom."

You are a very important person with a unique combination of talents, gifts and abilities. You have within you the ability to make a difference in the lives of so many people. There are people out there that you may or may not have met yet that need what you have to offer. Someone may have just had a major setback in his or her life and you will be able to *encourage* him or her. A family member may have just been verbally abused by her boss and you can show her *kindness*. A friend may have lost his job and you can *give* him money. And still another may have lost all hope, and you can increase her *faith*. You are uniquely you. There is no one else on the planet like you. Don't be selfish with your gifts and keep them all to yourself and your family. If you really want more out of life, then give more to others. As a bonus, when you give of yourself, you get ten times more in return.

Perhaps you don't know what your gifts are. The following exercise will help you to discover some of your gifts as well as the gifts of your spouse.

Part one—desires
Each of you should take out a pad of paper and write down all of the things that you would like to do with your life. What are the desires of your heart? Don't worry about being practical; just write down everything that comes to your mind. Spend a couple of days on this exercise and then exchange lists with your spouse.

"Everyone should carefully observe which way his heart draws him, and then choose that way with all his strength."
- Hasidic Saying -

Part two—attributes, skills and talent
Write down all of the positive attributes, skills, and talents that you see in your spouse. Be as specific as you can and give examples of each. This is the time for you to put on your private investigator's hat and look for all of the clues that will lead you to discovering your partner's talents, skills and desires. Watch your spouse and observe what he or she is good at. Notice how your mate interacts with other people. Listen to the stories that your spouse tells you about his or her dealings with others.

> **Darren and the talented little boy:** I (Darren) can remember kicking a soccer ball around with a boy about four years of age. Even though he had never played soccer before, his basic skills were very good. I could tell how much fun he was having trying to kick the ball past me. He was a thin kid full of energy. He had

a talent that if noticed and encouraged by his parents could develop into a skill that may gain him a college scholarship, an Olympic medal or even a professional career. Or he could be looked at as just a little boy burning off some excess energy. Why was it that I saw a soccer player when most people just saw a little boy running around on a warm summer day? I was looking for his talents.

The following is a list that you can use as a guide in helping you to identify your spouse's talents:

Leader	Encourager	Empathetic	Good Listener	Teacher
Artistic	Giver	Compassion	Wisdom	Serving Others
Kindness	Faith	Optimistic	Administration	Hospitality

Part three—encouragement
Make sure to continually look for areas of talent in your spouse. As you notice your mate using one of his or her talents, point it out and compliment your mate. Say things like,

- "Sally, you are a great listener. I noticed how well you were paying attention to Joyce when she was talking to you. You seemed to really make her feel better knowing that she had someone with whom she could talk to who really cared."
- "Bob, that was really great advice that you gave to Jarrod. You are a very wise man."
- "Debbie, that was an awesome meal you prepared for our guests last night. You really have the gift of hospitality. Everything was perfect and everyone had a great time."
- "Dan, you are really great with numbers and money. Have you ever thought of doing something along those lines for a living?"

When you discover what your spouse is good at and what he or she enjoys doing, make it a point to encourage him or her. Encourage your partner to use these talents and pursue his or her dreams. It should be your goal to be your mate's number-one supporter and fan.

Remember that your spouse has a lot more to offer you and others than what has been previously experienced. This is true even if you have been married for fifty years. We should always be experiencing growth throughout our life, expanding our horizons and making a difference in the lives of others.

*"What you do every day should contribute to giving your
life meaning. If it doesn't, why are you doing it?"*
- Don Hutcheson -

Different is good

One of the most common sources of confusion and conflict among married couples is the notion that our spouse should be just like us. They should think, act, respond, relate, believe and feel the same way that we do. Common comments are, "I can't figure out my wife" and "My husband doesn't understand me." Unfortunately, those two statements fit together hand-in-glove; they validate each other. Let's take a closer look at those two statements.

"I can't figure out my wife."

It is amazing to us how many men say that statement in one way or another. They are perplexed. They can't figure their wife out. Men will do something expecting a certain result, but get something completely different. And just when they think they have got it knocked, their wife throws them for a loop. They get frustrated, get into arguments and sometimes stop trying to figure their wife out altogether. They can't win. No matter what they do, it just doesn't seem to work out. Nothing they do is good enough.

"My husband doesn't understand me."

According to the previous statement, this statement must be true. If a man can't figure out his wife, then it is true that he doesn't understand her. This is a cause for much frustration and sometimes a feeling of loneliness for some women. They want to be understood by their husbands. She can't figure out why her husband doesn't understand her—after all, she always drops hints and she will even tell him what she wants from time to time. She wonders what it will take to get through that thick skull of his.

Genetic programming

How many times do we try to change our spouse only to end up frustrated? How often do we expect one thing, but get something totally different? Maybe you have even gotten frustrated or angry with your spouse because he or she didn't live up to your expectations. You try and you try, but you can't figure your spouse out. You suggest that your spouse read books or seek expert advice, yet after all of that, he or she still doesn't understand you. Many couples get confused and decide that they are incompatible. You are not incompatible; you are just different.

Who said that you had to figure your partner out or that he or she had to completely understand you? You and your spouse are different. You were designed for a slightly different purpose. Men and women have their own unique and different genetic programming. You do not need to be able to figure out these genetic programming differences, nor can you change these characteristics to make them more like yours. All you need to do is recognize these differences, respect and accept them, and learn how you can both benefit from them.

We all have different personalities

Not only do we have different talents, skills and abilities, but we also have different personality types. Our personality is a combination of our genetic makeup and our upbringing. Our personality makes us who we are. It makes us different and unique from everyone else. There are four basic personality types, and we are a combination of more than just one. The following is a brief description of each:

Sanguine. The Sanguine is the outgoing super-extrovert. These people are the cheerful and playful types. Having a good time and enjoying life is their motto. They tend to be relatively confident, make a good first impression and have a great outlook on life. They are oftentimes the life of the party. They can't wait to have fun. They are very charismatic and are never at a loss for words. They are great storytellers and people are drawn to them, however, they can also dominate a conversation, talk too often about themselves and are not very good listeners. They are restless, unpredictable and spontaneous to the point of lacking self-control. They tend to be naïve, childlike, and make emotional decisions (for example, they are often impulsive buyers). They can sometimes be a little overpowering and come on too strong.

Sanguine people are optimistic and rarely worry about the past or the future. They are very enjoyable, make friends easily, apologize quickly and are sympathetic, genuine and warm. It doesn't take much to amuse them or make them happy or excited; however, they can also become sad, angry and cry very easily. They are always smiling and friendly and love to share in others' happiness and sorrows. They enjoy being with people, but rarely keep in touch with them. They thrive on attention and approval. They are disorganized, always late, easily distracted and have a lot of unfinished projects.

Sanguine people will drop their clothes wherever they took them off, and they are constantly forgetting where they put their car keys. They don't always need closure and can even stop watching a movie three-quarters of the way through and not be concerned with how it ends. They are very hospitable and enjoy visiting and caring for the sick. They are the actors, entertainers, salespeople, public speakers, volunteer workers, leaders, foster parents, receptionists and athletes. The Sanguine is typically the last born or the youngest boy or girl.

Choleric. The Choleric is easily moved to express strong emotions. If you want results, the Choleric is the one to look for. Choleric people are the self-confident extroverts. They make decisions quickly and change them slowly. They are self-directed and self-sufficient. They are very optimistic and don't let fear get the best of them. They have a sharp mind and can think on their feet. They are intuitive and are a good judge of people. They have a lot of willpower, are organized, action and goal oriented, and are not easily discouraged. They rise above their circumstances and are not afraid of opposition—as a matter of fact they oftentimes welcome it. They will go to great lengths to prove themselves right.

There is no second place for the Choleric. They are great motivators and people want to follow them, however, they can be insensitive to the needs of others, have violent tempers and appear unemotional, apathetic and cold. They view tears as a sign of weakness. They wouldn't expect anyone to do something that they wouldn't do, however, they often make decisions for other people. They can be arrogant, unforgiving and revengeful, domineering, opinionated, prejudiced and hard to please. Cholerics are strong leaders, professionals, upper and middle level managers, attorneys, good athletes, administrators, heads of organizations, principals and high school teachers, executive assistants and visionaries. They tend to be firstborn or only children.

Melancholic. The Melancholic is more prone to sadness than the other personality types and can be relatively introverted. Melancholic people tend to be rather pessimistic, looking for the negative in things versus the positive, which would explain their rather dark mood. Melancholic people are perfectionists and pay close attention to details, which could explain why they are very hard on themselves and therefore are critical of others' imperfections. They are the ones that organize their closet according to color, style, season, etc. If you move something on a Melancholic's desk, it will be right back to its original spot before the end of the day. The opinions of others are very important to Melancholic people, and they fear rejection and ridicule. They are suspicious, sensitive and are easily hurt by others. They can have a violent temper when provoked and carry a grudge and/or seek revenge. For this reason, they can be difficult to get along with.

Melancholic people are very gifted, even genius-prone and gravitate toward creative, intellectual and/or analytical work. They are prone to deep intellectual and/or reflective thinking. When following their heart they will take on a career as an artist, musician, author, poet, fashion designer, engineer, accountant, architect, teacher (English, science, or math), chef, cosmetologist or interior decorator. They enjoy crafts, reading and watching athletic events (they would much rather watch than participate). They are self-disciplined, very thorough and hate leaving projects unfinished. They are theoretical types who are sometimes impractical and lack common sense. They are indecisive and hesitate to take on anything new. Melancholic people are extremely cautious regarding who they let into their world, but they are loyal and dependable friends. You can always count on them—they put others' needs above their own to the point of self-sacrifice.

Phlegmatic. Phlegmatic people are very introverted. They are easygoing, slow- paced and don't show a lot of emotion or empathy. They have a lot of friends, are good- natured, calm, dependable and pleasant to be around. They are the peacemakers, are diplomatic, passive and avoid conflict at all costs. The Phlegmatic tends to worry, be fearful and can lack self-confidence. They are good listeners, are not judgmental and only give advice when asked.

They can tend to be selfish, stingy, stubborn and have a superiority complex. They aren't as concerned with what others think of them and oftentimes lack tact. They have a dry sense of humor and rarely laugh out loud. Phlegmatic people seek stability and hate change. They can be pessimistic and discourage others from going against the flow. They plan their activities, are organized, efficient and dependable, however they rarely become leaders because they are indecisive and have the tendency to lack motivation. They are the super athletes, gourmet chefs, administrators, elementary teachers, counselors and administrative assistants. Phlegmatics tend to be middle children.

Most likely you and your spouse don't have the same exact personality mix. It is very possible that your personalities are very different, and in some cases the exact opposite. Not knowing and appreciating your differences can lead to a lot of frustration in your relationship. You may have even asked yourself, "Why can't my spouse be more . . . ?", "Why doesn't he or she do . . . ?", or "Why does he or she always . . . ?" What you are really saying is, "Why can't he or she be more like me?" The answer is, because your spouse is not you nor is he or she like you. Your spouse has his or her own unique personality. The differences in your personalities can be an awesome benefit to your marriage if you focus on their strengths instead of weaknesses.

> **Darren's view:** Donna and I are opposites in many ways. I am a results-oriented, self-directed Choleric with several Melancholic characteristics, while Donna is a compassionate, fun-loving Sanguine with some Phlegmatic characteristics. She is strong where I am weak and I am strong where she is weak. We are able to accept each other's weakness now that we have a better understanding as to why we act the way that we do.

If you are very much like your spouse, that can also be a challenge. Oftentimes the things that bother us the most about our spouse are the things that we don't like in ourselves. After all, if you don't like yourself, you will find it hard to like other people—especially people who are a lot like you.

> *"Each relationship you have with another person reflects the relationship you have with yourself."*
> - Alice Deville -

If you and your spouse have very similar personalities, you may have to focus on your weak points more than if your personalities were very different. Two Sanguines living together may have a lot of fun, but they can get into a lot of trouble if someone doesn't balance the checkbook and pay the bills on time or if they spend or give all of their money away. Someone needs to go against their basic personality and adopt some of the positive habits of one or more of the other personality types.

Our set personalities are no excuse for bad behavior

Our basic personalities may have been formed during our childhood, however, that doesn't give us an excuse to accept the negative and potentially damaging aspects of our personality. Saying, "I know that I get extremely angry at the drop of a hat, but that is part of my nature" is a cop-out. You shouldn't try and change your personality or become someone that you're not, but you should try to become the best person that you can be.

> *"Always be a first-rate version of yourself, instead of a second-rate version of somebody else."*
> - Judy Garland -

Identify and work on your weak areas. If you are a selfish and stingy Phlegmatic, start to give more to others and discover that you will end up receiving more than you gave in return. If you are a pessimistic Melancholic, make a daily habit of being thankful for what you have, focusing on the positive and trying to find the good in every situation. If you are a Choleric with an explosive temper, be very conscious of it and give yourself time to think things through before you act, react or say something that can damage your relationships. If you are a Sanguine who loves to dominate a conversation, you will be well served by concentrating on becoming a better listener. Changing our negatives into positives isn't easy and it will take time and a lot of effort, but the end result is well worth it.

The differences between the sexes

Not only do we each have different personalities, but there are also very distinct differences between men and women. This is old news; however, we often forget how different we really are. Just like our personalities, no man or woman fits 100 percent into any one category.

For a man, his primary need is more physical, whereas a woman's primary need is affection. He will show his love through physical intimacy, whereas she will equate love with a touch, kiss, hug, conversation and hearing that she is loved and appreciated. More will be discussed regarding these and other primary needs in the chapter entitled "Discover your spouse's desires."

You may have heard the saying that the only difference between men and boys is the price of their toys. When little boys get together they will almost always play games. When little girls get together they will talk most of the time. These basic tendencies don't change much as we get older. Men still need to play and women still need conversation. For that reason it is good for us to take a more active role in fulfilling at least part of this need. Men need to learn to be more effective communicators with their wives. Women need to let their husbands play golf or go fishing. You may even want to go with him every once in a while or discover other activities that you both enjoy and can do together. This is a great way for husband and wife to bond as long as you agree not to become competitive or critical with each other. Take a greater interest in your spouse's activities and you will find that the number and/or size of your differences will decrease.

Women are more in tune with their emotions, thoughts and dreams. Men are more inclined to be logical, detail oriented and factual. Men tend to be more focused on one task at a time and can sometimes lose sight of higher priorities. A man may get so wrapped up in his work that he forgets to look at the clock to realize that he said he would be home a half-hour ago. Everything that needs to be done is compartmentalized in his mind, and he quickly moves from one completed project to the next. His great focus makes him efficient; however, it also has a similar effect as blinders have on a horse. He doesn't notice everything that is going on in the environment around him. A woman, on the other hand, tends to be more multi-tasked. She is very aware of everything in her environment, which could in part explain her intuitive nature.

Men are more project and results driven, whereas women place a higher value on relationships. That would explain in part why the vast majority of romance novels are purchased by women. Most women love dramas, and most men prefer action movies. Women are also very interested in the lives of other people. A woman may not care to watch a sporting event on TV, but would love to go see one of her friend's children play soccer.

Women are nurturers and men are conquerors. Take the whole shopping experience, for example. It is no secret that most men and women have a different view of shopping.

Darren's shopping conquest: Most men cannot get away with this, but since I have good fashion sense and know what Donna likes, I will oftentimes pick up outfits for her. When I go into the clothier, I have a pretty good idea of what I am looking for. I look through everything very quickly to see if something catches my eye. If I see something that I like, I look for her size, then proceed to find a matching blouse and shoes. I can walk into the store and one half-hour later walk out with two new outfits in hand. Donna, on the other hand, will spend a lot more time and will even pick something out just to show me how ugly it is. I am so focused that the ugly articles of clothing don't even register in my mind.

Many women will continue that strategy at every store at the mall. For many women, shopping or talking to friends are an emotional release just like watching football, engaging in hobbies or taking on projects are for a man.

Men derive much of their sense of worth from what they do—their jobs, careers or projects. Women derive their feelings of worth from their relationships with friends, family and most importantly their spouse. Because women place such a high value on relationships, they are more in tune with the quality of relationships including their own. We will get asked often by women if our relationship is really as great as it seems. To this day, neither one of us has been asked that same question by a man.

Ask any man to rate his marriage on a scale from one to ten and you will find that his rating will be at least a point or two higher than what his wife would give it. He may think that his marriage is good because the "facts" tell him so. They live in a nice house, drive a nice car, have food on the table and clothes on their back, the bills are paid and their kids are well taken care of. She may think that their marriage could use a lot of work because her "feelings" tell her so. He rarely compliments her, he seems more interested in the basketball game than in her, he only gives her flowers when he has done something wrong and they don't spend much time together. So if he gives their marriage a nine while she rates it a seven, who is right? Just as a chain is only as strong as its weakest link, a marriage is only as strong as the lesser of the two opinions.

The differences in our upbringing

We all grew up in different surroundings, in different homes, and with different parents. These environmental factors played a major role in forming who we are today. Many of the conflicts that arise among couples can be traced back to the way in which they grew up. The following stories demonstrate how our childhood can affect our marriages.

Sally and John—fight or flight

Sally was raised to never yell at someone or lose her temper. Whenever her parents' discussions would get too heated, they would drop the conversation, give each other some space and time to cool off and then proceed in a calm manner at a later time. The absolute worst thing that one could do would be to yell at the other person. That would be extremely disrespectful.

John, on the other hand, came from a very expressive household. Everyone said what was on his or her mind and expressed his or her feelings with great emotion. Holding back one's feelings was a sign of mistrust. Heated discussions were the norm, and it was a sign of great disrespect if someone would walk out in the middle of a conversation (fight).

Sally and John fell in love and got married. Sally loves John's passion and John appreciates Sally's even-mannered calmness. The first time they get into an argument, however, John raises his voice and Sally, sensing that things could get out of hand, walks out of the room. This makes John even more upset, and he follows her speaking even louder. She knows that they need time to cool off and he knows that they need to talk things through. They both get frustrated and can't figure out why their spouse acts the way that he or she does.

This kind of problem can exist and cause frustration in a marriage for years, possibly even for the length of the marriage. One of the primary reasons that a conflict like this can continue for years is because we ask the wrong questions and come up with the wrong answers. We forget to put on our private investigator's hat and discover what it is that causes our spouse to act and react the way that he or she does. John may think that Sally is always trying to avoid confrontation and would rather ignore their problems than openly discuss them. Sally may feel that John doesn't care about her feelings because he is so quick to yell at her and get into a fight. The real reason for their conflict may be as simple as the way that each of them defines respect. Sally feels that it is disrespectful to yell at the people you love and care about, and John feels that it is disrespectful to walk out on a discussion with the people that you love and care about.

Scott, Kim and the money war

Scott's family was very good with money. They didn't make much, but what they had grew larger every year. Scott was taught that he needed to respect his money. He was led to believe that money was like a living thing and that if he didn't treat it well, it would leave. At the age of four, his parents opened a savings account for him. They then opened a checking account for him when he was nine years old and taught him how to write checks and balance the checkbook. Scott's Mom was in charge of paying all of the bills, and the family often talked about ways to save, invest and make their money work for them.

Scott's parents were very conservative and only bought the things that they needed with the exception of vacations. They didn't use credit cards, but preferred to pay cash for everything. Scott's Dad told him to be careful what he spent his money on and taught him about opportunity costs. He also told him that it was well worth it to spend his money on experiences and education. His family always went on great vacations and they had an extensive library. At least four times every year Scott's parents would get together to plan out their financial strategy.

Kim's family, on the other hand, were bargain hunters. They would often brag about how much money they saved at the mall that evening. They made a pretty good income, but never had anything left over at the end of the month. They would buy things that they wanted but really didn't need and would justify the purchase by saying that the item was 50 percent off or that they saved an additional 15 percent by opening up a store credit account. They had several credit cards and used them often. Kim's Dad was in charge of paying all of the bills, and the family often talked about how broke they were and how hard they had to work for their money.

Kim spent every penny that she earned and was a spontaneous buyer just like her parents (although she called it bargain shopping thinking that she was being frugal). She never balanced her checkbook, but always had a rough idea how much money was in the account. Every now and then she would receive an overdraft notice in the mail. Because her family spent everything that they made, they always went on budget vacations, if any at all. Her parents told her that it was a waste of money to spend a lot on a fancy vacation every year. Her Mom and Dad never invested in their companies matching 401(k) because they said that they couldn't afford it.

Scott was instantly attracted to Kim. She always looked great and was a sharp dresser. Every time they went out, Kim was wearing a new outfit. He loved how spontaneous she was, and they always had a great time together. Kim was impressed by how organized and in control Scott was. He was very good at planning their dates, was always on time and was the kind of stable man she was looking for. They got married a year and a half later. Shortly after they got married, one of Kim's credit card bills arrived in the mail. Scott opened the envelope and almost fell off the chair. "Three thousand, nine hundred seventy-two dollars! There must be some kind of mistake." He yells for Kim to come in the kitchen immediately.

Scott in a very upset voice asks, "What is this?" Kim couldn't figure out why he was so upset with her. She just bought a few things that she "needed". To keep the peace, Kim reassured Scott that she would pay the card off by the end of the year. However, old habits are hard to break. Not only was the card not paid off by the end of the year, but it was maxed out at five thousand dollars. Scott was furious. He thought of all the things that they could be doing with that money. He could be making 12 percent interest instead of paying 15 percent. He looked at the credit card as being a net loss of 27 percent on their money, while Kim wasn't worried because she could easily afford the monthly payments.

Scott expected Kim to be the one who paid all of the bills and balanced the checkbook because that was his Mom's job. Kim expected the opposite. Scott was always focusing on how to invest their money, whereas Kim looked for ways to spend it. Most of their fights seemed to be about money. She couldn't understand why he wouldn't let her buy the things that made her happy, and he couldn't understand why she took no interest in their financial future.

When in doubt—ask

Sometimes the best solutions are the simplest ones. In short, tell each other how certain actions and/or reactions make you feel. We are usually good at showing our feelings, but do a poor job of communicating them. Sally and John need to sit down and tell each other how certain things that they do make them feel and why. Scott and Kim need to sit down and go through their finances together. Scott needs to understand why Kim feels the compulsion to spend, and Kim needs to understand how her current spending is sabotaging their future financial well-being.

While opening up to your spouse in this manner, make sure that you listen intently and that you don't try to down play your spouse's feelings by telling your mate that he or she shouldn't feel the way that he or she does. Your spouse's feelings are his or her feelings, period. Once you understand your partner's feelings and your spouse understands yours, you will both be better equipped to work through your differences. Once you know what is hurtful to your spouse, you will be more conscious of not continuing that behavior. After all, by hurting your mate, you are only hurting yourself.

We are sure that you would agree that a marital relationship is a very complicated thing. We have different talents and abilities, we each have a different personality, men and women think differently, and we grew up in different environments. We have all of these differences yet we often think that we should be able to get along perfectly without much effort.

Irreconcilable differences

One of the most common reasons stated on divorce papers is *irreconcilable differences.* That floors us. There is no such thing as an irreconcilable difference. There are only unknown, misunderstood, unappreciated and God-given differences. All of the challenges that we face in a marriage can be resolved if you want to find a solution. It is possible to live in peace and harmony with someone who is the exact opposite of you. The question is, are you willing to take the time and effort to find this common ground? Not being able to get past our differences is a common sign of selfishness. We want our way and we are unwilling to change, adapt, compromise or sacrifice. That kind of attitude will never enable you to have an awesome relationship with your spouse, or anyone else for that matter.

"Love is what's left in a relationship
after all the selfishness has been removed."
- Cullen Hightower -

Is it a difference of opinion or a personal rejection?

Many couples don't realize that it is perfectly acceptable to agree to disagree. One person doesn't have to be right and the other wrong. It is possible for you to have different opinions and both be right. In order for one to accept this kind of disagreement he or she must not take it personally. Too often we take these disagreements or differences of opinion as a personal rejection. We forget that our spouse is rejecting our idea, not us. It is important that you see the difference.

A waitress at a café goes from table to table asking people if they would like a cup of coffee. The first person she approaches says no. The second does as well. The third person that she asks also rejects the offer. Does the waitress try to talk the customers into trying a cup? Does she take the rejection personally thinking that they must not like her or that she is doing something wrong? Does she get mad at the people because they don't want or like coffee? Does she think that there is something wrong with them because they don't want any coffee?

Accept the fact that you and your partner will disagree about many things. How you handle these disagreements will determine your peace of mind and the health of your relationship. The following are suggestions that you should try, in order of importance.

- **Everyone's happy.** This is the outcome that you should always strive for. It isn't necessarily the easiest choice, but it is by far the best. Think of a solution that you can both be happy with. You want to vacation in the mountains and your spouse wants to vacation on the beach. You want to go to Denver and your partner wants to go to the Bahamas. Instead of picking one over the other, pick a place that you would both love to visit. Perhaps you would both love to tour Italy.
- **You are both happy with your independent decisions.** You are picking out furniture for the house and you can't agree on the exact style and colors. You want contemporary and your spouse wants traditional. If you cannot agree on something that you both love, then perhaps you could agree that you would both get what you want. One room of the house is yours to decorate as you see fit and another room belongs to your spouse.

This is okay as long as neither of you dislikes the other's choice. Otherwise you could both lose because you can't stand that one room of the house.

- **You can both live with it.** Sometimes a compromise is in order. You think the kids should be home by 7:00 P.M. on a school night and your mate thinks that they should be able to stay out until 9:00 P.M. A compromise that you can both live with might be 8:00 P.M.

  In some situations a compromise can be the worst choice. It may cause you both to feel like you didn't get what you wanted. A compromise is perfectly acceptable if you both walk away feeling like you have won; however, it can be very unfulfilling if you both think that you have lost. There is almost always a win-win solution to every situation. It will take more time and effort to find it, but it will be well worth it in the end.

- **You decide to let your spouse have what he or she wants.** If a couple can't reach a decision using any of the above methods, then one of them can decide to forfeit his or her desires. This may sound like a bad thing, but if done with the right attitude, it can have amazing results. More will be discussed regarding this topic in the chapter entitled, "Discovering your spouse's desires."

The differences between the sexes and in our talents, skills, abilities, personalities and upbringing make life exciting. You can choose to become frustrated by these differences or you can recognize them as being part of what makes us human.

For you to understand your spouse and for him or her to understand you is not about figuring out *why* they are different, but rather to discover *what* these differences are and then learn to appreciate and live with them. Of course, this fact-finding mission is more fruitful when you and your partner are able to engage in an open and loving dialogue. How to experience this level of communication will be discussed in the following chapter.

CHAPTER 8

EXPERIENCING FULFILLING COMMUNICATION

Communication

When couples are asked what they think is most important in a good marriage, communication will undoubtedly be on their short list. Everyone would agree that communication is a very important part of any relationship, especially a marriage. We all know how to communicate, don't we? If we all think that we know how to communicate, then why is communication such a huge problem area in marriages today?

First of all, many people confuse communication with talking. Talking is a part of communication; however, it is not the most important part. Secondly, men and women are very different in the way they communicate. Unfortunately, these differences are not always known by the opposite sex and hence the reason for many communication problems. What makes things worse is the fact that we may not even know ourselves what we need from our spouse in the area of communication.

When listening to men and women talk about the communication side of their relationship, two very different stories are told. Many men say that their wife is always on their case or nagging them all the time. Many women on the other hand say that their husband never listens to them or doesn't understand them. These are obviously indications that we do not always know how to communicate effectively with the opposite sex. Fortunately, communication skills can be learned, and anything that can be learned can be improved upon.

The communication differences between men and women are evident even at a very young age. Give a little boy and a little girl a toy truck and you will notice how differently they play with them. The boy won't talk much. He will most likely make a lot of truck noises and sound effects. The girl on the other hand will carry on a conversation, especially when playing with other children. She may ask the imaginary driver where he would like to drive. She may even ask other kids if they would like to play with her.

Girls tend to gather in smaller, more intimate groups where everyone tries to get along well with each other, while boys gather in much larger groups and focus on competition. Older boys and girls also act differently toward the same gender if someone gets hurt. Their empathy skills are very different.

If you have both girls and boys, you probably already realize how different they are, yet we oftentimes forget that we still have our differences even as adults. We don't start out different and then end up the same.

The average woman speaks approximately twice as many words in a day as a man does. This would indicate that she requires more conversation than he does. Knowing this can help a woman to understand that if her husband doesn't seem to want to talk, it doesn't mean that he doesn't care about her. It might mean that he has already used up his daily word quota. At that point his conversation will be more for his wife's benefit than for his own.

Left brained versus right brained

Recent studies have shown in part why communication differences occur between men and women. These studies have shown that men listen with the left side of their brain, while women listen with both the left and right side of their brain. This is a very important distinction. Understanding why men and women communicate differently will reduce some of the frustration experienced during communication and enable us to give our spouse what he or she needs.

The left side of our brain

The left side of our brain is responsible for our logical and analytical thinking. This is the area where we process facts and figures. The left side of our brain allows us to analyze, debate and solve problems. We wouldn't have engineers, architects, doctors, astronauts, accountants or many other fields of discipline that require numbers, facts and figures if it weren't for the left side of our brain.

The right side of our brain

The right side of our brain is responsible for our creative thinking. This is the area where we explore our emotions and imagination. The right side of our brain allows us to create wonderful things. We wouldn't have artists, musicians, actors, poets, fashion designers or many other occupations where creativity, emotions and imagination are involved if it weren't for the right side of our brain.

No one is 100 percent left brained or 100 percent right brained. We all have a different mix of the two. It may make sense to think that two predominately left-brained people or two predominantly right-brained people would get along better than a couple who are opposites. One might think that they would have more in common and therefore relate better to each other. That is not necessarily the case.

Darren on the left and Donna on the right: Donna and I are very different. She is very right brained and I am very left brained. These differences complement us very well. Where I am weak, she is strong. Where she is weak, I am strong. The problems in relationships come not because people are different, but rather when partners don't recognize and appreciate these differences. We love the fact that we are so different. And since we allow each other to express ourselves freely without the fear of ridicule or judgment, we have evolved in our relationship. I have become more right brained and Donna has become more left brained. We notice our differences, appreciate them and even want to develop similar characteristics in our own personality.

It is great when you come to the stage in your relationship when you look at your spouse and say that you want to be more like him or her. This is the appreciation that is expressed in the Honeymoon Marriage.

What do men and women want?

Men and women want the same thing. They both want to be happy, feel loved, needed, and appreciated. Well, if husband and wife both want the same thing, then it should be no problem giving your spouse what he or she wants and needs, right? Unfortunately, what we want and need in order to feel loved, needed and appreciated may not be what our spouse wants and needs in order to feel loved, needed and appreciated. We have to learn how to communicate with our spouse in a way that gives our partner what he or she wants and needs. While it may be true that opposites attract, the differences in the way we communicate can cause more harm than good if not recognized. Learn what your partner wants and needs and you will greatly improve the quality of your relationship.

What women want

A woman wants her husband to listen empathetically without interruption. She wants him to understand her feelings and relate to the concerns of her day. She wants to know that her husband cares about her and will always be there for her. Women want men to listen with the right side of their brain.

A man, listening with the left side of his brain, hears his wife saying, "I have a problem and I would like you to solve it for me as quickly as possible." As soon as her husband hears the problem and figures out a solution, he interjects (interrupts) with his opinion. His wife takes his interruption (interjection) as a sign that he doesn't want to listen to her, that her concerns are not valid and that he thinks that she doesn't need to feel that way. Instead of feeling better by sharing her feelings, she may feel worse because the one that she loves the most is not willing to "listen" to her. She may even say, "You never listen to me." The husband, having no idea what that statement means, (thinking that he *is* listening to her) will disagree, and an argument is sure to follow.

This argument can have no winner because both parties are right and both parties are wrong but they just don't realize it yet. So what is a husband to do in a situation like this? Answer—give her his undivided attention. Try to understand her situation. Validate her feelings by saying, "I understand how you could feel that way." Don't interrupt her, or offer advice or a solution. In most cases, she doesn't want her problem to be solved. She just wants to share her life experiences with her husband in a way that makes her feel understood, respected, supported, cherished and loved.

What men want

Men on the other hand, want a solution to their problems, but only when they ask for one. A man wants to figure out his problems on his own. For this reason he may retreat to an isolated location, read the paper, work on a hobby or watch TV. Being alone or distracted helps him to better sort out his problems. The answer may come to him in the middle of waxing the car.

His wife cannot understand this action because when she has something on her mind she wants to talk about it. She may even think that he is avoiding her. Men and women think differently. Men try to find solutions and pride themselves in being able to figure things out. Perhaps that is why many men have a hard time stopping and asking for directions. They just assume that they can figure it out on their own. Their problems are also in many ways challenges or a mystery to be solved. You wouldn't tell the ending of a book or movie to someone that hasn't seen or read it yet, would you? Unfortunately, this is what many women do to their husbands. Until he asks for help, he is still working through the situation. His wife's offer of unsolicited advice may be taken as a direct attack on his ability to solve his own problems. He interprets her advice as saying, " You can't solve this problem on your own," or "I don't think you know what you are doing," or "I could do a better job myself." He wants to feel trusted, needed, appreciated and loved.

Direct versus indirect
Another potential area for frustration among couples is the manner in which they make their requests known. Most men are direct and to the point, oftentimes to the point of being blunt or lacking tact. A man may not consider how his wife will react or how his comments will effect her feelings. He may say something like, "That outfit doesn't look good on you" just as they are walking out the door to go somewhere. He may tell her that she is getting fat or any other comment that may be true yet requires a more delicate approach. He may fail to reassure her that he loves and appreciates her prior to offering constructive criticism. Men, make sure to offer your input at the opportune time. Give her love and affection prior to constructive criticism and handle your comments or requests in a much gentler manner than you would with one of the guys.

Women on the other hand can communicate in quite the opposite fashion. Many women are indirect in the way they make their needs known. They may not come right out and say what is on their mind, but rather drop hints, talk around an issue, or expect their husbands to know what they are thinking or how they are feeling. This causes a lot of frustration for women who are disappointed because their expectations were not met. When communicating with a man, a woman needs to spell it all out so that there can be no room for misinterpretation. Women, don't assume that he should know what to do, how to do it and how often it should be done. Tell him the way you would tell someone how to bake a cake—step by step, ingredient by ingredient.

Timing is everything
For the most part, men and women want the same thing. They just want it at different times. Women want suggestions and advice, but

not while they are talking. When they are talking, they want their husband to be a sounding board. After a woman is done talking, she will oftentimes feel much better. Women want to feel that they have been heard. Men want suggestions when they are talking, but not when they are silent. When they are talking, they want their wife to be an empathetic counselor or coach. Men want to be reassured that they are the best, can do anything, and that their partner is proud of them.

Also, make sure that you have your spouse's undivided attention before you start talking. One way that you can tell if you have your mate's undivided attention is to look into his or her eyes. You can usually tell if your mate is listening or not. Talk to your spouse while he or she is in a different room and your conversation might just bounce off the wall right past your partner. Your spouse might hear you, but he or she is not paying attention and will most likely not remember the conversation.

Listening intently

When you are with your spouse, be there in body and in mind. Give your mate 100 percent of your focus and don't be thinking of anything else that may need your attention. Undivided attention is what everyone longs for but few receive. This stems from our need to be understood.

Effective listening is one of the greatest skills one can ever hope to master. Talking is easy, anyone can do it. But effective listening is a skill that few people possess. Listening is hard work. It requires a conscious effort. To be an effective listener, you must truly want to know what the other person has to say. You must want to understand where the speaker is coming from, what he or she is feeling and thinking as well as why. Effective listening is the act of an investigator and not that of a judge. It is not your duty to determine if the speaker is right or wrong, but rather to hear why it is that he or she feels the way that he or she does.

Effective listening is free from interruptions and the feeling of being rushed. You cannot listen effectively when you are thinking of the next thing that you are going to say. Your focus has to be on the words that are coming out of the person's mouth and nothing else.

People love to spend time with good listeners. If people's listening skills are fine-tuned, they will even attract people to them. Good listeners will often hear, "I can't believe I'm telling you this. I have never told this to anyone before."

*"The reason why we have two ears and only one mouth
is that we may listen the more and talk the less."*
- Zeno of Citium -

Effective listening doesn't mean that you cannot talk. Just the opposite is true; however, your conversation will be directed toward what the other person is telling you. Your *effective listening* conversation can be in the form of questions. Questions cause the other person to open up to you even more. By asking questions, the other person will sense that you not only want to listen to him or her, but that you care about him or her as well. Once someone knows that you care about him or her, your conversation and even your relationship will go to a deeper level. That doesn't mean that your conversation should be an interrogation with a string of questions. It just means that you should care enough about the speaker and what he or she is saying that you can't help but probe deeper for even more information. Great effective listening statements would include,

- "Really? Tell me more."
- "How did that make you feel?"
- "What else did you do?"
- "That must have made you feel terrible/good."
- "I can understand why you are upset/excited."
- "That's great, congratulations! I knew you could do it. What are your future plans?"

Just make sure to be real. Effective listening requires sincerity. People can sense when you are sincere or if you have an agenda. Animals aren't the only creatures on the planet that have a sixth sense. We humans can also sense things above and beyond our sense of touch, smell, taste, sight and hearing. This sixth sense is often referred to as a gut feeling or our intuition. If the only reason you are listening to someone is because you are waiting your turn to get your two cents in, the other person will know it. Put aside your needs until your partner feels like he or she has been heard, then and only then is it your turn.

Most people if given a safe and caring environment eventually share their innermost thoughts and feelings, but not necessarily at the time that they happen. Men often time need time to come around and share their feelings. Maybe they want to think things through first or maybe they aren't exactly sure what they are feeling and don't want to come off sounding "dumb" by sharing thoughts that are not well thought through. This is foreign to many women because they tend to be more in tune with their feelings and take pleasure in sharing them as they happen.

At first contact, a woman may jump right in with, "You will never guess what happened to me today . . ." She will go into great detail right down to the way that it made her feel. A man may become perplexed by how quickly his wife equates an act with her feelings. He may even question the validity of her feelings by saying that he doesn't think the offender meant to hurt her and that she is just overreacting. While that may be a "logical" hypothesis, the fact of the matter is, she *does* feel the way she feels and she just wants to be heard. By being heard (her definition, not his), she will automatically feel better and be able to better ascertain whether or not her feelings are justified. This is her way of working through her problems.

A woman wants to speak and then come to her own conclusions, whereas a man wants to come to his own conclusions and then speak. We have to trust each other in our differences. A woman noting that her husband seems preoccupied and wants to be caring and nurturing may ask him what is on his mind or what is wrong. His response will be neutral at best by saying phrases like "nothing" or "I'm fine." For a woman to respond in this way might mean that she is upset with the person asking the question. For a man, he just hasn't had the time to mull over the events of the day enough to be able to know how he feels or if his feelings are warranted. Only when he has "figured it out" will he open up and share his thoughts. That is, if his wife will give him enough space and time to "work things out." If instead she presses harder by saying, "I know something is wrong, what is it?" this will most likely frustrate him, causing him to repeat himself or say something to push her away or cause her to back off. She in turn will take this as a sign that he doesn't care about her and that their relationship is in trouble. If she then fires back with her reaction (feelings) to his reaction, he may become angry and not open up at all.

Human beings can become very stubborn and angry, and arguments can oftentimes burn the communication bridge. If we understand that we act and react differently to the same type of situations, we can avoid many of these conflicts.

Grandma's wisdom: As mentioned before, my (Darren's) Grandma used to say to us, "Kids, don't fight. No one wins when you fight. If I ask Pa for something and he says no, no is no. I leave it alone. He will then come back to me and ask what it was again that I wanted. If we had argued about it, that would be the end, but I always get what I want."

When a man says that nothing is wrong and is challenged, he may dig his heels in and never open up. If he is allowed to retreat and think things through, he will oftentimes give his wife the open conversation that she wants, needs and deserves.

Be careful of how you communicate when you are angry
It is perfectly acceptable to talk to each other when your emotions are high as long as your emotions are directed toward someone other than your spouse. This requires a lot of self-control. Our normal reaction is to tell someone off as soon as we are hurt or offended by that person. It is wise to allow yourself a cooling-off period, a time when you can think about what you are going to say. Getting into a heated discussion backed by strong emotions can be very dangerous. It will almost always cause the other person to become defensive and lead to an argument or fight. Each person may even say harmful things that they don't really mean, and once you speak, you can never take back your words. That doesn't mean that you should suppress your feelings or not tell your spouse exactly how you feel, it just means that you need to make sure that the timing is right and that you have cooled off enough to carry on a civil and loving conversation.

> *"Anyone can become angry—that is easy. But to be angry*
> *with the right person, to the right degree, at the right time,*
> *for the right purpose, and in the right way—this is not easy."*
> *- Aristotle -*

Also, get rid of the notion that you always have to be right. We are all very different and unique. We need to realize that these differences are part of who we are and not some character flaw. Just because your spouse acts or reacts differently to circumstances or sees things differently than you doesn't mean that he or she is wrong and you are right. As mentioned earlier, there is nothing wrong with agreeing to disagree.

> *"Honest differences are often a healthy sign of progress."*
> *- Mahatma Gandhi -*

For communication to be effective, conversation needs to be somewhat on our own terms. Don't be afraid to ask for permission to talk, offer advice, etc. The following are some examples:

Susie: "How was your day?"

Mike: "It was okay."

Susie: "Would you like to talk about it?"

Mike: "Not really."

Susie: "Well, if you change your mind or want to talk later, you know I am always here for you. I love you."

Mike: "Thanks, I appreciate that. I love you, too."

Arlene: "I had an incredible day!"

Steve: "Really, how's that?"

Arlene: "I really need to talk to you about it, but it will take me quite a while to explain everything. Is now a good time?"

Steve: "I have a couple of things to do first and I am afraid that if I leave them unfinished I won't be able to give you my full attention. Would it be okay if we talk in an hour?"

Arlene: "That will be fine."

Steve: "Thanks for understanding. I love you."

Arlene: "I love you, too."

Later that evening . . .

Arlene: She tells the events of the day with great detail, incorporating her emotions as she paints the picture.

Steve: He hears the problem, analyzes the situation and formulates a solution but keeps his opinions to himself for now. "Wow, you have had an incredible day. I can understand why you feel the way you do."

Arlene: "Yeah, and that is only the beginning. You should have heard . . ."

Steve: He knows the solution and how she can solve the problem very easily but again just listens. "What else happened?"

Arlene: She continues her story.

Steve: "I know that you are able to work through this on your own, but if you would like my opinion, I would be more that happy to share it with you."

Arlene: "No, I feel much better. Thanks for listening to me. You are so wonderful."

It is difficult for most men to hear their wife tell them about her problems without offering a solution. It is almost unnatural for him to just listen and keep his opinions to himself until asked. It takes a conscious effort to develop these skills, and they will improve with practice. Likewise it is unnatural for a woman to allow her husband some time and space to come around and share his feelings. She will also improve her masculine communication skills with practice and by not taking his retreat personally.

> ***Our dinner celebration:*** I (Darren) recently hit a milestone in my life. Donna had prepared a surprise for me to celebrate the occasion. She took me by the hand, told me to close my eyes, and walked me into the dining room. I opened my eyes and saw a romantic setting for two—china, silverware, crystal, the works. The only light in the room was coming from the two candles that were placed in the middle of the table. She had also cooked a wonderful meal, better than any restaurant could prepare. As we started eating she noticed that I was a little preoccupied and asked if there was something wrong. I told her that I was fine, that I just had a lot on my mind. I didn't realize it until several days later that she never probed further to find out what was wrong. She knew that I would tell her before the night was over.
>
> After dinner she told me to go sit on the couch. When I walked over to the couch I found a congratulations card lying on top of a bag of almond kisses. What a nice surprise that evening was. About an hour or so later I told her what was on my mind and why I seemed preoccupied. Had she insisted on an answer during dinner, I don't know what I would have said. All of my thoughts were so jumbled in my mind that it took me a while to sort them all out.
>
> Yes, communication is important in a marriage, but what is more important is giving your partner what he or she needs when he or she needs it. During our candlelight dinner, I needed some time to sort things out and Donna gave me what I needed. Not to mention that the food was great as well (they say that the quickest way to a man's heart is through his stomach). There have been several times when I was watching television or working on a project that I turned the television off or stopped what I was doing so that I could give my wife my undivided attention. This act alone gave her 90 percent of what she needed. She needed to be reassured that she is cared for and valued more than anything else in my life. After that, the communication was just the icing on the cake.

The Honeymoon Marriage is filled with meaningful and timely communication. Say what you mean and mean what you say. Let each other know exactly what you want, how you want it, and how often. Don't pretend that your spouse can read your mind or your emotions. Be mature and secure enough in your relationship not to be afraid of offending your partner when you tell him or her what is on your mind. Listen when you are busy and talk when you are tired. Be aware of your mate's needs and place them above your own. Talk freely, listen intently and empathize often. Understand each other and thoroughly enjoy each other's company.

CHAPTER 9

LEARN THE LOST ART OF UNDERSTANDING BODY LANGUAGE

In the last chapter we discussed the importance of getting your partner's attention before talking to him or her. We even said that it was best if you looked into your partner's eyes while you were talking to make sure that he or she was with you.

Our lives are filled with so many distractions. Most of these distractions are external, however, many of them are internal—the thoughts that occupy our minds. Talking to someone in and of itself may not be enough to snap him or her out of a trance. Face-to-face, one-on-one communication is always the best way to fully understand and bond with another human being.

Recognizing the importance of nonverbal communication
You may have heard that 80 percent of communication is nonverbal. We don't know if the percentage is that high, but there is no doubt in our minds that our nonverbal communication is extremely important. What you see is oftentimes a clearer representation of reality than what you hear. "A picture is worth a thousand words."

Talking on the telephone is great, however, it is difficult to properly express yourself or relate to the other person over the phone. It is very important to be able to see the other person while talking to him or her. That way you can read your partner's body language. You can see the expressions on your partner's face, his or her posture and mood, and to what degree your partner is accepting what you are saying. That way you can feel like you are truly communicating with him or her and not just talking and listening.

For communication to be as effective as it can be, it has to be on a level that is deeper than just talking and listening. It has to be on the level of relating, understanding, and caring. It is not good enough for us to know that we have been heard. We want to know that we have been understood. And body language will tell you very quickly whether or not you are getting through to your spouse.

Getting good at reading body language takes practice, and it is an important component in the Honeymoon Marriage. It is important to know that your partner understood what you just told him or her. Otherwise you are setting yourself up for disappointment, frustration, and a potential argument.

We can usually tell if people are with us or not. Sometimes it is obvious by what they say. They will interrupt in midsentence, they will say quick words like yeah or uh-huh, they will jump in as soon as there is a pause, or they will quickly change the subject, usually talking about themselves. Some of the body language signs that people are not listening are when they become restless, they play with their hands or you lose eye contact with them (they start looking around, looking at their hands, or moving things around).

Show respect and listen to your spouse when he or she is talking to you. Be there in mind, body and spirit. As mentioned in the previous chapter, let your spouse know if the timing isn't right and set up a time that works best for both of you. If you notice that your partner isn't "with you" when you are talking, reel him or her back in gently. Say something like "You seem a little preoccupied. Would it be better if we talked at a later time?" After all, there is no point in talking if no one is listening.

If you are the kind of person who doesn't notice when your spouse gets a haircut, new outfit, or loses ten pounds, then you will definitely need to work on your perception skills. Observation is the first step toward nonverbal communication. You have to be paying attention in order to notice that something is different, that something has changed or that something isn't right.

Most people are too preoccupied with themselves to even notice changes in others. This preoccupation can limit the potential closeness that couples can achieve. Make a conscious effort to notice the subtle changes that take place in your partner and in your relationship.

While telling our spouse what we are thinking and how we are feeling is a very important aspect to achieving a close-knit relationship, we don't always think of offering this kind of information without a little coaxing. That is when it is important to notice your partner's body language, facial expressions and even the tone of his or her voice. Pay close attention to these nonverbal communication cues.

When you notice that something is off, ask questions in a very caring way. Questions like:

- "You seem a little distracted, what are you thinking about?"
- "You seem down, what's wrong?"
- "You seem flustered, what can I do to help?"

Questions like these show your mate that you truly care about him or her. The fact that you noticed, and that you were willing to put your life on hold in order to help your mate, can make all of the difference in the world.

Just remember not to push him or her. If your spouse doesn't want to talk about it, that's fine. Just the fact that you noticed may be all the support that your mate needs. Besides, sometimes conversation is overrated. All your mate may really need is a hug, smile, kiss, touch or a little time and space.

A word of caution: if you are the recipient of these kinds of questions be sure to share your thoughts and feelings. The worst thing that you can do is blow your spouse off by saying, "Nothing's wrong" when there is. If your spouse receives this reaction once too often, he or she will stop asking. Even worse, your spouse may think that you don't care about him or her enough to share what is on your mind, or may develop a "Fine, deal with it yourself" attitude. Don't desensitize your spouse. Tell him or her what is on your mind or say that you would like to talk about it later. Foster this kind of communication and it will bring your relationship to a much higher level.

The connection that you have with your mate can even evolve into a "sense" that you get when something is not quite right. This sixth sense or intuition doesn't even need an outward sign. You have a gut feeling. You just know. Listen to your gut feeling, it is usually right.

Actions speak louder than words
There is a saying that we heard quite some time ago that embodies the most important form of communication. It goes something like this, "What you do speaks so loudly I can't hear a word that you are

saying." The most important form of communication is in what you *do*, not what you say.

- If you say that you love your husband or wife, but you don't act lovingly toward him or her, your spouse won't believe you.

- If you say that you are sorry for being late and then you repeat this behavior, your spouse won't believe you.

- If you say that your spouse is the most important person on the planet to you, but you spend too much time with your friends, your spouse won't believe you.

- If you say that you trust your spouse, but you continually ask if your mate knows what he or she is doing, your spouse won't believe you.

- If you say that you care about him or her, but you continually forget your anniversary or your mate's birthday, your spouse won't believe you.

- If you say that you value your mate's opinion, but you argue with him or her regarding many of the things that he or she says, your spouse won't believe you.

- If you find your lover attractive, but you never tell your lover or pay him or her compliments, how will your partner know what you think?

- If you tell your mate that he or she is special, but you rarely do the small things that he or she likes, your spouse won't believe you.

Put your money where your mouth is. *Act* like your spouse means everything to you and he or she will believe you. Listen to your partner, hang on every word that he or she says and you will develop a closeness that you haven't felt in years.

Recognize when something has changed. Notice when your partner seems disappointed, upset, angry, frustrated or sad. Tell your spouse often how much he or she means to you and demonstrate it through your actions.

And never limit the number of times you say the most important words in the English language—"I love you."

SECTION 4

THE QUICKEST
WAY TO GET
WHAT YOU WANT

CHAPTER 10

DISCOVERING YOUR SPOUSE'S DESIRES

One of the quickest ways to get what you want from your mate is to give your mate what he or she wants. This principle has been taught for thousands of years, yet few people see the wisdom of this fundamental truth. It really makes sense when you think about it. Who do you feel like giving something to? Is it the person who is always selfishly taking *from* you or is it the person who is always unselfishly giving *to* you?

There are many terms used to explain why giving is the quickest way to receiving. They are all correct, however, a slight twist needs to be added to some of them when talking about the giving and taking relationship of husband and wife. The following are a few examples that you may be familiar with:

- **The law of the harvest.** You reap what you sow. This law has been recognized since the day mankind first planted seed. Plant corn and you will get corn. This law also applies to our actions. Plant an act of kindness and receive kindness in return. Honor your spouse and he or she will honor you. Judge and you will be judged. Plant love and receive love. Sowing is investing in your future. If you want a good crop, you will need to sow good seeds. If you want a good relationship, you will need to invest in your spouse.

- **The law of reciprocity.** This law is very much like the law of the harvest. There is a natural tendency to want to return a favor or give when you have been given to. The degree to which this tendency manifests itself varies from person to person. Have you ever received a gift from someone whom you didn't buy a gift for? How did that make you feel? You might say, "You didn't have to get me anything. I feel bad because I didn't get you anything." Most people have a natural tendency to want to give back. Give to your spouse and he or she will want to give to you.

How have you experienced the "law of reciprocity" in your life? Tell us your story by going to www.honeymoonmarriage.com and click on the keyword "law of reciprocity".

Revenge is the negative side of reciprocity and it can cause a lot of problems. When someone rips us off, we want to even the score. If someone tells us off, we want to tell him or her off. You may have heard someone say, "I don't get mad, I get even." No they don't. There is no such thing as getting even. As soon as you retaliate, the other person responds in kind. This kind of war can last a lifetime. It is better to adhere to the saying "Two wrongs don't make a right." If your spouse does you wrong, don't try to get even or punish him or her. That will only lead to more pain for both of you. Instead tell him or her how you feel and then seek a resolution.

- **The Golden Rule.** "Do to others as you would have them do to you." This phrase was coined by Jesus Christ as written in the best-selling book of all time, the Bible. It is an excellent rule and one by which we should live our lives. If you want someone to be nice to you, then treat him or her nicely. It only makes sense.

In a marriage, it is easy to think of you and your spouse as two independent individuals who share the same house and many of the same experiences. Because of that mindset, we oftentimes treat our spouse more harshly and with less love and compassion than we would want someone to treat us. We falsely think that our actions toward our spouse affect only him or her. There may have been some truth to that mindset when referring to your roommate in college; however, a marital relationship is much different.

When we enter into marriage, something very amazing happens. Two individuals come together and create a bond that links their hearts and souls together. The Golden Rule as it relates to your marriage is not just a principle of receiving back what you give, but rather a reminder that whatever you do to your spouse you are really doing to yourself. Do to your spouse as you would have him or her do to you because that is exactly what you are doing. Your spouse is part of you. When you hurt your mate you are hurting yourself. When you withhold from him or her you are robbing yourself. Give your spouse everything that you have and everything that he or she needs and you will be rich beyond compare.

In the last chapter we discussed our many differences. We have different personalities, different talents and abilities, different thought processes, we communicate differently and we have different needs. It is because of these differences that we should rephrase the Golden Rule to read "Do to others as they would like you to do to them." This has been called by some the *Platinum Rule* or the *Diamond Rule*, and it is the secret to getting what you want and need out of your relationship.

Giving someone a tennis racket for his or her birthday may seem like a great gift to you because you love playing tennis. But if the recipient of your gift has never played a game of tennis in his or her life and has no intention of ever doing so, your gift will have been a waste of money. We have all given and received gifts that weren't wanted. We do the same thing in our marital relationship. We give our partner what we would want or what we think our partner wants or needs instead of finding out what her or she truly wants and needs from us. Give your husband or wife what *he or she* wants and needs from you, and your mate will give you what *you* want and need from him or her. This will always work in a caring relationship as long as you take the time to find out what your mate's needs are.

- **The love bank.** This is a phrase that was coined by Dr. Willard F. Harley, Jr. in his best-selling book entitled *His Needs Her Needs*. The love bank is an excellent word picture that describes how our relationships work. In short, whenever you do something good or positive to or for your spouse you make a deposit. Every time you treat him or her poorly, you make a withdrawal. The author states that pleasurable interactions cause deposits, and painful interactions cause withdrawals. This philosophy suggests that as long as you are making significantly more deposits than withdrawals, your relationship will be a healthy one. And if your account is overdrawn, you are in trouble.

The love bank analogy is great because it is simple and you can relate with it. It is also something that you can be mindful of every time you interact with your spouse. Simply ask yourself if you are making a deposit or a withdrawal. The danger of thinking of your relationship as a "love bank" is in the value you give to your deposits and withdrawals. It is easy to view our deposits and withdraws in terms of a one dollar bill, a ten dollar bill, and a one hundred dollar bill.

Let's say that a slightly positive or negative interaction is worth one dollar, a stronger interaction is worth ten dollars, and an extremely negative or positive interaction is worth one hundred dollars. Using that thought process, when you have a slightly positive interaction ($1), a stronger positive interaction ($10), an extremely positive interaction ($100), and an extremely negative interaction (-$100), you might think your love bank balance would be a positive eleven dollars. Unfortunately, that is not how it works. In our experience, negative interactions weigh much more than positive ones. That is why a consumer will tell three people when he or she is pleased with a product or service, while telling seventeen people if dissatisfied. In our opinion, a more accurate valuation would be to give the three negative variants a value of five dollars, fifty dollars, and five hundred dollars respectively.

Dr. Harley also made a slight revision to the Golden Rule. He calls it the Marital Golden Rule.

"Meet your spouse's needs
as you would want your spouse to meet yours."
- Willard F. Harley, Jr. -

- **The emotional bank account.** This is a phrase that was coined by Dr. Stephen R. Covey in his best-selling book *The 7 Habits of Highly Effective People*. The emotional bank account is very much like the love bank with an emphasis on making the deposits that are important to the recipient. This of course assumes that you know what the other person wants or needs. You don't need to understand why your spouse has different needs than you, but you do need to know what those needs are. As mentioned before (and will be mentioned again), ask your spouse what he or she wants and needs. Don't guess or assume. That won't work and it will most likely keep you from getting what you want and need.

Dr. Covey also recognized that a negative withdrawal was much greater than a positive deposit. He pointed out the importance of apologizing when a withdrawal has been made. A sincere apology can minimize the effect of a withdrawal and get your emotional bank account back in the black again (that is, as long as there have been enough deposits).

Another thing to keep in mind is that your deposits do not collect interest. If you made a deposit of ten dollars a week ago and haven't made any deposits or withdrawals since, that ten dollars is now worth eight. Unlike money in the bank, a deposit that you make into your relationship will not increase in value. In a relationship, you are either gaining ground or you are losing ground. It is very important that you make deposits on a regular basis.

You can't pour water from an empty container, nor can you receive the love that you need from an empty mate.

Picture a car with its gas tank empty. You can't go very far on a quarter tank of gas, and to expect your car to go anywhere on an empty tank of gas is irrational. Are you and/or your spouse operating near empty? If so, you will never reach your desired destination—the Honeymoon Marriage.

One more analogy and then we will discuss how you can discover your spouse's desires. All of the above analogies are great, however, perhaps you can relate better to your own physiological need for food. If you do not give your spouse everything that he or she needs, you are emotionally starving your mate to death. That unfulfilled hunger will cause frustration, unhappiness, an affair or even divorce.

Don't let the well run dry
We all have basic needs that have to be met in order to live a happy and balanced life. We all have the need to be loved, appreciated, honored, respected, trusted, understood, accepted, encouraged,

admired, and as mentioned in the first chapter we also need unfailing devotion. These are all very important, but how do you know if you are meeting all of your spouse's needs? You guessed it—ask.

There are a lot of great books that you can read, classes that you can attend, and counselors whom you can visit, but the best place to get this kind of information is straight from the horse's mouth. Ask your partner what he or she wants and what you can do for him or her. This may be a little awkward at first but once you get started, the conversation will get easier. Your lover may even look at you a little funny at first if you are not already in the habit of engaging in such conversations. He or she may even think that you have ulterior motives. However, after discovering that you are asking out of genuine concern, your mate will be very receptive and will tell you what he or she wants.

Make sure that your fact-finding mission is done at a time and place where the two of you can be alone without any distractions. Prior to engaging in this conversation, reassure your spouse that you love him or her and that you want to have an honest and open conversation. Let your spouse know that you are not going to get offended, upset or hurt by anything that he or she tells you. *Do not* get defensive or offer a long list of things that you would like your spouse to change. This will kill an open dialogue in a hurry. Just listen, take notes and repeat back what your mate said in your own words to make sure that you understood him or her correctly. This is a great practice to get into for three very important reasons:

1. Sometimes we hear or interpret things differently than what our spouse really meant. You can't give someone what he or she wants if you have a fuzzy definition of what that is.
2. Your spouse will feel as though he or she was understood. Everyone wants to be understood.
3. This shows your spouse that you truly want to know how you can make your relationship better and that you care about him or her.

The first question that you should ask may be the hardest. If your husband or wife is honest and feels comfortable enough, his or her answer to your first question may shock you. Remember to stay cool, calm and collected. You mate's answer is how *he or she* feels, and it is correct. Ask your spouse to rate your marriage on a scale from one to ten, with one being you are on your way to a divorce and ten being the perfect marriage.

Remember that perception is everything, and your mate is telling you how he or she perceives things. This should be a time of growth, and where there is growth there are oftentimes growing pains.

Ask your mate what you could do to make your relationship better. Make sure to have a note pad and pen handy and write down everything that he or she says. After each point, repeat it back so that you are sure you know exactly what your partner means. Ask only once you are ready to honor his or her requests. It will do more damage than good for you to go through this exercise if you are not prepared to follow through. As a matter of fact, not following through on this kind of a commitment could be one of the most damaging things that you can do to an already stressed relationship.

Remember that this fact-finding mission is all about your mate. Don't fall prey to the temptation to unload all of the things that you want or that you want your spouse to do. You will get your turn in due time.

As soon as you get a complete list of your spouse's requests, pick one on the spot and decide to do it that day. Don't tell your partner what you have planned; just surprise him or her. Then pick another and do it the following day. Continue going down the list until all of the items have been addressed. It is important that you take immediate action, however, you are not in a race. It may take you several days or even several months to accomplish everything on his or her list.

If the two of you are reading this book together, then you can simply exchange lists. If not, we would suggest that you hold on to your requests until your mate asks for them or until you have consistently demonstrated your ability to meet your spouse's needs. Odds are your mate will ask for your requests once he or she sees your sincerity and commitment.

If you are not trading lists or if your spouse doesn't ask for your suggestions right away, be patient. Wait for an opportune time. Once your mate sees how much you care, he or she will be more receptive to your requests. Make sure that you have your partner's undivided attention and have set up an appointment in advance. When together, ask if it is a good time to talk. If your partner says no, then reschedule. Don't get upset, because if you don't have your mate's full attention, you have nothing anyway. If it is a good time, lay it all out in the open. It would be a good idea to write out your requests beforehand so that you don't forget anything.

Start by complimenting your spouse and telling your spouse how glad you are to be with him or her. Tell your partner that he or she makes you happy and that your requests will make your relationship even better. When making your requests known be very kind and gentle. Handle your requests with velvet gloves, being very conscious of your mate's feelings. Make sure that you give off the correct, relaxed body language. Look straight into your partner's eyes and show him or her that you genuinely care.

Be sure that your partner knows exactly what you want. Don't beat around the bush or drop hints. That will not get you to where you want to be, and it only leads to frustration, both yours and your mate's. Also, never fall into the trap of thinking that you shouldn't have to tell your mate what you want because he or she should already know what you want. This response is a very common yet unrealistic attitude.

After you have expressed your desires, ask for your partner's feedback. This is very important because there may be a reason why your spouse is not giving you what you want or need. There may be something that you are doing that stops your partner from acting the way you would like him or her to. Listen but don't get defensive. We know we have already said that several times, but it is so important that it bears repeating. Stay positive and upbeat. You may not want to hear some of the things your mate says or you may think that they are not true. You may even think that your spouse is way off base. That doesn't matter. Don't disagree with him or her, because that will only bring this potentially wonderful process to a screeching halt.

"Do you want to be right, or do you want to be happy?"
- Brian Tracy -

The art of gift giving
Giving and receiving gifts to and from each other can be fun. However, this can be a tense time in some marriages. One spouse or the other may be concerned that he or she might not get the right gift and that his or her lover may be disappointed. These may be valid feelings based on past gift-giving experiences. The receiving party didn't get what he or she had hoped for or wanted. When the receiver of the gift is disappointed, hurt, upset or even mad regarding the gift, there is something very wrong with the gift-giving ceremony. In some cases, the receiver may even punish the giver for getting it wrong. This is a very unhealthy situation that can turn what should be a fun, loving exchange into a dreaded experience. Who is at fault? As in everything, there is more than one side to the story.

Scenario 1

If Joyce told Paul that she wanted an eighteen-inch sterling silver necklace with matching earrings and what she unwrapped was a sweater, then Joyce may very well feel disappointed, hurt or upset. She may even get mad if this has happened more than once before. If Paul knew exactly what Joyce wanted and if it was within their means to get it, then getting her anything different is not the right thing to do. Joyce deserves to get something that she considers special from the man that she loves. Paul was in the wrong.

Scenario 2

If Joyce didn't tell Paul directly what she wanted and the sweater disappointed her, then Joyce was at fault. Joyce may have assumed that Paul knew what she wanted. She may have dropped several hints along the way. She may have left a catalog open on the kitchen table turned to the jewelry section and circled the items that she wanted. All of these hints or clues may have gone unnoticed by Paul. Joyce may even be hurt that Paul didn't care enough to "listen" to her or to try hard enough to figure out what she wanted. Paul didn't disappoint her on purpose. As a matter of fact he gets great joy from pleasing his wife. He never picked up on her hints.

Be direct

Hint and clue dropping are not effective ways to communicate to men. Men need the direct approach. Joyce may think that she shouldn't have to tell him what he should already know. After all she has been dropping hints for a week now. She may also think that if she has to tell him exactly what she wants and where to get it, then she may as well just get it herself.

Joyce is setting herself up for disappointment by not telling Paul exactly what she wants. Worse yet, she is setting Paul up as well. He wants to please her, but she is not making that easy for him. Paul on the other hand needs to discover what Joyce really wants. The best way to get it right is to ask. Paul should take the initiative as follows:

Paul: "Joyce, your birthday is coming up in a few weeks and I want to get something really special for you. Do you know what you want?"

Joyce: "No, I haven't really given it much thought."

Paul: "Think about it and let me know at least a week prior to your birthday so that I will have enough time to get it. If you would like it to be somewhat of a surprise, then write down several things that you would like and I will pick one. Make sure to be as specific as you can. I wouldn't want to get the wrong thing."

Joyce: "Thanks, Paul, for making my birthday so important to you. I love you."

Paul: "I love you, too."

Men give gifts very much like they communicate. They are problem solvers. As mentioned earlier, when a woman tells a man the problems of her day, her husband wants to jump into the conversation and solve her problems. However, she didn't ask for nor does she want her problems solved. She just wants him to listen, empathize and be supportive. If instead, he offers solutions and tells her that she shouldn't feel the way that she does, she will think that he never listens to her and that he doesn't care about her feelings. This exchange can take place during gift giving as well.

The perfect anniversary gift

In passing conversation, Sarah tells James that she hates their washing machine, that it's not big enough, doesn't work as well as it used to and that they need a new one. James places this statement in his memory banks to be retrieved at a later time. Several weeks pass by and he remembers that next month is their fifteen-year wedding anniversary. What could be a better gift than a new washing machine? She just said that she needs one. James then goes shopping for the "perfect" gift. He wants to buy her the best because she deserves it. He goes from store to store comparing the features and benefits of many machines. James picks one out and schedules its delivery for the day before their anniversary. "Boy will she be excited," James says to himself as his own excitement grows.

Sarah also remembers that their anniversary is coming up and begins to shop for James's "perfect" gift. After hours of shopping, she finds it. It is a silver-plated picture frame with side-by-side four-by-six-inch openings. She takes the frame to an engraver and has "Ours is a love that will last forever" engraved along the bottom. She then puts a wedding picture of them in the left side and a recent picture on the right. Sarah is impressed with her creativity and knows it will be the perfect gift. She can only guess what James must have gotten her. She thinks that a half-carrot marquis channel ring would be perfect. She drops hints and even leaves the jewelry catalog open with the ring circled on the kitchen table three days in a row. Here is what took place on their special day:

James: "Happy anniversary, Sarah!"

Sarah: "Happy anniversary."

James: "You will never guess what I got you for our anniversary." He is so excited he can hardly stand it. He walks her down to the basement and has her close her eyes. He then tells her to open her eyes as she stands in front of her new washer and dryer set.

Sarah: She has a disappointed look on her face.

James: He notices her disappointment and asks, "What's wrong?"

Sarah: "You bought me a washer and dryer for our fifteen-year anniversary?"

James: "Well, yes. Don't you like them?"

Sarah: "I thought that you would get me something special."

James: Now he is hurt. "This gift is special. It is exactly what you told me you needed. I spent days picking it out. What did you want?"

Sarah: "It doesn't matter."

We will let your imagination fill in the rest of the story. This is their special day together, yet they ended up hurting each other's feelings over a gift given in love. To James (or most men) getting a practical gift that will solve his problem or make life easier is the perfect gift. It only stands to reason that he would use that same logic when picking out a gift for his wife of fifteen years.

When buying gifts, remember the Platinum Rule, "Do to others as they would like you to do to them." James and Sarah gave each other something that they would appreciate instead of giving something that their spouse would appreciate. As a rule of thumb, men should never give household appliances to a woman for a special occasion. Some women many even take that as an insult. She may think to herself, "What kind of a gift is a washing machine? Great, now I can do his dirty laundry more efficiently." If he is the one that does most of the cooking, a new stainless steel cookware set may be the perfect gift, but not so for her. Women need to make their desires clear or they will not get what they want. Men are not mind readers and can be terrible at picking up hints. Be direct with a man and you will both be happier.

We have always received exactly what we wanted for our birthdays, holidays, anniversaries and Valentine's Day for the last fourteen years running. How do we choose the perfect gift every time without fail? The answer is very easy, but we want you to think about it before you come to a conclusion. The "perfect" gift that we give each other comes from the heart. It is well thought out and it portrays our love for each other in a very special way. Our perfect gift is each other. For us, that is all that we need. All that matters is that we are together on these special days. Anything else is just icing on the cake.

Until you get to that point in your relationship, think about what you would like to receive for your next special day. What would be the perfect gift for your next anniversary? Write down your answer and then give it to your spouse.

We all become somewhat complacent

Let's face it, once we become comfortable with each other we tend to become lazy in our marriage. We treat our spouse a little differently than we did when we were dating or after we first got married. It is this laziness or lack of understanding each other's needs that causes couples to say, "Well, I guess the honeymoon is over." What would happen if you treated each other the way you did when you were dating or when you first got married? Do you think it is possible that you would feel the same if you acted the same way toward each other? We would like to propose that you wouldn't feel the same. You would feel even closer and more in love.

We have heard many couples who have been married for over fifteen years say that they love each other more now than they did when they first got married. We love each other more today than we did when we first started dating over fifteen years ago. We even love each more today than we did on our honeymoon over twelve years ago. Are we just two oddballs? Was it that we got lucky and found our soul mate? Is it because we share all of the same interests? Are our personalities, mannerisms and temperaments the same? Or is this kind of relationship possible for anyone who wants it and is willing to do what it takes to get it?

Yes, we may be a little odd, but so are you. Yes, we do consider ourselves lucky to have each other, and you can feel that way about your partner as well. No, we have very different primary interests; however, we have found countless activities that we both enjoy and do together. No, our personalities, mannerisms and temperaments are very different, but we have learned to appreciate, respect and even capitalize on our differences. And, yes, you too can have what we have if you do what we do. We once heard a story about the great composer Wolfgang Amadeus Mozart. A student of his was marveling at Mozart's piano skills and made a comment something like, "I wish I could play as well as you." Mozart became very upset and said that anyone could play as well as he did if they practiced as much as he did. While it is true that Mozart had God-given abilities that not everyone else had, he still made a very good point. The point is, you shouldn't compare your relationship with that of anyone else. You should only focus on practicing as hard as you can at making yours the best that it can be. It is this practice and not luck that makes one's endeavor great.

You have the choice to either feed and nurture your relationship and watch it grow or you can deprive your mate of his or her love food and watch your relationship wither away. If it is that easy, why don't more couples practice Honeymoon Marriage techniques? Why don't they simply give each other what they so desperately need? It is possible that you don't recognize what your spouse's primary love needs are or you don't realize their level of importance.

Our primary love needs

As mentioned in the last chapter, a woman's primary need from her husband is affection and a man's primary need from his wife is physical intimacy. Let's take a closer look at these two needs.

Before we begin, notice that we said needs and not suggestions, wants, or desires. These two needs are not optional. These needs must be met in the proportion that your spouse requires. Every person and every couple have different requirement levels and that is why it is so vitally important that you openly discuss your marital needs with your partner. He or she is the only one who can tell you what he or she needs. It is important that *all* of our needs are met, however, we will focus most of our discussion on the two primary love needs.

Her primary love need is affection

Women need affection like a person stranded in the desert needs water. Affection is her *primary* need and it is a reassurance of her husband's love for her. She needs affection in order to create an intimate bond with her husband. Giving a woman the affection that she needs is really quite simple. Examples of affection would include a kiss, hug, kind loving words including "I love you", compliments, flowers, cards, love notes, touches, gifts, quality time, flirting, meaningful communication, etc. These and several other examples are discussed in the chapter entitled "Small things mean a lot."

Her desire for these affectionate acts is not a sign of childishness or insecurity. It is just the way she is wired. In the chapter entitled "Unleash the romance and passion in your relationship," we discussed a woman's need for romance. These "romantic" acts are interpreted by her as much-needed signs of affection.

> **Starved for affection:** Not too long ago, I (Darren) was under a lot of pressure, so much so that it affected how I was treating Donna. What made matters worse was the fact that I felt like she was partially responsible for what I was going through. I learned years ago that she needed a lot more affection than I did and I made it a point to give it to her whenever we were together. But for two days my affection for her was nonexistent. You might say that I acted cold toward her, emotionless. My actions toward her caused her to almost put up a defensive wall between us because it was causing her pain. I don't know why I acted like this toward her but I knew that my damaging behavior had to stop. On day two of my "coldness" neither one of us could sleep. We stayed up for hours and talked things through. We both apologized, and as talking and forgiveness have the tendency to do, my pressure immediately left. As I held her in my arms as we were lying in bed, she began to cry. When I asked her what was wrong, she said, "I missed you." What she missed was my affection.

The saying "starved for affection" is right on the mark. If a woman doesn't get the amount of affection that she needs, she will not feel fulfilled in her relationship and that will have a direct impact on how she responds to her husband.

His primary love need is physical intimacy

Little boys can be very affectionate. They may not be as affectionate as little girls, but they still like to be held, touched and pampered. As a boy gets older his need for and his displays of affection usually decline. Then at the age of thirteen or fourteen puberty hits and everything changes. Suddenly he is attracted to girls for more than just a playmate during recess. The thoughts of girls occupy his mind more than most other thoughts. He begins to experience the effects of the hormone testosterone in his body.

Testosterone is the hormone responsible for his deepened voice, muscular growth, increased growth of body hair, beard and of course his sex drive. It is an extremely powerful hormone. Testosterone is even synthesized (anabolic steroids) and used by many bodybuilders to massively increase the size of their muscles. Your husband doesn't just wake up one morning and decide that he wants to have sex. His strong sex drive is nature's way to ensure the perpetuation of the species. We hate to break down a man's sex drive

DISCOVERING YOUR SPOUSE'S DESIRES

into such primal language, but the facts are the facts. The testosterone coursing throughout his body creates his need for sex. He cannot help it. It is not a decision or a choice; nature has chosen this course for his him. Many scientific studies have been conducted regarding the effects of testosterone. Female rats, for example, when injected with testosterone attempt to mate like male rats.

Some women say that all their husband thinks about is sex. Well, testosterone is one of the few hormones that interacts directly with the brain. And believe it or not, our brain is our primary sex organ. Men produce four to eight milligrams of testosterone every day, which is at least eight times what a woman produces. That could explain why his desire to have sex can be at least eight times stronger than his wife's.

If a man doesn't get the amount of sex that he needs, he will not feel fulfilled in his relationship, and that will have a direct impact on how he responds to his wife. Men derive much of their feelings of love and acceptance from making love. It is also a way that he shows his love for his wife.

The man on a mission
The man who is on a mission to win over his lady has no problem showering her with affection. He goes out of his way to make her feel special. It doesn't matter what they do as long as they are together. They go for walks, go to the movies, go out to eat, go to sporting events, play with each other, etc. They even talk for hours, and as mentioned in the chapter entitled "Experience fulfilling communication," talking is one of her love needs. These acts of affection win her heart and after a while she falls madly in love with him.

Once he has her, these outward signs of his love and connection with her decrease. It isn't that he loves her any less, it is just that he thinks the "mating ritual" is over. During mating season, a male deer creates large amounts of testosterone. As a result, he spends much of his time pursuing females. Air Force studies have shown that happily married men have lower levels of testosterone than men who are single, recently divorced or are having marital problems. Perhaps that explains in part why a man's drive to "win over" his wife decreases after marriage. It isn't a sudden drop-off, but rather a steady decline.

The alluring qualities of a woman
Likewise women act differently once they have gotten their man. Men are very visually stimulated and women know it. A woman will

go out of her way to look good to attract and keep her man. She also takes an interest in the things that he likes. She will participate in activities that he enjoys even if these activities are not ones that she would engage in if she were not with him. This is great for him because it meets his need for a playful companion as will be discussed in the chapter entitled "Play with me—bringing out your inner child." She does all of the things that stroke his ego like telling him how great he is and showing him that she is proud to be with him. She will demonstrate her acceptance and trust in him by allowing him to choose what they will do and where they will go.

Once she has her man the hunt is over and she can go back to doing what interests her the most, which in many cases is not what they were doing together while courting. During the first part of their marriage she is a very willing sexual partner. She feels very close to him and wants to express her love in every way possible. After a while, her interest in sex fades. This is true for two reasons. First, her biological need for sex is not as strong as that of her husband. Second, she is no longer receiving the affection that she needs to get her in the mood.

Our natural tendency to reduce our level of "spouse pleasing" is no excuse for not meeting our partner's needs. How you act and react toward your mate is your choice. And as mentioned earlier, a beautiful thing happens when a loving couple strives to meet each other's needs. Conversely, a marital existence filled with bitterness, sorrow, loneliness and pain awaits the person who is only interested in his or her own needs and desires.

Cause and effect

We once heard that if a married couple put one dollar in a jar every time that they made love during their first year of marriage and then took out a dollar every time thereafter, the jar would never be empty. We're not sure how many couples experience that level of degradation in their sex lives, but the statement made a good point. What causes the honeymoon stage of a marriage to end so quickly?

The reason may be as simple as cause and effect. Take away or reduce the amount of affection a woman receives from her husband and her desire for sex greatly diminishes. Likewise, take away the amount of physical intimacy that a man receives from his wife and his outward display of affection diminishes. As a general rule, a man doesn't need affection as much as his wife nor does a woman need sex as much as her husband does, but unless each of them gets what they need, they will both suffer.

"Shallow men believe in luck.
Strong men believe in cause and effect."
- Ralph Waldo Emerson -

All human beings, men and women alike, make their decisions based upon the desire to gain pleasure and/or avoid pain. We also have an overpowering need for acceptance and consequently dread rejection. These are extremely powerful forces as they determine the choices that we make in life. When a wife's need for affection, communication/understanding, respect/honor, security/reassurance, a comfortable nest/financial stability, and a devoted husband is not met, she will experience the pain of an unfulfilled relationship. She may even feel rejected by her husband. When a husband's need for sex, trust, an attractive wife, acceptance, a playmate, admiration, and an encouraging and supportive wife is not met, he will also experience pain and rejection.

Subconsciously, we look for a way to get rid of this pain and rejection and replace it with pleasure and acceptance. Unfulfilled love needs *will* have an effect on your marriage. If you do not meet these and other needs, they may get met by someone else.

Don't let someone else fill the need

There are many stereotypes and misconceptions floating around regarding the cheating spouse. The following are some of the myths:

Myth #1: An affair is all about sex.
Myth #2: Mostly men enter into affairs.
Myth #3: The cheating spouse went out of his or her way to find someone else.
Myth #4: An evil person seduced him or her.
Myth #5: Unethical, immoral or promiscuous people commit affairs.
Myth #6: An affair could never happen to me.

All of these things can be true; however, an affair usually starts very differently. Let's take a look at the realities of an affair.

Reality #1: An affair is not about sex, or at least that was not the initial intention. Most affairs start just like many marital relationships did—as just friends. When the guilty party is caught, admits to the affair or leaves their mate to be with the other person, he or she will oftentimes say something like, "I never intended on having an affair, it just happened." The eventual attraction that leads to sex in an affair is oftentimes caused by a person allowing someone of the opposite sex to meet his or her love needs that have not been met by his or her spouse.

A woman not receiving enough tender loving care from her husband (or worse yet being treated poorly by him) is drawn to the man who compliments her and treats her with kindness, gentleness and respect. He is a good listener and she feels comfortable talking with him. She tells him about her problems and he does the same with her. He really understands her. She feels so good about herself every time they are together. She doesn't feel the pain, loneliness and rejection that she feels when she is with her husband.

A man who is not appreciated by his wife, who feels that his wife is not sexually attracted to him and is constantly belittled, is drawn to the woman who strokes his ego. Men are typically drawn to a woman through physical attraction, however, a wounded man can be equally attracted to the woman who will make him feel like a desirable man. The male ego can be easily bruised. They may meet at work or through a mutual friend and instantly hit it off and decide to meet for coffee later that week. They both have such a good time that they decide to meet somewhere every other week. No harm—no foul, after all, they are just friends. She decides to join the health club that he belongs to so that she can spend more time with her new friend. He is very happy that he has found a new playmate as well as a good friend. Over the course of time, one thing leads to the next until they end up sleeping together. Neither one of them had planned it, it just happened.

Reality #2: Men *and* women enter into affairs. The last we knew it took two to tango. We have not seen a national statistic, but out of all of the affairs that we are aware of, women committed 67 percent of them. That isn't a fair representation of the nation as a whole, but we think it still proves a point. Women also enter into affairs.

Reality #3: One doesn't have to look far in order to find his or her adulterous companion. As many as 50 percent of divorces are caused by a mate who met "the other person" either through or at work. They can be found at the health club, church, civic group, coffeehouse, restaurant or anywhere else people of the opposite sex spend time together. The other person can be a friend of the family, friend of a friend or even a friend of their spouse.

Reality #4: A person doesn't need to be "seduced" into an affair. You may think that it is harmless for a married person to regularly meet with someone of the opposite sex. You may see nothing wrong with meeting him or her for a cup of coffee, bite to eat or after-hours work project. You may be right, however, why would you want to take the risk that your friendship might grow into something more? That is one risk in life that you don't have to take.

Reality #5: Otherwise ethical, moral, even strongly religious people enter into affairs. Affairs don't discriminate. Rich people have affairs as do poor people. Fat, skinny, educated, illiterate, gorgeous, unattractive, moral, immoral, self-employed, unemployed, it doesn't matter. Everyone with feelings is susceptible.

Reality #6: No one is immune to the possibility of an affair. You say that it will never happen to you? We hope that you are right. But know this—one of the most commonly uttered statements by the wounded party is, "I never thought it would happen to me." Also know that you are not completely powerless. Treat your spouse as well as you can, meet all of his or her needs, avoid spending time alone with people of the opposite sex, and these things will help to prevent an affair.

We realize that this has been a very weighty section, but we wanted you to realize that there are consequences to all of your actions and reactions within your marriage. Don't be deceived into believing that you could never have an affair nor could your spouse. Since you are the type of person who is reading this book and will apply its principles, we think that your odds of this happening to you are greatly reduced. Just make sure to be on your guard and don't take your spouse or your relationship for granted. Also, know that not getting your needs met by your spouse is not in any way justification for having an affair. The phrase "It just happened" is simply not true. The road to an affair is paved with choices, choices you have complete control over.

We spent most of our time discussing the love needs of affection and sex because they are typically the strongest for most women and men respectively. Don't think that you are out of the woods by meeting these needs alone, however. There are many other love needs that are woven throughout this book that are also very important. Some have been called by their names, while others have been described by their actions. As mentioned earlier, every person's needs are slightly different and every couple's needs differ as well. Find out what your spouse needs, in what amounts, and how often. Your mate is by far your best resource for this kind of information.

Now let's move on to a lighter yet still important aspect of the discovery process.

What does your spouse really want to do with his or her life?
We started this process earlier by discovering your spouse's gifts, talents and abilities. We also brushed the surface of your mate's

goals, dreams and aspirations. We will now take that discovery process to a much deeper level. This is the "What does your partner want to be when he or she grows up?" level of discovery. What is it that really makes your spouse tick? What are his or her passions? What does your mate enjoy doing more than anything else? If your spouse could pick any profession, what would it be?

Perhaps one of the reasons why your marriage isn't as good as it could be is because either you or your spouse or both are involved in a profession that isn't tailor made for you. "What does a job have to do with my marriage?" you ask. Well think about it. You and/or your spouse spend as much if not more waking hours at work than at any other place. You may even spend more time with the people at work than you do with the people you would rather spend time with. Work plays a major role in our life and in our marriage.

Your mate may not hate his or her job, but something might be missing. Maybe your partner isn't passionate about what he or she is doing. Your partner may make good money, but maybe thinks that he or she should be making a lot more, or perhaps the money really isn't that important to your spouse. He or she might like the job but hate the commute. He or she may feel unappreciated, overworked, overstressed, under challenged or even bored. Maybe your mate wants out but feels trapped. All of these feelings can lead to job dissatisfaction, and job dissatisfaction is serious business.

Job dissatisfaction can bring a lot of tension into your marriage. It can even make your lover sick, very sick. It could even kill him or her! A study was conducted at the H.E.W. in Massachusetts to determine the primary causes of heart disease. The findings may shock you since heart disease is the number-one killer in America and it accounts for 7.2 million deaths worldwide every year. More than 50 percent of the people who have heart attacks *do not* have any of the common risk factors such as; smoking, overweight or obesity, hypertension or diabetes. The two most important factors for heart disease were found to be:

1. Job dissatisfaction
2. Self-happiness rating based on two questions:
   a. Are you happy?
   b. Do you love your job?

It is not a coincidence that more Americans die at 9:00 a.m. on Monday morning than at any other time of the week. It is extremely difficult to have a Honeymoon Marriage if you hate your job. Not being completely satisfied in your life's work can make you feel like you are not being the person that you were meant to be.

"Getting what you want will NOT make you happy.
What will make you incredibly happy
is becoming who you need to be."
- Vic Conant -

So how do we become who we need to be? How do we discover who our spouse needs to be and what his or her deep and oftentimes suppressed ultimate desires in life are? This discovery process will take a lot of time and soul-searching, and we need to continually ask ourselves if what we are doing for a living is bringing meaning into our lives. We all have different talents, gifts, interests and abilities and we have a deep desire to use them in our profession.

"I would rather be a failure doing something I love
than be a success doing something I hate."
- George Burns -

The following are some questions that you can ask yourself and/or your spouse to determine whether or not you should consider a different career path:

1. Are you passionate about your life's work?
2. Do you look forward to going to work?
3. Do you do what you want to do or what you are told?
4. Do you get excited at around 4:00 Friday afternoon?
5. On Sunday evening, do you start to look forward to starting work on Monday morning?
6. Is your life's work challenging, or do you get bored easily?
7. While at work, do you daydream of doing something else or being somewhere else?
8. Do you find it hard to get to sleep on Sunday night?
9. Do you get along well with your boss?
10. Are you using your current position only as a stepping stone to bigger and better things?
11. Do you have to travel a lot and spend time away from your family because of work?
12. Have you been promoted only to find that you are no happier than you were before the promotion?
13. Was money your primary reason for choosing your career?

14. Did you choose your career path because it was expected of you?

15. Do you find it hard to relax and get work off of your mind?

16. Do you regularly take an antacid?

17. Do you and your spouse get into arguments over work-related topics?

18. Does your husband or wife want you to get a different job out of concern for your marriage or your health and peace of mind?

19. Do you have the amount of vacation time that you need?

20. Are you earning what you are worth?

21. Are you working below your potential?

22. Do you find that it takes more than a week to unwind while on vacation?

23. Are you on call after work hours?

24. Do you dislike your commute to and from work?

25. Do you spend more time with your colleagues than you do with your spouse and children?

26. Do you come home from work and yell at your family members over insignificant things?

27. Has your job become your number-one priority in life?

28. Does your gut tell you that you should be doing something else?

29. Would you rather be doing something else, but the pay isn't as good?

30. Would you rather be doing something else, but you are concerned what others might think?

31. Is your profession adding to the quality of your life or taking away from it?

32. Are you respected and appreciated at work?

33. Does your occupation continually teach you new things?

34. Is your work environment a healthy one, or is there a lot of gossiping and negative conversations and attitudes floating around?

35. When you finish a work project, do you feel exhilarated or exhausted?

36. Do you have to cancel family activities because of work?

37. Are you allowed to be creative and think outside of the box?

38. Does your job allow you to be your true self?

39. Are you allowed to work the hours that allow you to capitalize on your body's unique chemistry, i.e., Are you a morning person or are you most productive later in the day?

40. Do you dream of winning the lottery so that you can do what you really want?

41. Are you looking forward to retirement?

42. Do you love talking to others about what you do?

43. Do you feel that your life's work contributes to the greater good of humanity?

44. Do you change jobs often?

45. Are you proud of what you do for a living?

No one can tell you what you should dedicate your life to doing, that is an answer that you must find within yourself. The chapter entitled "Discover who you are and who your spouse is" as well as the upcoming "Section 6—Money Matters" will get you thinking in the right direction and give you a few more suggestions along the way. In the end, it is you and you alone who knows the desires of your heart. Follow your heart.

> *"We have all been placed on this earth to*
> *discover our own path, and we will never be happy*
> *if we live someone else's idea of life."*
> *- James Van Praagh -*

CHAPTER 11

SMALL THINGS MEAN A LOT

Darren's cartoon wisdom: I can recall watching a cartoon when I was a youngster called the *Groovy Ghoulies*. It featured hip 70s versions of our favorite old time monsters including Dracula, the Mummy, Frankenstein, the Werewolf, etc. I believe the Frankenstein creature's name was Frankie. For some reason, I have never forgotten one of the lines that Frankie said often when referring to his dragon-like pet. With a Boris Karloff accent he would say, "It takes so little to make the poor creature happy." I believe that those words stuck in my head because they hold profound wisdom that applies to us human beings as well. When it comes right down to it, it takes so little to make us happy, yet we often miss all of the small seemingly trivial things that we could do to improve the quality of our life.

The health of a marriage is largely dependent upon a lot of small things rather than a few big things. The big house, luxury automobiles, exotic vacations and expensive jewelry may be enjoyable, but without the small things, they have very little meaning or importance in a marriage. The person who works ten to twelve hours per day and a half a day on Saturday or who travels all of the time and says that he or she are doing it so that his or her family can have a better life, may be missing the point. Trust us, your spouse and children want *you* more than they want new expensive stuff. Money is important and we believe that we should all make as much as we can as long as we have our priorities in line. And family is, or at least should be, your number-one priority.

We once heard a very successful multimillionaire say, "If you can't make the kind of money that you want to working just eight hours per day, then you are doing something wrong." Of course there may be temporary situations that require a lot of your attention and cause you to have to work extremely long hours, however, this should not be a way of life. Not if you desire the Honeymoon Marriage. If this overworked situation continues, you may want to consider other employment.

Make sure that you are sending the right signals to your family members, signals that tell them that they are more important to you than anything else. If you are spending more time making a living than you do with your loved ones, then you should consider asking yourself a very important question. Are you willing to do without some of the "stuff" in order to have a more fulfilling life with your spouse?

While we agree that we need to think big in order for big things to happen, sometimes we need to think small when it comes to our relationships. Remember the saying, "big things come in small packages?" In the Honeymoon Marriage, it is the small things that oftentimes lead to big results. Small things are the ones that don't require a lot of money, but are priceless just the same. Here is a list of several small things that can have a big impact on your marriage:

A kiss

A kiss is a wonderful expression of love and affection toward your mate. It may only takes a fraction of a second, but its effects are long lasting. The power of a kiss can be most effective when it is not expected. Giving your spouse a big kiss because of something that he or she did for you is great; however, showing your spouse this sign of affection for no apparent reason can be even better. You are in the middle of the grocery store and you suddenly get the urge to kiss your spouse. So you grab your mate and give him or her a big kiss square on the lips. This may shock your spouse a little, but it will definitely change the rest of your shopping experience. Most women would love for their husband to do this to them, however, some men will get a little embarrassed by this public show of affection. We have one thing to say about that. Men, get over it. A kiss is great; however, making out in public is obviously not appropriate. Other people don't like to see it either. There is a time and a place for everything.

When we demonstrate our feelings through a kiss, that action gets reflected back to us. The receiver feels more love from the giver and the giver feels more love for the recipient.

Darren on kisses: Every time I leave the house while Donna is still sleeping, I bend over and kiss her on the forehead. This almost always wakes her up as if she was the fairy-tale princess Sleeping Beauty. (By the way, that is exactly what I think of her.) When I kiss her in this way it not only touches her heart, but it also seems to deepen my love for her. Every now and then we even kiss each other on the back of the hand. We do this in environments where a kiss on the lips may not be as appropriate.

If you have a great relationship, a kiss is worth more than diamonds. Be stingy with your signs of disapproval and liberal with your signs of affection.

A touch

The human touch is a very powerful thing. It may not be as outwardly obvious as a kiss, but it can leave a strong impact on the one who receives it. A brief experiment that was done several years ago demonstrated the power of the human touch. The experiment was done at a big city library where the librarian was given very simple instructions. She was to greet and process everyone in exactly the same way with one exception; she was to touch every other person's hand as the person checked out his or her book. Standing outside the library was a person who was to survey the people as they exited.

The surveyor asked each person to describe what the librarian looked like, what kind of a person he or she was, and how they felt about the librarian. The people who were not touched could not even describe the librarian and could hardly remember the librarian's gender. They reported the librarian to be kind of cold and indifferent. The people who were touched, on the other hand, could describe the librarian in fairly good detail and thought that the librarian was warm and caring. When asked if the librarian had touched them, most said no. The people who were touched had a completely different experience just because of a simple touch even though they didn't even realize that they had been touched.

A study was done at the University of Miami in which a group of premature infants (preemies) were divided up into two groups, a control group and an experimental group. The investigator would stroke each of the preemies in the experimental group three times per day for ten minutes each. Those babies who were touched gained an average of 49 percent more weight per day than the babies who were in the control group even though they were given the same formula.

The human touch can even have healing properties. A touch can heal your mind, emotions and even your body. Some of the most interesting findings are discovered by accident, and the following is such a finding. Scientists at Ohio State University studied the metabolism of cholesterol in rabbits back in 1980. They fed the rabbits a diet that was extremely high in cholesterol. Surprisingly, there was one group of rabbits that did not get high cholesterol levels even though they were given the same high cholesterol diet. After much investigation, the researchers discovered that the only difference between these rabbits and the ones that were getting the high cholesterol and hardening of the arteries was in the way that they were handled by the person doing the experiment. Instead of just simply giving the rabbits their food, the person feeding them would take them out of their cages and pet, hug, kiss and talk to them. If this kind of human affection can have that kind of effect on animals, just think what it can do for your spouse. Think what it can do for your marriage.

Every time you walk by your spouse, touch him or her. Hold hands everywhere you walk. Do this and you are sure to get a lot of looks. Regardless of your age, people will think that you just started dating or that you just got married. So if other people think that, how do you think this behavior will make you think and feel? How do you think it will affect your marriage? We often get mistaken for newlyweds even though we have been together as a couple for over fifteen years and married for over twelve.

A hug

A hug, like a kiss and a touch, only takes a moment and is a necessary ingredient in the Honeymoon Marriage. A hug can bring comfort, show love and make someone feel safe. A hug can have healing powers. It can melt away unforgiveness, bitterness, sorrow and pain. It is one of life's affectionate wonders.

"Love comforteth like sunshine after rain."
- William Shakespeare -

Sometimes there is nothing that you can say or do that will make your partner feel better. At those times, a hug may be what the doctor ordered. You don't need to say a word, just hold your mate and let the healing begin.

A hug uses the power of the human touch yet is at least ten times more powerful. Depending upon your upbringing, this may be a difficult habit to get into. If you did not grow up in a family that showed their affection in this way, you will need to move out of your comfort zone somewhat. Whatever you do, don't go another day without giving your partner a great big heartfelt hug. It will do your spirit good and it will strengthen your marital bond.

> *"Give me all your love'n, all your hugs and kisses too.*
> *Give me all your love'n, don't let up until we're through."*
> *- ZZ Top -*

One hug a day may not be enough so make it a point to hug your spouse often, and as mentioned in the last chapter, ask your spouse how many hugs he or she requires.

A look

While it is said that the eyes are the windows to the soul, they can also be the reflection of the heart. The way you look at your spouse tells your mate what you think about him or her even if it is not on a conscious level. We once had a beautiful lady in her sixties tell us that she could tell how much we loved each other by the way we looked at each other. What you are thinking about your spouse when you look at him or her shows through. Most of us are rather transparent to the ones we love.

Do you look at your spouse with appreciation on your mind? Can your partner tell just by looking into your eyes how much you want to be with him or her? When you look at your lover does your heart beat a little faster? Do thoughts of passion enter your mind? If not, your spouse will pick up on the signals that you are sending and will respond in like fashion. Look at your lover as if you were falling in love all over again.

> *"A successful marriage requires falling in love many times,*
> *always with the same person"*
> *- Mignon McLaughlin -*

Stop and take the time to look your partner directly in the eyes and think only great things about him or her. Think about how wonderful your lover is and how lucky you are to have such a partner. Think of all of the romantic and passionate feelings you had in your early years. Think about how much you appreciate your partner's presence. Then tell your lover these wonderful things. Make it a habit to only think positive, uplifting things about your spouse throughout the day. These thoughts will eventually transform themselves into an outward expression.

The way you look and act toward your mate will change the way that he or she looks and acts toward you. And if your partner is not already the person depicted in your thoughts, don't falter, because he or she will become that person in time. When you look at your spouse, pretend that he or she can read your mind. That way you will only think the thoughts that you would want your mate to hear.

Give flowers

This is one of the easiest things to do, yet many people give it little thought. Flowers are an excellent representation of nature's beauty. The gift of flowers doesn't have to be romantic or given only to women, however, they are always an expression of appreciation and/or affection. Giving flowers is an extension of your feelings or emotions. If you give flowers to the host who invited you over for dinner, it is an outward symbol of your appreciation for your friend's hospitality and friendship. When you send flowers to a funeral home you show your respect and condolences. When you give flowers to your spouse, you tell your mate that you love and appreciate him or her and that he or she means the world to you.

Some men look at flowers as a waste of money because they wilt and die very quickly. Their practical minds may think that silk flowers would be better because they will last forever. Silk flowers are great as decoration, but they lack the living beauty necessary to show your feelings. If you are a man reading this chapter, please don't miss the point. Most people love to receive flowers, especially women. Make it a simple matter of budgeting $20 at least once per month to buy and give the bride of your youth an outward symbol of your love and appreciation. We realize that your wife wants this to be a spontaneous event, however, if you need to, schedule it in your day planner (Tuesday, October 12—buy flowers for wife). We can't think of another small purchase that can make a bigger impact.

Women, you are not off the hook. Your husband will most likely not be into flowers, so you will need to be a little more creative. What small outward sign of your affection could you give your spouse? Perhaps you could spend that same $20 (or more depending on brand and quality) to buy a sexy piece of lingerie. Remember that this gift is for him, not for you. You could save up your $20 per month to buy him a tool that he needs or wants. Small things mean more to a woman than a man, so you may even need to save up your money for several months. Most women would love to get a $20 gift from their husband every month, whereas a man would prefer a $240 gift once a year. We are sure that if you give it enough thought, you will come up with the perfect small gift.

Say "I love you"

No other three words in the English language can have a stronger impact on your relationship than *I love you*. Say them often and say them with feeling. These words are not spoken to inform someone of something that he or she doesn't already know. They are a gift given to the one that means the world to you. These words will strengthen your marriage. We start to believe whatever we hear repeated over and over again. This is true whether these words are only thoughts in your mind or spoken out loud by others. Saying "I love you" often is like adding strength and stability to the foundation of your marriage.

"A successful marriage is an edifice
that must be rebuilt every day."
- Andre Maurou -

The Honeymoon Marriage does not go one day without each partner saying those all-important words. Of course your words need to be backed by your actions or else they lose their meaning and effectiveness.

Just like the giving flowers example above, saying "I love you" over and over again may not seem logical to some men. A man may think, "I said it once, my wife heard me, nothing has changed, so why should I say it again?" To a woman, this thought process may seem ridiculous, but to a man, it may make perfect sense. As discussed in Section 3, men and women are very different. To expect a man to think like a woman or a woman to think like a man is setting yourself up for a lot of frustration. As a rule of thumb, women want to *feel* and men what to *know*.

Men—yes, your wife *knows* that you love her, however, she needs to *feel* that you love her over and over again. Do whatever you can do to make her *feel* loved every day. Give her at least ten loving touches every day. Tell her that you love her at least three times every day (before you go your separate ways in the morning, when you get home after work, and before you go to sleep at night).

Women—don't hesitate to tell your husband exactly what you want and need from him on a daily basis. Don't assume that he already knows or that he can read your mind. Tell him that you need to hear him tell you that he loves you every day. Tell him that you need him to compliment you often (Make sure that you have earned these compliments. This will be discussed in the "Look your best" segment later in this chapter.). Sometimes you will need to take what you want. Take his hand and hold it. Take his arm and put it around you. Hug him every time you need a hug.

Remember that your husband also needs to know that you love him as well. He will know this in part by the respect, appreciation and trust that you give to him. Another great way to show that you love him is let him know how proud you are of him.

Time

Most of us need to look at time differently. We can start by changing the words we use to describe it. All too often we use the phrase "spend time" when we really mean, "invest time." You *spend* time mowing the lawn. You *invest* time with your spouse. When you *spend* something there is a cost. This cost is called an opportunity cost. Time's opportunity cost is what you have to give up because you chose to spend time doing something else. If you spend one hour mowing the lawn, you gave up the opportunity to wash the car during that time. Investing is a completely different animal. You invest with the intention of receiving more in return than what you originally invested.

We are all familiar with investing money. You invest $100 in a mutual fund at 9 percent annual return and you end up with $109 at the end of the year. Investing time works in a similar fashion, although the return on investment is not always easily measured or predicted. Time with your spouse should be considered investment time. Invest as much time in your relationship as you can. Believe that you will receive a great return on your investment because you will. If you think of this time as an opportunity cost (I could be doing this or that right now) then your time is spent and you will not receive as profitable a return, if any.

In our busy society there is a lot of talk about quality time versus quantity time. In most cases this is our way of justifying not doing the things that we should be doing. If you are *spending* time, then quality-focused time is very important. If you are *investing* time, why would you want to sell yourself short by only investing a little? If your definition of quality time is being there in the moment or that your mind is not wandering or thinking about other things, then we agree that quality time is very important. If quality time is your way of making yourself feel better for only spending half an hour talking with your mate on Tuesday evening because other things took a higher priority, then quality time should be eliminated from your vocabulary.

You can't rush your relationship-building experience. Time is very important even if it is just sitting next to each other holding hands and not saying a word. From now on, think of quantity time as being a key ingredient in the Honeymoon Marriage.

Chivalry

Some think that chivalry is dead. Well, it is alive and kicking in the Honeymoon Marriage. Chivalry is an outward display of courtesy, graciousness, generosity, and even honor. It is typically thought of as gentlemanly acts toward women, however, it doesn't have to be. Chivalrous acts are selfless acts where one offers to do the small things for others. Traditional examples would include opening the door for your spouse, pausing to allow him or her to enter a room first, offering to carry something for your partner, etc. By doing these small things, you are showing your partner how important he or she is to you. You are honoring them in a small yet important way.

These chivalrous acts can be expanded to include doing household chores or anything else that your spouse normally does. Chivalry is attempting to make someone else's life a little easier instead of only being concerned for your own needs and desires. We have all heard the phrase, "He bent over backwards to help them." When was the last time you bent over backwards to do something special for your spouse?

Be on the lookout for ways to be courteous, gracious and generous to your partner. Look for ways to honor your spouse as someone who is more important than the President of the United States.

"Genuine love is honor put
into action regardless of the cost."
- Gary Smalley -

Plan a picnic

It is tough to beat the experience of spending time in the great outdoors. There is something about nature that causes you to relax and recharge your batteries. Depending on where you live, this activity may require a little planning. The perfect day for a picnic is on a sunny afternoon.

Instead of going to a restaurant for lunch, put on your play clothes, drive to a park, and have a picnic. Bring plenty of Frisbees and balls for the kids to play with. As a side note, a picnic is an excellent idea for date night. While the kids are off playing (or at a friend's house or the baby-sitters, in the case of date night) you and your spouse can enjoy each other's company and take in a lot of fresh air and sunshine. Don't be shy; make sure that the two of you get in some playtime of your own. Frisbee's weren't created for just kids, you know.

While sitting on the blanket, talk about all of the beautiful things that you see all around you (don't forget to include your mate—that will score you major love points). Talk about how thankful you are to be alive and to have each other to share your life with. Take in deep breaths of fresh air. Dream about what your life will be like in the future. Enjoy each other's company, relax, and clear your mind of all of the pressures of life.

Praise

We live in a negative culture that always tries to find fault in everything. Just read the paper or watch the news and you will find story after story of what people did wrong. Unfortunately, very little attention is paid to those who have done something praiseworthy. The saying, "no news is good news" is not far from the truth. Let's face it, bad news sells. It seems as though it is easy for us to find fault in others, but it takes a conscious effort to find or at least notice and acknowledge the good and praiseworthy things people do.

Finding fault in one's spouse is a common pastime in many marriages. In order to have the Honeymoon Marriage, you must try and overlook your spouse's faults and focus on what he or she does right.

"Let me be a little kinder,
Let me be a little blinder
To the faults of those around me,
Let me praise a little more."
- Edgar A. Guest -

Go out of your way to find what your mate does well and compliment him or her on it. You may not realize it now, but your spouse does so many things right that if you went out of your way to notice them and then compliment your spouse, you would be complimenting your mate every day. Wow, how do you think you would feel if you received compliments from your spouse every day? It would feel great, wouldn't it? When you praise your spouse, be sincere and be specific. It is fine to say, "you are the world's best husband," however, it is even more meaningful if you say, "I really appreciate your always taking such good care of the lawn. It looks fantastic. You are the world's best husband." Also, make sure to praise your spouse in front of others. This will make your mate feel special like nothing else can.

Avoid people who engage in spouse-bashing conversations. They have a disease that, if caught, can damage your marriage. No one likes to be the oddball and stand out in the crowd; however, you need to redirect the conversation or leave. Guard your mind, because whatever you let into it will affect your life. This will be discussed in great detail in the chapter entitled, "Expanding your mind—the pursuit of knowledge and wisdom." We know of a really great guy who has been treated very poorly by his wife ever since she started hanging around a group of husband-bashing women. Needless to say, their marriage is less than perfect and he feels like he can do nothing right. Would you willingly jump into a pit of venomous snakes? If no, then stay away from people who will poison your mind and surround yourself with like-minded people who have what you want.

Watch the sun set
If you are fortunate enough to live by a large body of water or flat land and can watch the sun set or rise, don't take it for granted. Watching the sun set or rise is an awesome sight. It is without a doubt one of nature's crowning glories. Make it a point to watch it as often as you can and don't rush the experience. The more time we take to marvel at the beauties of nature together, the more it nurtures our spirit and our relationship. If the body of water near you has a shoreline that you can walk along, then you have really got it made. Walks along the beach while holding each other's hand during a sunset are priceless.

If you have never experienced this with your spouse, then save up your money and plan a weekend get-away where you can. There are some things that you cannot afford to miss, and this is one of them. During our last trip to Hawaii, we spent a week on the island of Kauai. The island was small enough that we could watch the sun rise and set all in the same day. What an awesome experience that was! We can't wait to go back there and do it again. It was by far the most relaxing and romantic vacation we have ever had.

Phone when you are going to be late
This is a very simple act that shows mindful consideration for others. The last thing that you want to do is start the rest of your day together on the wrong foot. Arriving late without letting your spouse know ahead of time is not a courteous thing to do. Would you show up an hour late for a very important business engagement without calling to inform the other participants that you will be late? We hope not, and you should show that same kind of consideration for your husband or wife.

Waiting for someone to show up is no big deal when you know when to expect them. So let your spouse know that you are going to be late as soon as you know that that is a possibility. Then be there when you said you would. If you have to call often to inform your spouse that you will be late, then your priorities are misaligned. Make sure you are late as rarely as possible, but if it is going to happen, call and let your spouse know and apologize whether the delay was within your control or not.

Go for walks

Exercise is good for the body, mind and the emotions. Going for long walks together is a great way to reenergize your marriage. It is preferable that you walk outside so that you can take advantage of the fresh air and remove the "closed-in" feeling that you have had throughout the day. Going for a walk at the mall is good as well, however, you will tend to walk a lot slower (limiting your workout potential) and there are a lot of distractions. We have had some of our best conversations while walking. Our conversations have been even better when walking through a park, alongside a river, or though wooded areas. The more natural the setting and the fewer the distractions the better. Many of the thoughts and plans for this book and for our life came to us while we were walking.

"All truly great thoughts are conceived while walking."
- Friedrich Wilhelm Nietzsche -

Walking together is a good time to relieve the pressures of the day. Say whatever is on your mind. Be patient with each other because the conversation may lean toward the negative side at first. Your negative conversation should gradually move toward the positive. It is beneficial to talk about your challenges, but don't dwell on them for too long. Get the weight off of your shoulders and then focus on the positives in your life. This positive conversation should at times gradually move toward forward thinking. Talk about your exciting future together. Talk about all of the exciting things you will experience in your future life together.

"Grow old along with me. The best is yet to be."
- Robert Browning -

It may take you several walks to move from negative conversation to positive conversation. That is perfectly acceptable. There may be a lot of things that you need to work out as a person and as a couple. Make sure to listen intently and do not interrupt the other person. If you go for an hour walk and your spouse talks for the whole hour, that is OK—don't worry, you will get your turn. It may take several more walks before your conversation moves from positive dialogue to future planning and focusing on the exciting times ahead. This transition is a balancing act. You need to talk about your exciting future together, but you also need to live in the moment. While it is true that today's plans and activities determine tomorrow's reality, don't give up today for the sake of planning for tomorrow.

Take time to smell the roses. Enjoy the experience of being together. Notice all of the beautiful things around you. Every walk shouldn't be for the primary purpose of exercise. Slow down every once in a while and soak in all that nature has to offer. Stop and give each other a hug and a kiss. Hold hands while you walk. If you are too busy to go for a daily walk, then you are too busy to have a Honeymoon Marriage. Your daily walk is definitely time invested, not time spent.

If you have small children, pull them along in a wagon. If they can ride a bike, have them ride alongside you. If they want to walk let them walk with you. Your walks can be as short as twenty minutes or as long as several hours, whatever works for you at the time.

Going for a bike ride
Walks are great because they can cause you to slow down a bit and have great conversations, but when it comes to exercise, we prefer to go for a bike ride. Bike riding can give you an excellent low-impact workout. Running is okay but it can be a little rough on your joints. You can also take in a lot more scenery on a bike since you can cover more land in the same amount of time. And don't forget the wind in your face.

With a nice leisurely bike ride you can also combine exercise with a picnic. Just add a saddlebag to your bike or carry a small backpack and you can ride to your little picnic hideaway. There is one drawback to riding bikes as a couple. One of you will most likely be a faster rider than the other. If you are the faster rider slow down and never push the other person unless he or she wants to be pushed for exercise purposes. You are not in a race, so take it easy and enjoy your surroundings and each other.

A massage
We have already covered the importance of the human touch, however, you can take the power of the touch one giant step forward by giving each other a massage. A massage is an awesome stress

SMALL THINGS MEAN A LOT

reliever. It is also a very selfless act and an outward expression of your love for your partner. The shoulders are a good place to start since a lot of our tension is stored up in these muscles. A good shoulder massage can be done in almost any environment and should be done often.

Take classes or read books covering the topic. Learn where the pressure points are and how to give a proper massage. But don't wait to become fully educated, start today. Your spouse will tell you where the tension is and will greatly appreciate your time and effort. If you are on the receiving end, remember not to be selfish and make sure to return the favor.

The signal of love

When we started dating we created a hand signal that meant "I love you."

Signaling*:* One day I(Darren) was driving behind Donna and she stuck her hand through to sunroof opening and gave me the "I love you" signal. No matter where we are as long as we are within eyesight of each other we can say, "I love you."

How awesome to be able to express your love for each other when it is not convenient or appropriate to talk. Create your own unique hand signal. If you cannot think of one, learn how to say, "I love you" in sign language. Then make sure to use your new talent often.

Let dinnertime be quiet time

Our lives are filled with so much noise that we eventually don't hear it anymore. We all need a break from external or artificial noise. Make sure that you set aside quiet times to be experienced throughout the day. One of these times should be observed during dinner. Make sure to turn off the radio and TV while eating dinner. Your focus should be on the family unit and not on current affairs. This is a time when you can discuss each other's daily events. Enjoy your time together and be thankful that you have a roof over your head and food on the table.

Birthday month

We all like to be pampered on our birthday. We get to decide where to go, what to eat, and what to do. It should be a day of celebration and appreciation, not just a day of gift giving. The day goes by so quickly that before you know it you are back to life as usual. We like to extend the feeling of being King or Queen for the day into the whole month. We call it our birthday month. The whole month is reserved for the birthday person to have the first say as to what he or she would like to do each day. These events don't have to be anything extravagant, just a touch more special than the average day.

Go camping

Perhaps you can see a theme being created. Some of your most meaningful experiences can be free or at least very inexpensive. Many of these experiences entail spending a little more time with Mother Nature. What makes nature so great is all of the things that it doesn't have. There is no phone, no fax machine, no boss, no television, no radio, no one ringing the doorbell, and no traffic. Camping can be an inexpensive getaway and one that can be done whenever the weather permits. You can stay in a cabin, use a motor home, bring a pop-up trailer, or pack up the family car with gear and sleep in tents. We prefer to rough it and go backpacking. It is a neat feeling to know that everything that you need to survive the weekend is strapped to your back. Backpacking is also great exercise.

If you are not quite that adventurous, any of the abovementioned methods will do just fine. Regardless of which method you choose, make sure to go for hikes and build a campfire every night. We have already covered the benefits of going for a walk so let's focus on the campfire. Campfires are great any time of year; however, they really come in handy on those cool fall nights. Spending time around the campfire is the perfect way to end the day. Gather close, talk, tell stories, sing, and last but not least, roast marshmallows. No camping trip is complete without the ritualistic roasting of the marshmallows.

> *"Remember that a good marriage is like a campfire.*
> *Both grow cold if left unattended."*
> *- H. Jackson Brown, Jr. –*

Camping can bond a family together like no other activity. If you want to create memories for your children that will last a lifetime, then go camping with them.

Go to an art gallery or museum

This can be a lot of fun and it also enables you to learn more about your partner's likes and dislikes. Living just outside of Chicago allows us the opportunity to have great cultural experiences. Even if you live in a small town, make it a point to travel to the nearest cultural center in your state and take advantage of these great attractions. Eight years ago when we lived in Wisconsin, we visited a paperweight museum in a small northern Wisconsin town. That's right, a whole museum with nothing but paperweights. We had a great time. Visiting an art gallery is also a great experience. Who knows, it may even ignite a creative spark in you or your partner.

Attend a play, opera, ballet or the symphony
This is the cultural experience at its finest. It is great to see a well-made film or listen to music on a high-end sound system, but nothing can compare to a live performance. The sound, the sight, the whole experience is wonderful. This "small thing" will be more expensive and require more planning than many of the others, but the experience is well worth it. We once heard that there are two things that are always worth spending money on. One is education and the other is experiences. We couldn't agree more. Save your money, book a baby-sitter and make it a night to remember.

Go to concerts
No matter what category of music you enjoy, there is a band traveling throughout the country putting on live concerts. Nothing can replace the energy of a live concert. This activity may even bring back memories of when you were dating (yes, there are still groups that play all of your big band favorites).

Give cards
This is a wonderful inexpensive way of reaffirming your love for your mate. We're not talking about cards that commemorate a holiday, anniversary, birthday or other special event. What we are talking about is a card that is given just because you care. It is spontaneous and unexpected. Make sure to write something special on the inside of the card to add that special touch. Remember that men love to hear how proud you are of them, how much you appreciate them, and anything else that will boost their ego. Women love to hear how much they mean to you, how special they are, how lucky you are to have them and that given the chance, you would marry them all over again.

Write love letters
Love letters are also great and can be as short or as long as you would like. You may even want to give poetry a shot. Even if you do a lousy job, your lover will appreciate the effort. Writing down your feelings for someone else is not only great for that person, but it is also great for you as well. When you write a letter, your total focus and attention is directed toward what you will say and how you will

say it. Through the writing process, you might even uncover some loving feelings that you hadn't felt in a long time.

Darren's love note: Just today Donna was in the office on the phone with the door closed. I was working out and between sets I thought of something that I wanted to tell her. I didn't want to wait because I thought that I might forget. So I wrote a love note, stuck it on a thin book and slid it under the door. About fifteen minutes later she came out smiling from ear to ear. It took me twenty seconds to write, ten seconds to deliver, but it made a full day's worth of impact.

To add a little spice and excitement, hide some of the notes and letters where you know your lover looks every day. Go out of your way to demonstrate how much you care and love your mate.

Whisper sweet nothings

Years ago we heard that if you wanted to get someone's attention that you should whisper. That didn't make any sense to us but we tried it several times anyway. To our disbelief, it worked. We are not sure exactly why it works, but it does. Maybe it is because we whisper when we tell someone something that we don't want anyone else to hear, which causes others around you to become curious. Curiosity gets the best of us and we want to be let in on the secret.

We can't stand the fact that someone knows something that we don't know and is keeping it a secret. Just tell your spouse that you have picked out his or her birthday present and that it is awesome, but refuse to tell him or her what it is. See if that doesn't drive your mate crazy. Likewise, the person receiving the whisper feels special that you picked him or her to be the one to hear your secret. Whisper sweet nothings in your lover's ear. There is no doubt that it will make your mate feel special.

Work together

Every household has its share of chores. Whenever possible, do them together. Wash the car together instead of taking it to the car wash. Prepare the meal together. Wash the dishes while your partner dries them. Have your spouse rake the leaves while you put them in the bags. This allows you to have great conversation, and time seems to go by much faster as well.

Pet Peeves

We all have things that get under our skin. Most of these irritants are insignificant, yet we allow them to bother us and affect our marriage. These small things may include the following:

- Squeezing the tube of toothpaste in the middle versus at the end
- Placing the roll of toilet paper so that the sheets fall behind versus in front of the roll
- Throwing dirty clothes on the floor versus placing them in the laundry room
- Hanging clothes in the closet so that they all face to the right versus the left or facing both directions
- Channel surfing vs. finding the program that you want to watch and staying there
- Leaving the toilet seat up, and countless other things that you and your spouse know all too well

There are, however, two things that you can do to rid yourself of this constant source of annoyance.

First, if you know that one or more of your habits bothers your spouse, you can choose to stop doing it. You are an intelligent adult with the free will to do anything that you choose. You have the ability to achieve great feats. You may be able to raise a family, run a household, become a middle manager at a Fortune 500 company, start your own business, rebuild a Chevrolet 327 small block, organize a major event, operate complicated machinery, or even become a U.S. Senator, but you can't remember to squeeze the tube of toothpaste at the end instead of the middle?

Come on, you just don't want to change, and that is not the right attitude to have if you want the Honeymoon Marriage. Decide to change, focus on it and then make it happen. Remember, small things mean a lot.

Second, you can learn to accept your spouse as he or she is. No, your mate is not perfect, but he or she is yours for now and for always. Stop taking these personal mannerisms so seriously. In the overall scheme of things, these habits are really not that important. Don't keep nagging your spouse every time you see something that isn't done the way you would like it to be done. The next time your spouse commits one of these small acts, take on a new attitude. Think about the situation differently. The next time he or she throws an article of clothing on the ground, smile, pick it up and put it where you want it and say to yourself, "I love Jim so much. What would he do without me?"

*" The art of being wise is the art of knowing
what to overlook. "*
- William James -

It is ironic that some of the things that widows and widowers miss most about their spouse are some of the things that drove them crazy when they were together. All of these small things make us unique. Learn to appreciate each other's uniqueness.

Volunteering
Volunteering is one of the biggest small things that you can do. Anytime you selflessly give of yourself; you get a lot more back in return. If possible volunteer together as a couple. It is also great to involve your children in this process. The earlier they learn the importance of helping others, the better. Where you volunteer your time and energy is your decision. Go with the first thought that pops into your head, it is usually the right one.

Volunteering can be very therapeutic. It is easy to think about all of our problems during the course of the day. It is even easier when we have idle time on our hands and are in our everyday environment. Unfortunately, our attention tends to gravitate toward the negative if we are not careful. We can start to think of all of the things that we don't have instead of being thankful for all of the things that we do have. Our self-talk can consist of phrases like, "I wish that . . . ," "If only . . . ," "Why does this always happen to me?" etc. This negative focus can have a snowball effect where one negative thought leads us to think about another, which leads us to think about another, etc. These unpleasant thoughts can lead us to feeling sorry for ourselves.

Spending time with people who are less fortunate than yourself is a great way to take your focus off of your problems while simultaneously making you feel a little more fortunate to have the life that you lead. There is nothing like a little perspective to get us out of the rut of thinking that we have it so bad.

Volunteering will make you feel better about yourself, and when *you* like *you* just a little bit more, others will as well. It is amazing how an improved sense of self-worth can cause others to treat you differently. When you see yourself as being more valuable, so will others. Your increased sense of self-worth will also cause you to look harder to find the value in others. Helping others, being more grateful for what you have, focusing more on the positives and less on the negatives and feeling better about yourself will undoubtedly improve the quality of your life and your marriage.

Celebration and rewards

Rewards and celebration can go hand in hand with praise. You should look for reasons to celebrate and reward yourself, your spouse, your children and others. If you only celebrate the big things in life like birthdays, anniversaries, promotions, weddings, graduations and major accomplishments, then you are missing out on one of life's basic pleasures. While it is good to celebrate all of these things, we should also celebrate the small things as well.

A good example of this is with parents of eight-month-old infants. Somewhere between seven and eleven months, little Jimmy decides that he wants to try and walk. He pulls himself up and stands up holding on to the furniture. He takes one or two steps and then immediately falls down. The celebration begins. Mom and Dad are so excited that little Jimmy is almost ready to walk. They grab and praise him for his accomplishment. Several days later he walks the full length of the couch holding on for dear life. Another celebration is in order. A few days after that he stands next to the furniture and watches as they hold their arms out motioning for him to come to them. He lets go of the furniture, sways back and forth as he catches his balance, takes one or two steps forward and falls down. Yet another celebration is in order.

Why get all excited and celebrate? After all, he hasn't even walked yet. We celebrate because he is moving forward in his progression. Unfortunately, we are not always so free to celebrate our own small steps forward or the progress of others. We reserve the celebration for the big event. We aren't satisfied with the fact that we took our first steps or even that we have started to walk. It is no big deal when we start to jog, run and then sprint. Sometimes we won't even celebrate until we have won first place in the one hundred-meter dash of life.

It is good to have goals, plans and high expectations, however, if you reserve the celebration until you have arrived, you may miss out on the enjoyment of the process. You may even get frustrated along the way and give up altogether. Learn to acknowledge and celebrate the small accomplishments in your life and do the same with others. When we were writing this book, we celebrated every twenty-five pages or so. When we hit one hundred we made a night of it. Even though the book was a long way from being complete, we acted as though it just became a Best Seller. Our excitement caused the next twenty-five pages to be written with considerably less effort than it took to write the first twenty-five.

It really is true that life is a journey and not just a destination. Make sure to reward yourself, your spouse and your children at various stages along the way. The reward doesn't have to be big or expensive. It is not the reward itself that matters but rather what it stands for. Some of our most prized awards cost less than a dollar. A blue ribbon doesn't cost that much, but it sure can make you feel awesome. Look for occasions to reward your spouse. Show your lover how proud you are of him or her. Ask what your mate would like to do to celebrate and then go do it. A little celebration and a small reward can go a long way toward helping you reach your goals whatever they may be.

Adjust and adapt
Oftentimes the difference between success and failure is in the daily tweaking or adjustments that we make. A ship set out to sea has to make several course adjustments in order to reach its final destination. The best chefs taste their creation several times to make sure that it has the flavor or balance that they are looking for. If something is slightly off, they add to it until it is just right. The same thing needs to be done to your marriage. You need to be constantly making minor adjustments in the way you treat, respond, relate and act toward your mate. Keep in mind that these adjustments start with you. Don't look at all of the things that your spouse could do a little differently, but instead focus on yourself. In many cases we get instant feedback from our spouse every time we do something. If your mate reacts negatively, don't think to yourself, "What is his or her problem?" After all, in a marriage "your mate's problem" is now "your problem" and you need to make the necessary adjustments or add the needed ingredients to give it the flavor that you are looking for.

"When we are no longer able to change a situation,
we are challenged to change ourselves."
- Victor Frankl -

We can be very stubborn and unwilling to change our ways. We expect our spouse to change, but we are hesitant to change our own behavior. In short, we are selfish. Selfishness and marriage mix together like oil and water. If you want the Honeymoon Marriage, then you need to make adjustments to your thinking and your actions throughout your marriage. We oftentimes think that if we keep doing what we are doing that somehow things will change for the better. One of the greatest minds of all times calls this kind of behavior insanity.

*"Insanity is doing the same thing over and over again
and expecting different results."*
- Albert Einstein -

If your partner's favorite flavor of ice cream is chocolate, would you always buy him or her butterscotch because that is your favorite? If years later your mate develops a taste for orange sherbet, will you continue to buy chocolate ice cream? Those may seem like silly questions, however, that is exactly what we do every day in our married life. If your wife says that you never listen to her every time you try to offer advice and solve her problems, then you need to just listen and empathize with her. This will let her know that you understand and care for her.

If your wife loves to get flowers every once in a while, but you think that they are a waste of money, then you need to stop trying to understand her and just buy the flowers. If your husband doesn't want to talk about his day right when he gets home from work, then you need to give him some space and down time before attempting to carry on a conversation with him. If your wife needs to hear you tell her that you love her, stop trying to think logically that she should know that you love her, and tell her that you do and that you appreciate her as well.

Not only do we need to make adjustments in order to live a fulfilled married life, but we also need to adapt to each other's differences. Stop trying to change your mate or hope that your mate will change. Accept your lover the way he or she is, appreciate the fact that you are two completely different human beings, and learn to adapt to your differences. By adapting, we don't mean to always conform to your mate's way of thinking or doing things. That, of course, may rob you of your individuality. By adapting you realize that differences are a fact of life, and you figure out how *your mate's* needs can fit into *your* life as a married couple.

If your husband watches football as a form of emotional release, allow him this time. If your wife has to go through every rack in every store at three different malls just to find one blue blouse, then allow her this experience, as it may be her emotional release. If you grew up in Miami and moved to Chicago in January, you would need to adapt to the cold weather or freeze to death. Don't let your marriage freeze to death. Learn to live with each other's differences and needs.

Look your best

Most people are familiar with the business world's slogan "dress for success." We know that one should be well groomed and try and look his or her best in order to make a good impression on clients, customers and managers. It is no secret in the business world that if one wants to be promoted into management, one has to look the part. Once a person gets the promotion, however, he or she can't start showing up for work in a T-shirt and jeans. It doesn't work that way. The manager has to always look the part and always try to make a good impression.

As discussed in the chapter entitled "Dating your spouse—rekindling the flame," you tried to look your best when you first started dating. You wanted to look good in an attempt to win your spouse over. Now that you have your spouse, you still need to act that way. Do you look sharp during the week and then let yourself go on the weekend? If you are a stay-at-home caregiver, how do you look when your spouse comes home from work? Do you look like you went out of your way to impress your mate, or do you look like you really don't care what your mate thinks of your appearance? This is an especially important area for women because men are turned on through sight, whereas affection and touch turn on women.

This may be a tough pill to swallow, but how do you look today compared to how you looked when you first got married? Of course we are only talking about things that you have control over. We are not talking about gray hair, the balding man, or the woman who is developing wrinkles around her eyes. In our opinion these are beauty marks, a sign that the two of you are maturing together. What we are referring to is how you dress, groom and take care of yourself.

Are you twenty-five to thirty pounds heavier today? Are you sending signals to your spouse that he or she is so important to you that you want to always look good for him or her, or do you treat your appearance as though it is not that important now that you are married? Don't fall into this dangerous trap, and if you already have, climb out as quickly as you can. There is a lot of competition out there. Prepare to meet it head on. You put forth quite an effort to get your mate and it is your responsibility to put forth at least as strong an effort to keep him or her. The last thing you want is for your spouse to be surrounded by sharp people of the opposite sex all day, every day and then come home to you who is looking less than desirable.

Women in particular will go to great lengths to look their best for their wedding day. Why not continue that effort throughout the marriage?

Looking our best: Darren is in better shape today than he was when we got married twelve years ago, and I (Donna) am on target to be there in about three months. No it's not easy, but your mate is worth it and so is your marriage.

Use common sense and don't be afraid to ask your spouse what he or she wants.

Whiskers: Darren likes to give his face a break and not shave once or twice a week. For me that is no problem because I (Donna) love it. Someone else's wife may be different. She may find an unshaven face to be unattractive. In other words, look the way that you know turns your spouse on because if you don't someone else might.

Avoid temptation

This next suggestion may seem extreme. All we are telling you is what we practice and what has allowed us to have a Honeymoon Marriage. Avoid spending too much time with or being alone with someone of the opposite sex. Many of the affairs that destroy marriages start out very innocently by one or both parties. Your relationship with this person may seem harmless. You enjoy his or her company and all you ever do together is talk. This is especially dangerous for women.

As mentioned earlier, most women feel that their husbands don't talk to them enough. They oftentimes equate talking with caring and are drawn to the person who will listen and understand them. There is a lot of competition out in the world and there are even people who would try and steal your mate away from you. These people prey on struggling relationships and are masters at their trade. They will compliment and be kind to the wife who feels neglected or unappreciated by her husband. Perhaps she is lonely and doesn't have many close friends; he'll be there to comfort her.

She looks sharp and flirts with a man's ego. She tells him how smart and talented he is. An already wounded man or woman is vulnerable to this kind of attention. A good way to keep this from happening is to make all efforts to avoid compromising situations. If you need to spend time with someone of the opposite sex, then take someone else with you, preferably your spouse.

The power and importance of a kiss and a hug were discussed earlier. It is important that we use caution and better judgment concerning with whom we share these signs of affection. There are a lot of hurt and lonely people out there who are looking for love in all the wrong places. It is best to err on the side of caution than to inadvertently give someone the wrong idea. Relationship and age are big factors regarding with whom and how we kiss and hug others. Relatives can be the recipients of all the forms of affection that we care to give. This would include a kiss, hugs, telling them you love them, etc.

There are two basic types of hugs. One is the full embrace or the bear hug. The other is the one-arm hug. The bear hug needs no explanation. The one-arm hug is an appropriate way to hug someone of the opposite sex that is not a family member. The one-arm hug is done using only one arm, and contact with the other person is typically made at the shoulders and neck as you lean toward the other person to give them a hug. The exception to this rule is when it applies to people your parents' age or your children's age. We have been using the one-arm hug for years, and it is not in any way a signal to the other person that we don't care about him or her. We would venture to say that most people don't even notice or give it much thought.

Also, listen to each other. If one of you feels uncomfortable about the other spending time with someone of the opposite sex, or picks up on someone's flirtatious signals, then respect your partner's judgment and remove yourself from the situation. Many men are oblivious to these signals, so women, make sure to protect your relationship and men, trust your wife's judgment.

Ask for ways to improve your marriage
This has already been discussed, but it warrants repeating. How would you react if you worked hard for an employer for years, and your boss never told you how well you were doing or what areas of improvement were needed and then one day fired you? After the initial shock, you would probably ask your boss why your were being fired. How would you feel if he or she told you that it was because you weren't doing things correctly or efficiently enough? You would probably get defensive and become very angry, hurt or even betrayed. It is not fair to expect someone to do the right things if he or she doesn't know what the right things are. The same thing is true in your marriage. We are not talking about constantly pointing out what your spouse does wrong and how you would like him or her to change. That can be very damaging to your relationship. As a married couple ask each other for input and do not offer unsolicited suggestions.

Listen to music

If music can calm the savage beast, then think what it can do for we more civilized creatures. Music touches us on an emotional, spiritual and even intellectual level. The calming effects of mellow or inspirational music make it an excellent end-of-the-day experience. Many Americans have a stressful day at work followed by the commute home, dinner at a busy and loud restaurant or eating while watching TV, a brief conversation with each of the family members and end the day with the highly negative evening news.

They then find it difficult to get to sleep, don't have a sound sleep or wake up feeling less than refreshed. They may not feel it now, but that kind of a lifestyle will eventually catch up with them, and when it does, it won't show much mercy. Listening to soft, slow or inspirational music helps us to slow down, relax and ease our way into a good night's sleep. We prefer to listen to acoustical guitar, harp or soft piano music. Snuggling close to your lover and listening to classical or spiritual music accompanied by a hot mug of your favorite noncaffeinated herbal tea with just a touch of honey is an excellent way to end the day.

Avoid sarcasm and disempowering jokes

Be careful not to make jokes about your spouse's shortcomings. Having a laugh at someone else's expense is not a good habit to have. These seemingly harmless remarks can have a damaging effect on his or her sense of worth and it will definitely affect the quality of your relationship. Sarcasm and harsh remarks should also be avoided when referring to each other. Sarcasm is derived from the Greek word *sarkazein*, which means "to tear flesh." Sarcastic comments can cut deep, and they have no place in the Honeymoon Marriage. Think of your relationship as a magnifying glass in front of a mirror. Whatever you project into it is magnified and then reflected back to you. Be kind to each other and follow the age-old adage, "If you don't have anything nice to say, then don't say anything at all."

Consistency

Consistency is another really big small thing. Consistency is one of the best-kept secrets to achieving success in any area of life. Anyone can do something once, twice or every now and then, but the person who is consistently doing the right things will reach new heights in his or her life. Once there, he or she will continue to grow and move forward. If you truly desire to have an incredible marriage, then you need to be consistent. Your spouse won't be that impressed if you phone that you will be late one day but forget to do so the next time it happens. Helping your spouse with the dishes once is good, but if you really want to score points, do it often. Hug and tell your mate that you love him or her every day, not just when you feel like it. Buy your wife flowers for every birthday and every Valentine's Day. Go out on a date at least once a month. Invest quality time in your marriage every day. Always say "thank you", "please" and "I appreciate you."

"Gratitude is the most exquisite form of courtesy."
- Jacques Maritain -

Continuously look for reasons to praise your spouse. Don't let your mate's irritating habits pass by you one day and then get all hot and bothered about them the following week. Eliminate the Dr. Jekyll and Mr. Hyde routine of being patient and caring one day and then exploding in anger the next. Compliment your mate often. Consistency builds trust in a relationship, and trust is the foundation of intimacy. Our hope is that you consistently apply the principles described in this book to your life and your marriage.

The combination of all of the "small things" listed above adds up to be a very powerful package. Doing these things may even make you feel like you did when you first got married, perhaps even better. People may even mistake you as newlyweds.

Six months ago we spent some time in Hawaii. On our flight to Hawaii, a flight attendant handed us a bottle of champagne, two wine glasses and said, "Congratulations! This is our treat since you are on your honeymoon." When we told her that we had been married for eleven years, she couldn't believe it and told us to keep the gift anyway. As you can see, the small things don't just mean a lot, they mean everything. For they are the outward expression of our inward feelings and they create wonderful experiences that will last in our memories forever. Please don't wait for the feelings before you act. Act now—the feelings will follow.

We would enjoy hearing about the small things that make a big difference in your marriage. Go to www.honeymoonmarriage.com and click on the keyword "small things" to tell us your story.

CHAPTER 12

THE ATTITUDE
OF LOVE

There is a saying that an attitude is a small thing that makes a big difference. We think that it is best described as a big thing that makes all the difference in the world. Psychiatrist Dr. Karl Menninger said, "Attitudes are more important than facts." This is true because your attitude is determined by how you perceive a fact. How you perceive a fact can regulate how you will feel about that fact. And how you feel will determine how you act and react.

Rain, rain go away, come back some other day

It was my (Darren's) birthday weekend and Donna and I had planned on going hiking through the woods, checking out a waterfall, sitting alongside a lake armed with a picnic basket full of goodies. We woke up early that morning to the sound of rain. We both love the sound of rain, however, it would put a damper on our outdoor plans. Since it was raining we decided that we would do a little shopping, catch some lunch at a great Italian restaurant, hang out and have a great time. We could then go hiking the next day as the chance of rain was much less. We did just that and had a wonderful time. The next day it rained ten times harder than the day before. It was raining so hard that the roads started to flood, and it continued to rain for the rest of the day. Day two of the indoor activities.

We had a great time! It was one of the most enjoyable weekends that we have had in a long time. While shopping, we bought my birthday chair. It is from that chair that I write this account. All of our plans were spoiled by the weather, so what made this birthday so great? Our attitude. Our attitudes were more important than the facts (rain). We could have complained and had a bad attitude, but instead we had a blast.

"The greatest discovery of my generation is that human beings can alter their lives by altering their attitudes of mind."
- William James -

Of course a rainy birthday is really no big deal, plans or no plans. What kind of attitude should one have if something a little more serious should happen? The answer of course is to have a good, optimistic attitude. The converse will not make your circumstances any better. As a matter of fact, a bad attitude can only make things worse.

Our honeymoon experience

Things don't have to be perfect in your relationship in order to have a Honeymoon Marriage. As a matter of fact the perfect marriage is impossible. It is impossible for two imperfect people to come together in an imperfect world and develop the perfect relationship. However, if you have the right attitude, focus on the positive rather than the negative and consciously try to improve your relationship, then you will find that life with your partner can really be quite wonderful. We'll bet that if you were to look back at your honeymoon, you would remember that it wasn't perfect either. There were things that went wrong, and all of your plans may not have turned out exactly as you had wanted them to. Perhaps the weather didn't cooperate, your reservations got messed up, you or your spouse got sick or any number of other less-than-ideal circumstances. Even though things weren't perfect, it didn't seem to matter that much. Your primary focus was on your spouse, not your circumstances. You were able to overlook these less-than-perfect events as you looked forward to having a great time and starting a wonderful life together. Everything was new and you expected great things to happen.

Honeymoon fun: We had a blast on our honeymoon. Money was tight so we planned a budget honeymoon. Donna was still in school and I (Darren) was barely making enough money to support one person. I was working in Greenville, South Carolina, at the time so we planned a week at Myrtle Beach. A few things happened that week that could have put a damper on the rest of our honeymoon stay.

While driving to Myrtle Beach, we ran out of gas. (I had a bad habit of running the car to almost empty before filling it up.) Cell phones were not the craze back then, so we locked up the car and went for a little walk. We weren't exactly in a heavily populated area, so we decided to stop at the next house that we could see and ask to use their phone. We walked across a field to a farmhouse, knocked on the door, explained our situation and asked to use their phone. These very nice strangers offered to drive us to the gas station, then dropped us off at our car and we were off and running.

We arrived at our hotel much later than planned, so we checked in and went straight to bed. Around 2:00 in the morning a fire had started in our hotel. The alarms went off and everyone evacuated the building. We were all standing outside staring at the building wondering what was going on, since we didn't see any flames or smoke. Fortunately, the fire was small and was contained to just one or two rooms. After we found out that all was clear, we stayed outside for a few minutes holding each other's hand. The beach is so wonderful at night. The moonlight and stars were just bright enough for us to make out the white turbulence of the waters as the waves crashed against the shore. The sounds of the waves hitting the water and the beach had a calming effect on us, almost hypnotic. Had it not been for the fire, we would have missed a unique moment with each other.

While at Myrtle Beach, we purchased an inflatable mattress/raft. It was about queen size with a pillow top and recessed areas the size of soda cans throughout. We were floating about fifty yards off shore and enjoying a very relaxing day. Later that afternoon the waves started to increase in size. The surfers were out and they looked like they were having a great time. So I (Darren) decided that we should join them. I still have an adventurous streak in me that comes out now and then. I had done some boogie boarding earlier that week and got a feel for how to ride a wave. We paddled out about eighty yards from shore, then turned the raft so that our heads were facing the shoreline and waited for the next big wave to come in. I told Donna to pull up on the front end of the raft as hard as she could so that we wouldn't take a nosedive into the water when the next big wave came along.

A huge wave came from behind us and we knew that this was the one. We both pulled up on the front end and braced ourselves for the ride of our lives. The timing was perfect and we road the raft all the way to shore. Wow, what a rush! We were both excited and of course we wanted to do it again. We paddled back out and waited patiently for the next big one. By this time it was getting late and high tide was starting to come in. The waves were getting even larger than before. Finally, our wave had arrived. It was coming up fast and it looked as though it was going to be twice the size of the wave we had ridden earlier. We pulled up on the front end and held on for dear life. The wave kept getting bigger, and bigger and bigger. By the time it reached our little raft it had already peaked. I thought that we would have to pull up as hard as we could in order to ride this one—but it was too late for that. The giant wall of water crashed down and swallowed us up like Jonah's whale. We were both held under the water by its force and couldn't tell which way was up. We kept struggling until our heads finally broke through to the surface of the water. We were under the water for about fifteen seconds, but it seemed like an eternity. We almost drowned and were very thankful to be alive. The rest of our water time that week was spent at the pool.

On our way back home after the honeymoon was over, we made a wrong turn that took us two hours out of our way.

The abovementioned events could have caused us to have a bad attitude or at least be disappointed that everything wasn't going in our favor. But since it was our honeymoon, these things didn't really seem to matter that much. We focused so much on the good things that the bad things seemed insignificant. Was our honeymoon perfect? No, but it was still awesome and we had a great time loving each other and enjoying life. The same thing can be true in your marriage. Things will not always go the way you had planned for them to. You will travel over some pretty rocky roads in life. You will run out of gas, get knocked down by the wave of life and take a wrong turn or two. Through all of these things, stay close to each other and know that this too will pass. Focus on all of the good around you and be thankful for all of the things that you have. Cherish each and every day as you cherish each other. Live your life together with a honeymoon kind of love.

Darren and the pink slip: Five months ago I was downsized from my position as a sales manager for a Global Fortune 500 company. The company had already cut approximately 10,000 employees several months earlier and was planning on cutting 11,000 more. Yours truly was part of the second cut, as was my boss's boss.

Three days after I was given the proverbial "pink slip," we spent part of the day with our friends Amy and Steve. They had a lot of great things happening in their lives, and we were happy to share in their excitement. They had just gotten back from their one-year wedding anniversary getaway and had just put down the earnest money on a beautiful new home. We went to the model with them and they gave us a tour with great excitement and pride. As we were heading to the restaurant later that day, they asked what was new with us. I told them that I was downsized on Thursday.

Amy's response said it all. "That must be very exciting for you guys." She was right; the thought of new beginnings was exciting. Our friends knew us well enough to know that we have a great outlook (attitude) on life.

We believe that everything happens for a reason. We know that our position in life will continually get better as we get better. This is true because the choices that we make today will end up becoming tomorrow's reality.

As you educate yourself and strive to improve every area of your life, you make better decisions today, which will lead to a better tomorrow. This cycle can continue for as long as you demonstrate the discipline required to make better choices. And it is your attitude that allows you to continue down this narrow path, a road less traveled, if you will.

> *"Two roads diverge in a wood,*
> *and I—I took the one less traveled by,*
> *And that has made all the difference."*
> *- Robert Frost -*

We will go into greater detail regarding how this potentially terrible situation was turned into a awesome opportunity and how you can do the same in the chapter entitled "Nurturing your spirit—the road to inner peace."

In life it is always best to focus on what you want rather than what you don't want. This is true because what you focus on the most will eventually become a reality. Our minds are very powerful in that they can transform thought into reality. You may be in perfect health, but if you think that you will get sick and focus on that thought long enough, the odds are that you will get sick. Although there was nothing wrong with you initially, the symptoms that have developed are very real.

This is known as a psychosomatic illness. You have probably heard of the placebo effect, where an ill person can take a placebo (sugar tablet) thinking that it is a powerful drug and that person's health improves. As long as the person believes that he or she will be cured by that wonder drug (sugar tablet), he or she oftentimes is. Some studies have shown that as many as 33 percent of patients who take a placebo get better.

You can see from these two examples that what you focus on can materialize. Therefore, don't focus on all of the bad things about your marriage, instead focus on how you want it to be, thereby creating in your mind a clear mental picture. Start treating your partner as though he or she is already exactly the way that you would like him or her to be. Treat your mate as though he or she is giving you everything that you need in your relationship. Your new attitude toward your lover will speak louder than words and you will begin to see a positive change in your relationship. The universe has a way of giving us back what we give out. It is a cause and effect relationship.

"It is our attitude toward life that
determines life's attitude toward us.
Our attitude tells the world what we expect in return."
- Earl Nightingale -

Your attitudes are the feelings or emotions that you have toward a given situation, and it is your attitude that determines your level of success in every area of your life. Can you see how important having a positive attitude can be? That doesn't mean that we ignore negative situations, we just look at them differently. Look at the negative thoughts that you have toward your marriage, your spouse and love as being temporary hurdles. Know that all of these areas of your life can improve and believe that they will. Look at the negative briefly and only in order to generate a game plan on how to make it a positive. You have probably heard the saying, "when life hands you a lemon, just add some sugar and make lemonade out of it." That is a very simplistic example, however, in principle it can be effective. Where do you need to add some sugar in your marriage?

People who have good attitudes tend to be proactive and take charge of their life. They look at things as they are and discover ways to make them better. Take a look again at the things that you wrote down as being "negative." The first question that you need to ask yourself is, "What can *I* do to make this situation better?" This is an empowering question where you take control and take responsibility for your marriage.

Avoid asking yourself disempowering questions that make you feel helpless and stuck in your current situation. Disempowering questions are ones like, "Why do these things always happen to me?" "Why does he/she always treat me like this?" "Why doesn't he/she compliment me, hug me or say that he/she loves me as much as I would like him/her to?" The problem with disempowering questions is that they give you disempowering answers. These answers can be even worse than the original problem. If you ask yourself why your spouse doesn't compliment you, your mind will come up with an answer. That answer will most likely not be the correct one. Your disempowering answer may be because he or she thinks that you are not attractive.

Asking disempowering questions and getting disempowering answers is a downward spiral that makes you feel more and more trapped and helpless. After all, these answers are only true if you think that they are.

"The easiest person to deceive is one's own self."
- Edward Bulwer-Lytton -

Adopt the following attitudes and a greater sense of happiness is sure to follow. Repeat them out loud to yourself every morning and night until you believe without a shadow of a doubt that they are true.

- I have the ability to improve every area of my life, especially my marriage.
- I look at the negatives in my marriage as only temporary challenges that we can overcome and believe that these negative areas will eventually become the most positive.
- I am a lovable and attractive person.
- I love my spouse more today than I did yesterday.
- I am an enthusiastic, energetic and fun-loving person and people love to be around me.
- I always look for ways to make my marriage better and act on an idea as soon as it comes to me.
- Today I will discover what my spouse wants and needs and I will give it to him or her without expecting anything in return.

Developing a positive mental attitude is a lifelong process. Ridding yourself of your negative attitudes is not easy. Negative thinking and negative attitudes have been a lifelong habit for many people and it will take time and mental discipline to change this thought process. It is very important that you give this area of your life the attention that it deserves because the better your attitude is, the better your marriage will be.

A great marriage is not easy even though some couples make it look that way. You need to understand that your marriage is either getting better or it is getting worse. Nothing stays the same. Purposely looking for and focusing on the positive in every situation is an excellent first step. A powerful second step is to concentrate on eliminating the negative thoughts that go through your mind every day. More will be discussed regarding the power of our thoughts in the chapter entitled "Expanding your mind—the pursuit of knowledge and wisdom."

Develop the attitude of expectancy

An amazing thing happens when you expect great things to take place in your life. It is almost as though you become a magnet attracting success to your life. The stronger your expectancy, the stronger the magnetic force that you give off. This stronger magnetic force in turn brings a greater level of success. Expectancy can also be looked at as faith or belief. Faith is the belief in things yet unseen. It is complete trust without doubt or question. Are you expecting to have a great marriage or are you still unsure? Are you hopeful, but in the back of your mind you are preparing yourself just in case things don't work out? If so, that is not the attitude of expectancy. That is the attitude of "it might work out," and that attitude will never bring you ultimate success.

> *"If one asks for success and prepares for failure,*
> *he will get the situation he has prepared for."*
> *- Florence Scovel Shinn -*

Prepare for success. Become certain without a shadow of a doubt that you will have the Honeymoon Marriage, for that is the key that will unlock the realm of possibilities.

The attitude of love

The music group *DC Talk* has an excellent description of what love is. In one of their songs they say that love is a verb. Webster's dictionary defines a verb as being a word functioning to express existence, action or occurrence. Contrary to popular belief, love is not a feeling. Love is an action.

Have you ever heard someone say that he or she has fallen out of love with his or her spouse? Perhaps that explains how you feel. That comment is made with the attitude that there is nothing that can change the way the person feels. That simply is not true. If someone fell in love and then fell out of love, then he or she can fall back in love again. That is true 100 percent of the time and we can prove it. Better yet, you can prove it to yourself.

We know of a few millionaires who made over one million dollars, lost it all and then made it back again. How did they do it? They did it through their actions. As mentioned in the chapter entitled "Discovering your spouse's desires," it is all a matter of cause and effect. One becomes a millionaire by taking certain actions. Millionaires can also lose their money because of their actions. And they can get it all back again by simply doing the actions that got them the million dollars in the first place.

Every action that you take has its consequences, either good or bad. If you have gained something desirable and then lost it, you need to ask yourself three basic questions.

1. What actions enabled me to gain this important thing?
2. What actions caused me to lose it?
3. What actions do I have to take to get it back again?

Now let's rephrase these questions to address the one who has fallen out of love.

1. What actions caused me to fall in love with my spouse?
2. What actions caused me to fall out of love with my spouse?
3. What actions need to be taken in order for me to fall in love again?

Before we answer these questions, let's take a look at the meaning of the word *love*. Love is derived from the Latin word *libere*, which means "to please." Not knowing that simple truth can cause one to feel frustration, loneliness and emotional coldness, and it can even lead one to believe that he or she has "fallen out of love." Notice that the definition says "to please" and not "to receive pleasure." That is a very important distinction. In our marital relationships we often put the cart in front of the horse and then wonder why we aren't going anywhere. If you demonstrate the actions of love toward your mate, the feelings of love will follow. That strategy worked for you before and it will work for you again. It is a simple case of cause and effect.

Now answer the first and most important love question above. The answer to that question is so important because it is also the answer to the third love question. How did you act toward your spouse before and shortly after you realized that you were in love with him or her? Start acting that way toward your mate again and the feelings of love will follow. They may not come as quickly as they did the first time, but they *will* come again.

When you start treating your partner like you did when you first fell in love; your partner will start to act differently toward you as well. It won't happen overnight, but if you are persistent and have faith, your feelings and your relationship will be revitalized. The reason that this is true is because deep down you both want the same thing. You both want to be happy together. No one enters into a marriage hoping that several years down the road they will be miserable living with each other. You and your mate both decided that you wanted to "feel" the way that you did before you got married for the rest of your lives. Do the things that caused you to fall in love with each other and the feelings of love will follow. Start today. Don't wait until you feel like it. The attitude of true love is doing the *acts* of love even when you don't have the *feelings* of love.

"Love is patient, love is kind. It does not envy, it does not boast, it is not proud. It is not rude, it is not self-seeking, it is not easily angered, it keeps no record of wrongs. Love does not delight in evil but rejoices with the truth. It always protects, always trusts, always hopes, always perseveres. Love never fails."
- 1 Corinthians 13:4-7 -

SECTION 5

YOUR GUIDE TO ACHIEVING PERSONAL EXCELLENCE

NOURISHING YOUR BODY— EXPERIENCE BETTER HEALTH, MORE ENERGY AND GREATER SELF-CONFIDENCE

"The body is a sacred garment. It's your first and last garment;
it is what you enter life in and what you depart life with,
and it should be treated with honor."
- Martha Graham -

You may think that it is odd to find a "health" chapter in a book about achieving marital bliss. We're sure that you think that good health is important, but you may have never considered it as having an impact on your marriage. The fact of the matter is, everything that you do to and for yourself has outward consequences. These outward consequences in turn affect your relationship. We believe that in order for you to have the best marriage possible, you must strive to be the best that you can be in every area of your life, and that includes your health.

We have heard countless stories describing how improved health has changed people's lives. These positive changes have even affected their relationships. That is true because of the cause and effect relationship that we discussed earlier. Any time that you improve one area of your life, the positive effects spill over into other areas of your life as well. We recently watched an episode of *Everybody Loves Raymond* where Raymond's wife Debra was uncommonly frisky. Three times in one week—Raymond was beside himself. These events corresponded with her aerobic classes. Since he had never experienced that much affection from his wife, he started to get suspicious. He played out several scenarios, one of which was the thought that she had ulterior motives. In the end, Debra told Raymond that working out and getting into shape made her feel better about herself, which in turn made her feel better about "other things" as well. Yes, this example was played out through a situational comedy, however, we have seen similar scenarios played out in real life as well.

The pure and simple truth

When you take good care of yourself, you feel better. When you feel better, other areas of your life improve, including your relationships.

There is a lot of truth to the saying "You cannot give what you don't have." It is difficult if not impossible to love someone as much as you should if you don't love yourself. We're referring to a healthy true love for yourself, not a prideful, arrogant self-infatuation. If you don't like yourself, you will have a hard time liking others. If you don't respect yourself, you will not have a healthy respect for others. This chapter is about respecting yourself by respecting your body. It is about aspiring to the age-old adage of becoming healthy, wealthy and wise. Being as healthy as you can *is* wise. After all, what good is a pot of gold if you don't have your health? Improve your health and you will improve your marriage.

> *"It's a funny thing about life; if you refuse to accept*
> *anything but the best, you very often get it."*
> *- W. Somerset Maugham -*

How important is your health? On a scale from one to ten, where would you rate the importance of good health? How much is your health worth? It's priceless, isn't it? Do you act like it's priceless? If we offered you $1 million to carry on a lifestyle that had an 85 percent chance of giving you a degenerative disease like cancer or heart disease, would you take us up on our offer? How about $10 million? $100 million? That may sound like a crazy question, yet many Americans are doing it for free. The question is, are you one of them?

Contrary to popular belief, we are not getting healthier as a nation. We are eating poorly, getting fatter, under stress and becoming more prone to degenerative diseases. Even young people are starting to look and act older than they should. Not too long ago we were walking in a mall with a young couple in their late twenties early thirties. Without exaggeration, the young man had to sit down every fifteen to twenty minutes and rest. His lack of energy and stamina will possibly affect his job performance, his self-esteem and his relationship with his wife and family. As you know, kids love to run and play, and they really love it when adults play with them. How can he run and play with his child if he can't even walk for an hour straight? What do you think life will be like for him when he is fifty? If he doesn't change his lifestyle, he may not see his fiftieth birthday.

We have seen fifty-year-old men and women act as if they were seventy. We may be living longer as a nation, however, that doesn't mean that our quality of life is improving, especially in our later years. Getting older doesn't mean that our bodies have to automatically start falling apart. There isn't a self-destruct mechanism that is wired into our DNA. Man knows no disease that comes simply through the passing of time.

Recently at a party we overheard four men talking about how great their high blood pressure and cholesterol medications were. What? We expected to hear something like, "How about that Bear-Packer game?" Or, "How's the job treating you?" Not trading medication names. Something is drastically wrong with this picture. Two of the four had already had bipass heart surgery. This isn't the way things are supposed to be, and it isn't the way things have to be.

By now you may be thinking that this chapter doesn't apply to you because you are in great shape. You may be right, however, don't fall into the trap of thinking that optimal health is simply the absence of disease. Please reserve judgment and read through this chapter with an open mind. Even if you have excellent health, maybe you will pick up a few pointers that can allow you to help someone else who is headed down the wrong path.

"Health is a state of complete physical, mental,and social well-being, and not merely the absence of disease or infirmity."
- The World Health Organization -

Americans are living longer than ever before. However many of us are aging faster. What about the quality of life in those later years? Is it your goal to live an extra ten years just to spend them in a nursing home? It sounds like a rhetorical question, but we have to ask it. How would you rate your current health on a scale from 1 to 10, 10 being the best shape you could possible be in? Where do you want to be six months from now? If you are a six now, would you like to be an eight in six months? Write down your goal right now and post it where you will see it and be reminded that you must start improving your health today. We will give you tips a little later on exactly how to reach your target.

Our goal in this chapter is to let you know that it is within your control to be in the best shape of your life and that you don't have to be a statistic. You don't have to be zapped of energy, get sick all of the time or die of a degenerative disease. Just because your parents had cancer doesn't mean that you will get cancer. Twenty to thirty years ago scientists believed that degenerative disease was primarily genetic. If your mom had arthritis then you will most likely get arthritis. Today, scientists have determined that getting a degenerative disease is approximately 80 percent lifestyle related. We like that statistic much better, how about you? In other words, you have control over your health.

Some people would consider us health nuts. We have always considered ourselves to be health conscious. We exercised, avoided fried foods, limited our red meat intake, rarely ate eggs or other high cholesterol foods and took our vitamins. Almost three years ago we started to take a closer look at health and nutrition and we were shocked at what we had discovered. Almost everywhere we turned all of the signs were pointing in the same direction. In the next several minutes, we will share with you some of what we discovered.

Get your highlighter and pen ready because you will want to take some notes.

First let's take a look at some startling facts.

The top four causes of death in America

#1 Heart disease. Approximately 1 out of 2 Americans will die of heart disease. According to the World Health Report 2000, 7.5 million people died of heart disease! Don't think that heart disease is a man's problem. It's not. Contrary to popular belief, heart disease affects about as many women as men. Many people think that breast cancer is the biggest killer among women. In reality, 32 percent of women die of heart disease, while 4 percent die of breast cancer, 5 percent of lung cancer, 2 percent of colon cancer, and 11 percent of all other cancers. Heart disease is a major concern for both men and women.

#2 Cancer. Some estimates state that as many as one out of every three Americans will get some form of cancer. According to the World Health Report 2000, 7.1 million people died of cancer.

#3 Stroke. According to the World Health Report 2000, 5.5 million people died of stroke.

#4 Adverse reactions to properly prescribed medication. By trying to cure the leading causes of death, we have created the fourth largest cause of death among Americans over the age of forty. This trend does not have to continue; there is an answer.

Heart disease, cancer, and stroke alone claim more lives every year than the entire population of New York State. Drugs are not the answer, as you can see by number four above. And are the billions of dollars spent each year on medication curing diseases or just getting rid of the symptoms?

Unfortunately, there is more.

- 151 million people have diabetes. There are also a lot of people who have diabetes and don't even know it.
- Approximately 25 million North Americans have osteoporosis.
- Over 350 million people have some form of arthritis.
- Alzheimer's—This is the disease that gained much media attention because of former President Ronald Reagan. 216,000 people died of Alzheimer's and other dementias in 1998.
- Obesity—Although not a disease, obesity has a major impact on the health of millions of Americans. In the United States and in other industrialized countries, more people are overweight and/or obese than are of normal weight. Americans take the cake. We are the fattest people who have ever walked the face of the earth. If you don't believe that, just ask a foreigner who is visiting America for the first time. We promise you that the visitor will be in shock as to what he or she sees. Reports show that up to 30 percent of kids are obese.

And the list goes on. According to the Center for Disease Statistics, these diseases will kill more than 80 percent of us. We don't like those statistics. Remember earlier we said that acquiring these diseases was largely within our control? According to research done in the field of anti-aging medicine, 30 percent of our genes are hardwired—things like your hair and eye color, for example. We have at least some control over the other 70 percent.

These statistics are staggering, yet when it comes to optimal health; most Americans are driving the wrong way down a one-way street with their eyes closed. Everything is okay as long as they don't crash. Unfortunately, if they continue down that path, they *will* crash.

Darren's health seminar: Last year I gave a health seminar at a huge Health Plex. While handing out invitations to the presentation with two friends, I heard ignorance speaking loudly. The headline that I used was "Is your health in danger? Discover how you can avoid, delay or even reverse degenerative disease." One man in his mid-fifties took the invitation, scanned it over and then turned around and said, "Do I look like my health is in danger?" That is like going to your jeweler and holding a one-karat diamond six feet in front of her and asking if it is a flawless diamond. Because this man looked fit, he thought he was immune to degenerative disease. Another lady said, "No thanks, I feel pretty good."

Don't wait until you "feel" bad before you take a proactive approach toward your health. When do most people discover that they have cancer? They go in for a checkup because they don't feel good. By that time it may be too late. People don't catch cancer one day. It's not a virus. It can grow silently in a person's body for years until it gets bad enough that he or she notices that something is wrong. Prior to someone's first heart attack, the person will most likely not "feel" that he or she has heart disease. One cannot "feel" his or her arteries slowly building up plaque.

Unfortunately, most of the time, money and research that is invested into finding cures for these diseases is not getting us to where we need to be. Most of the world's efforts are spent trying to find a cure, less effort is devoted to early detection, and relatively little attention is given to the area of prevention. It is time to get back to conventional wisdom.

Remember the saying, "An ounce of prevention is worth more than a pound of cure"? Why don't we believe that anymore? We want to take a pill whenever something is ailing us. Can't sleep, then take a pill. Have high blood pressure, then take a pill. Have a headache, then take a pill. How much time is spent asking ourselves, "What is causing me not to be able to sleep well," "what is causing my blood pressure to be high and how can I lower it," or "what is causing my headaches?" In many cases you will find the cure by finding the cause.

Let's say that you had a fly dilemma in your backyard. These swarms of flies were becoming a big problem; many of them were even getting into the house. Your first question is "How can I get rid of the flies?" So you go to the store and look for fly killer. You pick out a spray can that says that it kills flies in seconds. Finally, you will be rid of your fly problem. You go home and spray every fly that you can see. Sure enough, they are dropping like flies. Several days later you notice that the flies are back in full force. What's going on? You thought that you had taken care of the problem. So off to the store you go. This time you ask one of the workers which spray is best for killing flies. You want the strongest most potent spray on the market. Now you'll show those pesky flies. You spray and they drop. Job complete.

A couple of days pass and you notice a couple of flies, but no big problem. The next day you walk into the backyard and you cannot believe your eyes. Not only are your flies back, but there are more now than ever. It is time to pull out the big guns, so you call the exterminator to rid yourself of this problem once and for all. The exterminator comes and investigates the situation. You ask him if he can kill the flies. He tells you. "Sure, I can kill the flies, but unless you get rid of that pile of garbage, they will just come back again."

You see, the flies were not the problem, they were just the symptom of the problem. The garbage was the problem. Until you know and address the cause, you will never get rid of or avoid the symptom.

The four areas of optimal health
The following are four basic areas that you need to focus on in order to achieve optimal health. An improvement in all four areas can cause you to become more productive at work and at home, increase your energy level, increase your level of self-confidence, improve your relationships and even help you to delay, avoid or even reverse degenerative diseases.

1. Exercise
2. Stress management
3. A healthy balanced diet
4. Nutritional supplements

Exercise
Exercise is paramount to living a healthy life. Our bodies were designed for movement. Not many of us work hard on the farm like we did two hundred years ago. Machines are now doing the physical part of many jobs. Many of us work at a desk or stand on our feet for most of the day. And even if you do get a physical workout at work, it is oftentimes coupled with stress. The kind of exercise that we are referring to is not tied to a stressful situation, nor does it cause stress. When done properly, exercise will reduce your level of stress and improve your quality of life.

Adapting an exercise program for many can be a major lifestyle change. Many of us sleep for eight hours, get ready for work, drive to work, sit at work for eight hours, drive home, eat dinner, watch television/listen to music/read a book, go to bed. Then we repeat that same cycle over and over again. Our bodies need exercise. They were designed for movement and not just movement from the couch to the refrigerator. The phrase "use it or lose it" speaks directly to exercise.

If we don't exercise, we lose a lot more than just muscle mass and our ability to run up and down the stairs without losing our breath. We eventually lose our quality of life. Let's focus on some of the many benefits of exercise. The following list describes some of the benefits of adopting a strength and aerobic exercise program.

- Strengthens heart function
- Improves sleep
- Lowers blood pressure
- Help relieve depression, tension, anxiety and stress
- Improves self-confidence
- Improves posture

It is important that we do both cardiovascular and resistance training. Resistance or weight training becomes even more important as we age. Weight training can increase bone density, the opposite of osteoporosis. Another bonus to increasing one's muscle mass is that muscle burns fat! While it is true that aerobic exercise burns more calories than weight training, adding muscle mass is like turning up the thermostat to your fat-burning furnace.

An increase in muscle mass raises the resting metabolic rate, the amount of calories the body burns at rest in a day. It is estimated that our body can burn an extra 50 to 90 calories per day for every pound of muscle we gain. Increase muscle mass by ten pounds and you could burn off an extra 500 to 900 calories per day. That is equivalent to jogging six miles per day, seven days per week. Women, don't worry about becoming muscle bound. Ten pounds of muscle takes up about as much space as three pounds of fat. In fact, an extra ten pounds of muscle can burn a pound of fat in one week, which is 52 pounds of fat per year.

If you are overweight, dieting alone can be a very difficult way to lose those extra pounds. Add an exercise program to your healthy eating habits and the weight will come off much more easily. Being in great shape will increase your energy level and stamina, and it will put a bounce in your step. As an added bonus, being in great shape makes you more attractive to the opposite sex. Do you feel like your mate is not as attracted to you as you would like him or her to be? There is something you can do about that, and it all starts with exercise and getting into shape. Not only will you look better, but you will also feel better about yourself. You will feel like getting out more and showing off the new you. This higher degree of self-confidence is also very attractive. You can't see it when you look in the mirror, but it is there all the same and others will notice it. When you look good, live healthy and start to feel great about yourself don't be surprised if your romantic life skyrockets.

> **Darren's workout:** I (Darren) was working out the other day and Donna was staring at me. She had one of those looks on her face. You know the look, the one that says, "I like what I see." It broke my concentration so I asked her, "What?" "Nothing," she said as she smiled and walked away. Why was she so turned on by watching me work out? Because she liked the idea of me looking my best for her. Let's just say that she never looked at me like that when I was sitting on the couch watching television.

Not only is a thinner waistline more attractive, but it can also lower your risk of heart disease. According to the Journal of the American Medical Association, women with a waist measurement of thirty to thirty-two inches had twice the risk of heart disease as women whose waist measurement was less than twenty-eight inches. Women with a waistline over thirty-eight inches had more than four times the risk of heart disease.

Two of our favorite workout video series are The FIRM® and USANA Health Sciences Lean Team system. Both do a wonderful job of combining weight training and aerobics.

If you would like to receive free information regarding our nutritional and exercise program, please go to www.honeymoonmarriage.com and click on the keyword "healthy body."

Stress management

Are you and/or your spouse stressed out? If so, you are not alone. Many people say that they are under too much stress. What makes matters worse is that most of these people have a feeling of helplessness. They think that their unhealthy level of stress is outside of their control and consequently feel trapped. Unfortunately, this feeling of helplessness can itself cause stress. The two biggest problems with unmanaged stress are:

1. Stress can become an endless loop where one stressful event causes another one to happen, which causes another and so forth.
2. The effects of stress are additive in nature, where one stressful event builds on top of another.

This stress cycle can get out of hand in a hurry, and it can snowball into much larger problems. Let's say that your spouse is working on a project at work with an upcoming deadline, placing him or her under a lot of pressure. That pressure causes your mate to get into an argument with his or her boss, which adds to the stress. Traffic is terrible on the way home from work. Normally that doesn't bother your mate, but considering the events of the day, it really gets under his or her skin. Halfway through the commute someone cuts your mate off and he or she has to hit the brakes in order to avoid an accident. Now your mate is really fuming. He or she gets home and starts yelling at you for no apparent or justified reason. You get into an argument, which increases the stress level. Now you are both mad at each other and avoid further conversation. That evening all your mate can think about is how poorly he or she was treated at work and the upcoming work deadline. This internal dialog causes even more pressure. You are both still mad at each other because of your earlier fight and you decide to go to bed angry.

Money pressures can cause a person to feel stuck at a job he or she hates or that he or she has to get an additional job, which in itself causes pressure. Problems in a marriage can cause arguments, which can in turn cause more problems. You get the picture.

If not met head-on and dealt with properly, that cycle can continue through to the next day, week, month or even longer until something gives. That something can be your job, your health or even your marriage.

As far as your health is concerned, the following is a list of some of the disorders that can occur or get worsened due to stress:

Muscle tension	Allergies	Hypertension	Viral infections
Ulcers	Cancer	Bacterial infections	Loss of sex drive
Osteoporosis	Arthritis	Digestive problems	Chronic Pain
Diabetes	Depression	Asthma	Cardiovascular disease
Nausea	Fatigue	Migraine headaches	Magnesium depletion

Stress is unavoidable. It is a part of life just like eating and sleeping are. Webster's dictionary describes stress as a physical, chemical or emotional factor that causes bodily or mental tension and may be a factor in disease causation. You know what it is and you know what it feels like. In order to handle your stress, you must first identify what is causing it. Stress comes from the following four basic areas:

1. **Social stress** would include death of a loved one, financial pressures, job pressures, family demands, arguments, deadlines, etc.
2. **Environmental stress** would include air pollution, water pollution, food pollution, noise pollution, traffic, severe weather, etc.
3. **Physical stress** would include sickness, poor nutrition, lack of sleep, lack of exercise, too much exercise or physical labor, smoking, alcohol, etc.
4. **Mental stress** is caused by your internal dialog as well as how you interpret the above stresses that come into your life.

According to a study conducted at the University of Washington, stressful events are not only accumulative, but each event has a varying impact on our health. In other words, some stresses are more damaging to your well-being than others are. They categorized the top forty-two stress-causing events and found the top four in order of magnitude to be:

1. The death of a spouse
2. Divorce
3. Marital separation
4. The death of a close family member

Remember that one stress will add to another. Your relationship with your spouse is a major contributing factor to your level of happiness and your risk of developing stress-related symptoms or illnesses. This book is designed to help you minimize your level of marital stress, hence improving your marriage, which will in turn lower your overall stress level and consequently improve your health.

Once you have identified what is causing your stress, you are better equipped to handle it. The following are a few tips that can help you to better manage your stress:

1. Write it down. Write down all of the things that are causing stress in your life. Include things that have changed recently, even though you may not think that they are causing stress. Every change brings with it a certain level of stress. Once you have written down each stressor, prioritize them according to their level of impact on your state of mind with the first being the one that causes the most stress on your life. Remember that a smaller stress repeated several times can be just as stressful as a big stress that happens periodically.

2. Ask what you can control. Decide whether or not you have any control over the circumstances that are causing your stress. Deal with the things that you can control and stop worrying about the things that you cannot. Too often we spend time and emotional energy stressing over things that we have little or no control over. Letting go of this negative emotional habit is not an easy task, but it is essential to your overall sense of well-being.

The other mistake that we make is thinking that we have no control over stressful situations when in fact we do. This is where the power of asking yourself the right questions comes in. These questions are called empowering questions because they empower you to improve the quality of your life. An example of an empowering question would be "What can I do to improve this situation?" Keep asking yourself that question until an answer comes to you. More will be discussed regarding this powerful technique in the chapter entitled "Expanding your mind—the pursuit of knowledge and wisdom."

It is also a great idea to seek advice from someone that you trust and respect. A person who is not emotionally involved in your situation can oftentimes see the answer much more clearly than you can. Don't be afraid to ask other people for their advice. You don't have to come up with all of the answers on your own.

3. Learn to say no. A common cause of stress for some is over-committing. Only take on the tasks that you can deal with at that time. Be bold enough to say no when you know that you are already too busy. This is an especially difficult thing to do when dealing with worthy causes. It is very easy to become over-committed by volunteering your time to work on civic, religious and/or charitable projects. Just because it is a worthwhile cause doesn't mean that you should sacrifice your health or place the activity above other family priorities.

4. Delegate. If you have too many tasks that need to be completed, think of someone else that may be able to do them for you. Sometimes our need for control and/or perfection can cause a lot of unneeded stress in our lives. We oftentimes want to do it all by ourselves or even take on the world instead of living a balanced and tranquil life.

5. Be patient with yourself and your circumstances. Know that everything will work out to your benefit and that you have the ability to figure it out and better your situation. You are only trapped and helpless if you think that you are.

6. Live healthy. Living healthy will better enable you to cope with the stresses of the day. Eating the right foods and avoiding the bad ones, taking high quality nutritional supplements and getting enough rest will strengthen your immune system and increase your stress tolerance level. You remember the saying "It was the straw that broke the camel's back." Stress can be defeated on two fronts— (1) you can reduce or limit the amount of straw that is placed on your back, or (2) you can strengthen your back.

Exercise as mentioned earlier is paramount to achieving optimal health. It is also one of the best stress relievers known to man. If you will not exercise for any other reason, exercise for your peace of mind.

7. Choose how you will act and react to stressful situations.

> ***Darren and the big truck:*** The following is an example of an environmental stress that I (Darren) experienced a year ago. I had just pulled out of a tollbooth when a semi started to merge into my lane. I had nowhere to go, so I slammed on the brakes and swerved off the road. I looked around and noticed that I was less than one foot away from a three-foot drop-off. Instead of getting angry at the semi driver (and possible chasing him down like I have seen so many people do), I was thankful that I didn't go over the edge or get into an accident. It took a while before my heart rate slowed back down to normal, and after that I was fine. It didn't bother me the rest of the day.

You can't always control the stressful events that enter into your life, but you can control how you view them and how you react to them.

8. Be aware of your negative thoughts. This will be discussed in great detail in the next chapter. In short, focusing on all of the negatives in your life will increase your stress level. Focusing on all of the positives in your life will decrease your stress level. Release negative disempowering thoughts quickly. Be thankful for all of the positive things in your life and know that things could be worse. Gratitude and focusing on the positive are great stress relievers.

9. Love yourself and love others. The actions and feelings of love are extremely powerful. Love can melt away stress. Start by building yourself up instead of tearing yourself down. We are often our own worst enemy. You need as much support as you can get, and that support starts with you. Focus on the good things about you. Remember the times in your life when you felt good about something that you did. You are awesome even if you don't realize it.

The love that you share with others is equally important to the love or self-esteem that you have for yourself. It can be a natural reaction to retreat from family, friends and community when you are under a lot of stress. Don't climb into your cave, but instead love others and let them love you. Share your burdens with each other and you will discover a great release.

Be your partner's best stress reliever. Share your concerns with each other. Give your partner encouragement by building him or her up, giving compliments, telling your partner that he or she is strong and will get through this in time and will make the decisions necessary to improve his or her circumstances. Your support is extremely important. It will help to relieve your mate's stress and it will improve your marriage. Give your spouse love in all of the ways that you know how.

10. Apply relaxation and stress management techniques. These would include but are not limited to quiet time, affirmations, visualization, prayer, massage and laughter. Our favorites are visualization, prayer and laughter. It is difficult to vividly hold a tranquil image in your mind, release your cares through prayer or engage in laughter and be stressed out at the same time.

Final thought regarding stress

Marital friction is without a doubt one of the largest potential causes of stress in one's life. Of course, having a great marriage doesn't mean that you are out of the woods. When speaking with happily married couples, we found that job-related issues were their number one concern. This was the most evident in dual-income households. In single-income households or where one partner worked only part time, the stress levels of both husband and wife were much lower. Many of these stressed couples felt like they were trapped. They didn't see the light at the end of the tunnel or a way out of their situation. Some even said that their situation had always been that way and that it would continue to be that way.

We discovered that the core reason for their stress was not necessarily work, but rather money. The reason they were both working, working at jobs that they didn't like or under circumstances that were stressful and/or commuting long distances wasn't because they wanted to, it was because they thought that they had to. That simply is not true. You or your spouse can stay at home (or work from home) if that is what you want. You can work at a job or have a career that you love and work with wonderful people. You can have a short commute or even be your own boss if that is your desire. You can even work half as many hours and make twice as much money.

We will show you how all of this is possible in Section 6 entitled "Money Matters."

The point is, you have choices and you don't have to live in a continual state of tension. As previously mentioned, most heart attacks happen among men on Monday morning. If you are highly stressed at work, dislike or even hate your job, then we would like to encourage you to do some soul-searching. If you hate your job, then you shouldn't be there, period. If your job is very stressful, then you need to discover how to manage or eliminate that stress, or get a different job. We don't care how much money you make or the position that you hold. Your health is much more important than your job.

A health balanced diet

Remember the age-old sayings, "you are what you eat," and "an apple a day keeps the doctor away?" There is a lot of truth to those sayings. However, do we really believe that they are true? Could it really be that simple, and if so, why don't we take a more proactive approach to our health and pay closer attention to the foods that we eat?

For many of us the answer is not that simple. Our lives revolve around food. The act of eating is not done purely out of the need for sustenance. We link eating with many emotions. We eat to celebrate a wedding, anniversary, promotion, accomplishment, graduation, baptism, bar mitzvah, confirmation, birthday, etc. We eat to make us feel better when we are lonely, depressed, hurt, stressed, etc. We turn to food to give us comfort. Hence the term "comfort food." In that sense it is almost like a drug. Unlike a drug or alcohol, we need food to survive. We can use our willpower, counseling or a twelve-step program to help us get off of harmful dependencies. And to stay off, we avoid these harmful substances. Food is a little different. We can use our willpower, go to counseling or join a health/diet program, but we cannot avoid food. For many, once they start eating, their willpower goes out the window. We know that we can say that we are not that hungry, but once we take a bite of something, we have no problem eating quite a bit.

Some of the deep-seated emotional ties that we have with food come from our past experiences. Our earliest experiences with food involved being held by our mothers while we ate. As children, we were rewarded and even bribed with food (and not health food by any stretch of the imagination). "If you are good, then we will take you to Joe's Burger Joint." "You and all of your friends get to go to Billy Bob's Pizza Play House for your birthday." We also comfort our children with food. "It's okay, let's go in the house and take care of that skinned up knee and then we can go and get you an ice cream cone." It is no wonder that we have a difficult time focusing on food as nourishment when our subconscious mind links food with pleasure or the relief of pain. It is understandable that it can be hard to control what and when we eat.

Our eating habits are strongly connected to our emotions, and we can prove it. While eating, tell someone that what he or she is eating is bad for him or her. You will most likely get an emotional or irrational response. "Well you have to die of something." Does that comment make sense given the fact that most people don't want to die and some even fear death? Very few people will be curious or concerned and ask for more information. On the other hand, tell someone that you have read a study that shows that using XYZ motor oil can reduce engine life by 30 percent and may even cause premature engine failure, and the person will most likely avoid that oil. After all, why take the chance, they paid a lot of money for that car.

When some people find out that we don't eat meat, they react very defensively toward us. They act as though we are going to break into their bank account and steal all of their hard-earned money. Some will even tell us why a vegetarian diet is bad for us. Why would people act so defensively, even borderline hostile, toward us if all we are doing is sharing with them our food preference? Could it be that deep down they know that they are not eating as well as they should, but are not willing to change? We believe that anyone who wants to know the truth and is willing to keep an open mind will find volumes of information that will point him or her in the right direction.

The information that follows is designed to give you an overall education regarding the foods that we eat. These facts will enable you to make healthier choices regarding your health and your diet. It is important that you not only adopt a diet that is healthy, but that it is one that you can live with on a daily basis. What we are suggesting is a well-rounded diet consisting of as many raw and whole foods as possible. The closer your food resembles that which grows from the ground or on a tree, the better it is for your body. The more we handle, process, cook and change the forms of these original foods, the less nutritious they become. We hope that you will see that the primary purpose for food is to nourish your body and sustain your health and energy levels. Many have forgotten that in recent years and look at food as nothing more than something that tastes good and fills up their stomach.

Remember the "food pyramid" that you were first shown in grade school? The U.S. Department of Agriculture (USDA) created the "food pyramid". The USDA recommends that we eat six to eleven servings of bread, cereal, rice and pasta per day compared to five to nine servings of fruit and vegetables. While it is true that whole grains are very important to our health, most of the food groups that are listed in that category and are consumed in America do not include whole grains or their valuable health benefits.

In the opinion of many health experts, these two categories should be reversed. We should be eating more fresh fruits and vegetables and less bread, cereal, rice, and pasta. The main reason for this is that the grain group that most Americans consume is highly processed, void of most fiber and contains too much salt, sugar and preservatives. This nutrient deficient, highly processed, high-glycemic (carbohydrates that are quickly absorbed, cause a rapid rise in blood sugar, and are stored as fat if not used by our muscles) food group is partially responsible for making us the fattest nation on the planet.

Several years ago low-fat diets were in vogue. They preached that fat made you fat. People started counting fat grams in an effort to lose weight. Many people started losing weight. Some were even experiencing health problems because they eliminated the fat in their diet altogether. We need fat in our diet in order to stay healthy. Since reduced fat diets were helping people to lose weight, many food manufacturers jumped on the "fat free" bandwagon and started to produce fat free foods. The marketing campaign worked. People started buying these prepared and processed foods like crazy. People were watching their fat grams but they were still gaining weight. Come to find out, these fat free foods contained more sugar, salt and other additives than their fat-filled counterparts in order to improve their taste. They also contained highly refined simple carbohydrates like white flour. You guessed it; the increase of sugar and white flour was causing people to gain weight.

Numerous studies have shown that too much fat in our diet is a major contributing factor in many diseases including breast cancer and heart disease. Fat in and of itself is not the problem as long as you are eating the right kind of fats and in the right amounts. There are good fats and there are bad fats. The bad fats are known as saturated fats and they are found in animal foods such as meat and dairy products. Preferable fats are known as unsaturated fats and are found in grains, legumes, nuts and seeds. One's fat intake should be limited to 20 percent of his or her total calorie intake. We get our fats from almond butter, nuts, seeds, avocados, flaxseed oil and pumpkinseed oil. We avoid animal fats.

Recent fad diets have made the consumption of carbohydrates taboo. They state that carbohydrates (the bottom tier of the food pyramid) should be avoided because they make you fat. They also encourage the elimination of sugar from one's diet. Substituted in their place are all the vegetables and high protein/high fat foods you would like. There is no doubt that this kind of a diet can help you to lose weight, however, most Americans will ignore the vegetable suggestion and jump right into the no carb/high protein/high fat part of the diet. It isn't carbohydrates that are bad; it's the wrong kind of carbohydrates. Dark green vegetables, lima, navy, pinto and white beans, long cooking oatmeal, whole rye, whole wheat, barley, apples, grapefruit, oranges, kiwi and strawberries are great carbohydrate sources.

Eliminating or drastically reducing a whole food group is not the answer to long-term healthy weight loss. Besides, a diet heavy in animal fats and animal protein is far from being healthy as will be discussed later. The simple fact that the *Journal of the American Medical Association* states that vegetarians have up to a 97 percent lower risk of having heart disease proves that a diet heavy in animal products and light in whole grains, vegetables, and fruits can be risky.

The healthiest diet is one that consists of as many whole foods as possible. We eat a lot of carbohydrates every day and we are far from being overweight. We also eat our fair share of fats. The key to lifelong weight management and good health is to eat the right kinds of carbohydrates, proteins and fats. Our diet consists of approximately 55 percent carbohydrates, 30 percent protein and 15 percent fat.

Why whole foods? Because they contain more of the good stuff and less of the bad stuff. According to Gary Null in his excellent book, *Get Healthy Now!,* each year, well over $500 million worth of chemicals are added to foods. In 1978, the average American consumed ten pounds of chemical additives. According to the Food and Drug Administration (FDA), there are over three thousand substances that are being added directly to our food. These chemicals and additives can have an adverse affect on your health. Do you read the labels on the products that you buy? If not, then you don't know exactly what you are putting into your body. One safe rule to use is the following: if you cannot pronounce it or it isn't something that you yourself would add to your food, then don't buy it.

Another reason to stay away from many processed foods is because of what a friend of ours calls the three white poisons; sugar, white flour and salt. Just read the ingredient labels on the foods at the store. The first ingredient in almost every popular cereal on the shelf is bleached enriched white flour. The second ingredient is sugar even in non-sugar-coated cereals. Sugar not only promotes cavities, but it also weakens our immune system. Our immune system does a lot more than just help us fight off colds. Many scientists believe that we all have cancer cells in our body and that a strong immune system is able to destroy those cells. The average American eats one hundred sixty pounds of sugar a year. And of course sugar is empty calories that will cause you to gain unwanted pounds.

The first ingredient in bread, even many wheat breads, is bleached enriched white flour. How can we get away with taking out vital nutrients, replacing them with synthetic versions of some vitamins at a fraction of the amount that we took out, and then call the end product enriched? Also, these chemical vitamins and minerals are added before baking, and when they are heated to 350 degrees, many if not all of the vitamins and minerals are destroyed. About the only thing bleached white flour is good for is making papier-mâché.

For centuries, people ate whole-wheat bread. Then almost overnight milling practices changed, separating the bran and germ, producing refined white flour void of a host of vitamins and minerals, particularly vitamin B. The same is true with white rice. Rice in its natural form fed the world for thousands of years until man stepped in and refined it into white rice. White rice became the staple food for millions of Asians, which caused many medical problems including protein deficiencies and beriberi, a thiamine deficiency. The original food pyramid, developed at the turn of the century, addressed these protein deficiencies causing Americans to eat more meat and other animal products. Malnutrition rates subsided; however, heart disease and other degenerative diseases and health conditions took their place.

Unfortunately, most Americans still eat those high levels of animal products and many of our diets contain an excess of processed foods. Red meat is usually the one with the bad rap. Surely chicken is okay, isn't it? Well, chicken is still high in cholesterol but it is lower in fat. Most of the chickens that are eaten today are not the same as they were in the past either. Chickens are "raised" by the tens of thousands in huge buildings and are not allowed to see daylight. They are kept in tight quarters not allowing them to move. They are given growth hormones that cause them to grow so fast that their legs often cannot support their weight. They are sprayed with chemicals and given medication to help control disease. The story is the same or even worse for pigs and cattle. Instead of making meat the focal point of your meal, reduce its portion and exchange it with a leafy dark green garden salad, fresh vegetables, brown rice, and whole grain bread.

If you're going to eat meat, eat the kind of meat that your grandparents or great grandparents used to eat. These animals are raised naturally without the aid of growth hormones or other chemicals, and many are even fed organic foods. These farmers raise their livestock to be healthy, not unnaturally big in a fraction of the time. The meat will cost more, but your health is worth it. The fewer the chemicals you put into your body the better.

What about dairy products, after all, "it does a body good," or does it? It seems ironic that 25 million North Americans suffer from osteoporosis or brittle bone disease in a land with such a high consumption of dairy products, which are supposed to be full of calcium. In fact, most of the Asian world does not consume dairy products yet osteoporosis is rare. Mammals need their mother's milk for nourishment, and we humans are no exception. Humans are, however, the only mammals that continue to drink milk as adults and we are the only mammals who drink another species' milk. The milk that is consumed today is not the same as it was years ago either. Today we pasteurize our milk to kill bacteria. Pasteurization also kills the live enzymes in the milk, which we need to help your bodies absorb calcium. Besides, calcium isn't as effective unless we consume adequate amounts of magnesium. The synergistic effects of various vitamins and minerals will be discussed later in this chapter.

Many people are even allergic to milk without them even knowing it. The mucous associated with dairy products slows or inhibits digestion. Milk is also high in sugar. Along with allergies, milk can also cause or lead to nausea, diarrhea, colic, bloating, asthma, increased frequency of colds and flu, acne, ear infections, and a host of even more serious conditions. Rice, soy and almond milks are great healthy alternatives. We prefer soymilk and ricemilk.

If reducing or eliminating animal products from your diet seems unnatural, consider the following example from Harvey Diamond, "You put a baby in a crib with an apple and a rabbit. If it eats the rabbit and plays with the apple, I'll buy you a new car." We are really herbivores by design and carnivores by choice. Our anatomy and digestive system more closely resembles that of the primate family (herbivores) than that of the cat family (carnivores).

If you think that kids are growing up quicker these days, you may be right. Studies have shown that young girls raised without the consumption of animal products reach puberty at about age sixteen, compared to about age eleven or less for girls who consume meat, dairy and eggs.

So what about protein? Protein is one of the six major nutrients required for good health along with carbohydrates, fats, vitamins, minerals and water. But we don't need as much protein as many people think. Americans are way over-proteined. The recommendations of the amount of daily calories to be provided by protein according to the Food and Nutrition Board of the USDA is 6 percent. The percentage of calories of protein in spinach is 49 percent, broccoli is 47 percent and tomatoes are 18 percent. The average American consumes over 100 grams of protein every day, which is two to three times the amount experts now say is necessary, depending on the weight of the individual. Unless you are a serious weight lifter, body builder or competition athlete, you may want to consider the amount of protein you consume.

Too much animal protein intake has been linked to osteoporosis. This is true because the phosphoric acid and sulfuric acid in meat needs to be neutralized by calcium, which is pulled out of our bones. As a matter of fact, the average measurable bone loss of female meat-eaters at age 65 is twice that of female vegetarians at age 65. Other causes of osteoporosis are diets high in caffeine, sugar and refined carbohydrates, cigarette smoking, lack of exercise, alcohol use and phosphates found in sodas. So you thought that can of soda was harmless. Other studies have linked excessive protein to causing toxins to be developed in the colon, arthritis, kidney damage and some forms of cancer. And animal foods have been linked to an increase in arteriosclerosis and heart disease.

Is there a safer way to get the protein that our body requires? Absolutely, sources of it grow from the ground everywhere. Protein is comprised of amino acids, which are the building blocks of our body. There are eight essential amino acids that our body needs and must get from the foods that we eat. All eight of these amino acids can be found in fruits and vegetables. Nuts, beans, seeds, whole grains and legumes are also excellent providers of protein. We prefer soy protein rich in isoflavones, which have the added advantage of protecting against cancer and promote heart and bone health.

America's children are starting to get diseases once reserved for adults, diseases like Type II diabetes. Even osteoporosis is now being considered a pediatric condition. It is no surprise when you look at the foods we feed our children or allow them to eat. How much nutrition can be found in a cheeseburger, soda and fries? On the other hand, how much harm can be done by that same meal? The average teenager drinks over three cans of soda per day and 10 percent of them drink over seven cans. Up to 33 percent of our children are obese. Only 1 percent of our children meet the USDA's

Food Pyramid guidelines. Many children do not even meet the Recommended Dietary Allowance (RDA) of vitamins A, C, E, B6, iron, calcium and zinc. Are you setting a good example for your children?

Do you eat five to nine servings of fruit and vegetables every day? Do you eat your vegetables raw or cooked? Do you grow your own produce or do you buy it at the store? Fruits and vegetables are a great source of fiber and antioxidants like vitamins A and C. And antioxidants have been linked to fighting the effects of free radicals which cause many of the before mentioned degenerative diseases. We will talk more about antioxidants later. If you do eat five to nine servings of fruit and vegetables every day, congratulations, you are on the right track.

Eating ample amounts of fruits, vegetables, whole grains, rice and conservative amounts of protein (focusing on reducing the amount of animal products consumed) coupled with regular exercise may have been enough to promote optimal health one hundred fifty years ago. But things have changed. Our world has changed and our food has changed. Just over a century ago, 97 percent of Americans were farmers. We ate fresh food from our own fields. Today very few of us grow our own food, relying on a long distribution path before it finally ends up on our dining table.

Most of this food contains chemical fertilizers and toxic pesticides. Some of our nation's soil is depleted of its original minerals. As a matter of fact, a bowl of spinach grown in 1948 contained about 150 milligrams of iron. Today, that same bowl of spinach contains only about 2 milligrams.

Remember the saying, "an apple a day keeps the doctor away?" Well let's assume that this apple is organically grown and contains no chemical fertilizers and no toxic pesticides. How much time has elapsed from the time the farmer in Washington picks the apple to the time you eat it? The farmer picks his apples and loads them into bushel baskets. The next day he brings them to the market where a buyer purchases them. The buyer sends the apples to a local distribution center where they are washed and packaged. They are then sent to a regional or national distribution center. From there they are shipped to your grocer. The grocer puts the apples on his display and waits for you to come in and buy them. Since we no longer go to the market every day, we buy a week's worth of apples.

How much time has elapsed from the time the apple was picked until the last one leaves your refrigerator? Is the vitamin content the same as a tree-ripened apple? Oftentimes produce is picked before it is ripe so that it will last longer in storage and transit. What about that healthy glass of orange juice? According to the manual supplied by our juicer, orange juice must be consumed within 15 minutes of juicing. After that it starts to lose its nutritional value. Also the fruit and vegetable juices purchased in the stores are pasteurized (cooked). Any time we cook produce we can lose approximately 50 percent of its vitamin content. Canned and frozen produce is even worse, losing as much as 95 percent of its original vitamin content.

Environment

As if all of that wasn't enough, our environment has also changed. Many of the toxins that we are exposed to every day were not around one hundred years ago. Chemicals and pollutants in our food, air and water place higher demands on our immune system. Over 100,000 toxic chemicals can be found in our environment.

If you are a smoker, then you are creating your own personal polluted environment. It has been estimated that smoking kills 307,000 people in the United States each year. Quitting isn't easy, but it is never too late to stop. Just two years after stopping cigarette smoking, one's risk of heart attack returns to about average and one's risk of developing lung cancer drops by about 33 percent. Deciding to stop smoking is one of the quickest ways to improve one's health.

The condition of our drinking water is the easiest to monitor. Avoid drinking tap water. Fluoride may prevent cavities, but you don't want to drink it. Chlorine and other chemicals can be used effectively in swimming pools, but you don't want to drink those either. We recently saw a TV commercial advertising a laundry detergent that kept your clothes looking new wash after wash. They advertised that your clothes wouldn't fade because this particular detergent neutralized the chlorine in the water. Our clothes fade because of the chlorine in the water? What do you think the chlorine does to your body?

Tap water may contain over a thousand chemicals. In some areas of the country you can even smell the chlorine in the tap water. A high-quality water purification system can filter out these and many other contaminants. We use a water purifier manufactured by the Amway Corporation. We found it to be one of the best purifiers available. It is listed with the NSF International and is effective in the reduction of thirty-one contaminants, most by over 99 percent. Using a filter is a step in the right direction; however, you need pure water, not just filtered water. Distilled water is also a good source of clean water; however, in the long run it is much more expensive than a water purification system.

There are many other pollutants that we are exposed to that are difficult if not impossible to avoid. For that reason we need to ensure that we have a healthy immune system. The best way to build up our immune system is through optimal nutrition. And the only way to guarantee optimal nutrition is through the use of the highest quality nutritional supplements.

Nutritional supplements

Are you currently taking nutritional supplements? You probably won't hear your medical doctor recommending nutritional supplements. That is because most are doctors of medicine, not doctors of nutrition. We find it very interesting that only 30 percent of doctors recommend supplements to their patients, yet 70 percent of them take supplements.

Many people used to think that they got all the nutrition that they needed from the foods that they ate. Nearly 70 percent of Americans no longer believe that and are taking nutritional supplements to round out their nutritional needs. Nutritional supplements used to be looked at by many as an insurance policy. These people realized that they were not eating all of the foods that the USDA recommended on a daily basis. After all, five to nine servings of fruits and vegetables does not exactly fit into the average American's lifestyle of eating on the run. As a matter of fact, the USDA surveyed 21,500 people and discovered that only 3 percent actually ate healthful, balanced diets daily. And of the 21,500 people in this survey, not a single person received the RDA recommendation of the ten most important vitamins and minerals regularly. Today nutritional supplements are looked at as not just an insurance policy, but they are looked at as being absolutely necessary for optimal health.

Not all nutritional supplements are created equal. What should you look for in a nutritional supplement?

First, every vitamin and mineral must be in the correct amounts. Most nutritional companies design their product after the RDA. The RDA was developed by the government to prevent deficiency diseases like scurvy, rickets, pellagra and beriberi. Pirates come to mind when we think of scurvy. As a matter of fact the term "limey" was coined after British sailors who developed scurvy while out at sea. It was found that scurvy, a vitamin C deficiency, was cured after feeding these sailors limes. Well, we don't know about you, but we are not too concerned about dying from rickets. We are concerned about avoiding heart disease, cancer and the other deadly degenerative diseases.

Much research has been done all around the world that points to the need for higher levels of nutrients than those called out by the RDA. This is especially true in the area of antioxidants, the champions over oxidative stress. Oxidative stress comes from everyday life and living, environmental pollutants, exercise, foods, smoking and alcohol. Oxidative stress produces free radicals, which cause degenerative disease and premature aging.

"The most important medical discovery of the last half century concerns two substances called 'free radicals' and 'antioxidants.' Free radicals have been linked to (at last count) about 60 diseases . . . we now have evidence that antioxidants can stop and (in some instances) even reverse the damage done by free radicals."
- Dr. Robert D. Willix Jr. -
Healthy at 100: 7 steps to a Century of Great Health

The best defense against these free radicals is the use of optimal amounts of antioxidants. Three of the main antioxidants are vitamin C, beta-carotene, and vitamin E. So what are the optimal daily amounts of these three substances?

Vitamin C—1,000 mg to 1,300 mg
Beta-carotene—16,000 IU to 25,000 IU
Vitamin E—400 IU to 450 IU

But just taking vitamin C, beta-carotene, and vitamin E is not enough. We cannot forget about the other thirty-two essential vitamins and minerals. The abovementioned levels are for people who are already in good health. Others with certain diseases may require greater amounts.

Second, all of the ingredients must be balanced and in the right form. Many vitamins and minerals have a synergistic relationship. In other words, they are much more effective when combined with the correct amounts of other vitamins and minerals. It has also been found that certain nutrients supplied in isolation can sometimes result in a deficiency of another nutrient. Some substances can even be toxic in higher dosages. Vitamin A in the form of Retinol can become toxic in amounts greater than 5,000 IU. A preferable form of vitamin A is beta-carotene, which is converted into vitamin A in your body, as you need it.

Vitamin D supplementation should not exceed 400 IU per day and iron (ferrous or ferric forms) should not be taken at all unless recommended by a doctor. Also, some supplement manufacturers use the cheapest synthetic forms in their products. The ingredients must be in a form that can be absorbed and then used in the body, otherwise known as bioavailable. Not only are some supplements not bioavailable, they don't even dissolve. Some are passed right through your system. Nurses call them bedpan bullets. Those who pump out septic tanks and clean port-a-johns can even tell you what brand they are because they can still read the manufacturer's name on the tablet.

Third, the product must be laboratory tested and quality guaranteed. A product's claims are meaningless if not backed by compliance with established standards such as the U.S. Pharmacopoeia (USP) Good Manufacturing Practices (GMPs), used by the pharmaceutical industry. Check to see if your supplements are listed in the *Physician's Desk Reference* (PDR). Just ask your doctor, he can look it up for you.

The Food and Drug Administration (FDA) in America does not regulate nutritional supplements. They are considered a food product and have as much regulation as pastry treats.

According to world-renowned immunologist and microbiologist Dr. Myron Wentz, "I began testing health supplements in my analytical laboratory to measure their nutritional balance and their effectiveness in promoting and sustaining a healthy life. Many of the products I analyzed were not only nutritionally unbalanced, but had incorrect and misleading labels. It was not uncommon for a product to show 400 milligrams of a particular ingredient on the label, and after analysis to find that it actually contained only 50 milligrams. My research proved many times that what consumers thought they were buying and what they were receiving were two different things."

If you want to be as healthy as you can be, then you need to take the highest quality nutritional supplements available. Don't sell your health to the lowest bidder.

According to Lyle MacWilliam in his manual, *Comparative Nutritional Supplements*, he found that the top three highest performing supplements to be manufactured by:

1. Usana Health Sciences
2. Source Naturals
3. SportPharma

These brands were selected after analyzing over four hundred U.S. and Canadian nutritional products. If you want to know which supplements we take, go to www.honeymoonmarriage.com and click on the keyword "nutritional supplements."

Water

We already discussed the importance of drinking pure water. Now let's take a closer look at this all-important substance. How important is water? It is the most important element required by your body second only to oxygen. You can live for weeks without food; however, you cannot live for more than a few days without water. Our bodies are made up of 72 to 83 percent water. Lose 20 percent of your body water and you will die.

Many Americans live in a constant state of mild dehydration and don't even know it. You don't have to feel thirsty to know that your body needs more water. As a matter of fact, when you feel thirsty, it is too late, you are already dehydrated. Studies have shown that drinking adequate amounts of water every day can eliminate up to 70 percent of health problems. Drinking adequate amounts of pure water is one of the easiest and least expensive ways to keep healthy, yet very few Americans even know how much water they drink every day. How do you know you are getting enough if you don't even know how much you are consuming? How do you know you are getting enough if you don't even know what enough is?

Most of us have heard that we need eight to ten eight-ounce servings of water each day. That requirement is higher when exposed to a hot environment, or exerting yourself physically. According to the International Bottled Water Association, only 34 percent of Americans drink eight or more eight-ounce servings of water per day and nearly 10 percent don't drink water at all. The best way that we have found to ensure that we drink enough water is to measure it.

We bought a six-pack of purified drinking water in twenty-four-ounce bottles. We then took a permanent marker and marked the numbers 1, 2 and 3 on top of the caps. We then had two sets of three bottles each already marked and ready to drink. When the bottles are empty, we filled them back up using our water purification system and put them back in the refrigerator. When we get up in the morning we take bottle number 1 out of the refrigerator, when that bottle is done, we take out bottle number 2, and so forth. That way we know that we are getting at least 72 ounces of pure water every day. We also carry water bottles in the car and take one with us when we go walking, even if it is just to the mall. Water is too important to your health to treat it lightly.

Pure water is the best and you will develop a taste for it over time. You will even prefer it to other beverages after a while. We used to love the taste of sodas, but now they taste like we're drinking pure sugar. They even leave an aftertaste in our mouths that is less than desirable. Beverages that contain caffeine and alcohol do not count toward your eight to ten servings since they have diuretic properties. Avoid drinking beverages that contain sugar. Not only will sugar cause the release of insulin into the blood, but it also forces the body to take water out of the cells to help dilute and digest the sugar. Drink fruit juices sparingly because they contain high levels of sugar. When it comes to fruit, it is best to eat the fruit rather than drink its juice.

Some people say that they cannot drink a lot of water because it makes them have to go to the bathroom a lot. That's the point! Drinking water and its subsequent elimination is one of the ways our body cleanses itself. Remember when you were sick as a little child and the doctor suggested that you drink a lot of fluids? The idea was to flush the toxins out of your system.

Drinking adequate amounts of pure water is even more important during and after working out or receiving a deep muscle massage. This is true because these activities release toxins from our muscles and they need to be flushed out of our body. After all, you wouldn't want these toxins to stay where they are, would you? Drink water and drink it often. It is one of the easiest and least expensive things that you can do to improve your health.

You were only given one body and it is your responsibility to take care of it the best that you can.

Exercise, living lean, stress management, a healthy balanced diet, nutritional supplementation and plenty of clean water are the ingredients to a healthier, more energetic and confident you. This new and improved you will bring a new dynamic to your relationship. Improve you, and you improve your marriage.

You have now finished the first chapter to the healthy, wealthy and wise trilogy. The next two chapters will address the knowledge and wisdom side of the triangle, and "Section 6: Money Matters" will deal with the wealth component.

EXPANDING YOUR MIND—
THE PURSUIT OF KNOWLEDGE
AND WISDOM

"People have more options than they think they do.
But most people spend more time planning their vacation than
thinking about what they want to do with their lives."
- Bob McDonald -

The whole package
We are, without a doubt, very complex beings. Our bodies perform hundreds of functions without us consciously being aware of them. The human psyche, comprised of the mind, will and the emotions, has the ability to create and transform our reality. Our body, mind, will and emotions all come together to form a truly unique and powerful package. Every part of this package works together to form what we call our life. All of these parts are interrelated and each one has an effect on the others.

Holistic approaches to solving problems in the human condition have been practiced throughout the world for thousands of years. The modernized western world is also standing up and taking notice of this age-old practice. We are starting to see an increase in the popularity and acceptance of holistic practices. It wasn't that long ago that the family doctor used to ask a lot of questions during the patient's visit—questions like When did the symptoms start? What changed in your life right about that time? How's the job treating you? How are things at home? How much sleep are you getting? If they were really progressive they might have even asked about diet. Today doctors either don't have the time or don't think that it is important to talk to their patients, let alone get to know them. In some cases, patients are almost treated in an assembly-line fashion, where it almost seems as though efficiency and productivity are more important than the person. The cure to our ailment is thought to be in a pill or a shot. Every person is treated in a similar fashion. A pill or a shot, next. A pill or a shot, next. A pill or a shot, next.

The industrial age is partially to blame for this mindset. The industrial age was the age of the machine. Men and women ran machines and in many cases were looked at as machines themselves. If a machine would go down due to a broken part, the part would be repaired or replaced as quickly as possible, the machine would be started up, and then put back into service. After all, products needed to be pushed out the door as quickly as possible. That's fine for a machine, however, we are not machines. If we try to just fix the "broken" part and then put our lives back into service, we have missed the bigger picture. What caused the part to break in the first place? How has the breakage affected other areas of one's life? What can be done to keep it from breaking again or so often? How can one become stronger so that problems don't reoccur? Who else has experienced this kind of a symptom, no longer experiences a problem, and what can I learn from this person?

All of the medicine, treatments, exercise and healthy eating, may not be able to fix what's "broken" if our negative emotions are out of control. All of the willpower one can muster may not be enough for a person to lose weight if there is something in his or her psyche that is keeping the person fat. We need to look at the *whole* person in order to fix the *whole* problem.

About a year ago, we along with a group of about one hundred people spent the day with a peak performance expert. He gave several powerful demonstrations of how complex we humans are. He told us that he knew of two pressure points in the body that could control our level of strength. The pressure point for strength was in the middle of our forehead, whereas the pressure point for weakness was right behind the earlobe. These pressure points only needed to be touched very lightly in order to be effective. He then had us all partner up with the person next to us. We were to take turns putting one arm straight out to our side parallel to the ground. The other person was to touch his or her partner on the forehead and then try to push the partner's arm down. The person with the raised arm was to resist as hard as he or she could.

Most people had a very hard time pushing their partner's arm down; some couldn't even budge the arm. Then we were to touch our partners behind their ear and repeat the exercise. The results were amazing! Arms were falling quickly throughout the room. My partner's arm was falling almost solely due to its own weight. We switched partners and repeated the exercise. The results were the same. When surveyed, about 90 percent of the room said that they could notice a big difference depending upon which pressure point was touched. The instructor then told us, "Your experience of strength and weakness was created by your mind. Last week I told my students that touching the forehead causes weakness and touching behind the ear causes an increase in strength." That was just a small example to demonstrate how interrelated our mind and body is.

Later that evening a small group of us stuck around as he offered some advanced training. He asked us what one thing we would like to change in our lives. Several people volunteered their requests, and he addressed each one of them one at a time. He was also a trained hypnotist and proceeded to tell everyone how to breathe and relax as he recited very calming and tranquil phrases. Now we had seen hypnotists cause people to quack like a duck and do goofy things before, but this was the first time we have ever witnessed one uncover the reason behind a destructive behavior.

There were several people in the room who wanted to lose weight. One by one he discovered the "fat-producing" foods that they were hooked on. He proceeded to tell them that every time they would think of that food, it would taste awful and make their tongue crawl and that they would have no interest in that food. After these people came to, just the mention of that food caused them to cringe. The look on their faces caused the rest of us to break out in laughter. Did they end up losing weight? Only time would tell. We were informed that this new program (thinking that their favorite fat-producing foods tasted awful) could be overwritten and that each person could end up right back to where he or she started unless the person continued to link an undesirable outcome to these foods.

So far nothing too impressive. Instead of quacking like a duck, they acted like eating chocolate ice cream was as pleasant as sucking on a lemon or eating dirt. But then something really amazing happened. There was a young lady in her thirties who wanted to lose weight. She had been overweight most of her adult life and no diet ever seemed to help. The instructor asked her if she had always had a weight problem, and she said that she was pretty thin until her late teens. He then asked her when the last time was that she thought she really looked good and to describe what she looked like. He then put her back into a hypnotic state and went back to that time. She described herself in great detail as though she was looking at a picture.

She had worked very hard to get into great shape and was wearing a really sharp red dress that made her look fantastic. Come to find out, she still had the dress in her closet even though she hadn't been able to fit into it in years. He asked her why she was all dressed up and looking so fine. She told him that she was going out with a girl friend and wanted to look her best just in case they ran into any cute guys. To make a long story short, she did attract a guy, dated him, got married and had a very painful relationship that ended in divorce. The reason she couldn't lose weight was because she linked being thin and looking good to attracting a man, which in turn would lead to a painful relationship. She associated being thin with the feeling of pain. This strong emotional state controlled what she ate and how she looked. Every effort that she made to lose weight would be sabotaged. That evening she discovered for the first time why she couldn't lose weight for all of those years and how she could solve her problem. She realized that being thin didn't cause her pain, picking the wrong guy did.

These examples show the power that our mind and emotions have on our body and our behaviors. In order for us to live up to our full potential and to live the most happy and abundant life possible, we need to take a holistic approach toward personal excellence. We need to focus on every area of our lives. The decisions that you make regarding the nourishing of your body, the expanding of your mind, the controlling of your emotions and the nurturing of your spirit, will determine the quality and happiness of your life and your marriage.

In this chapter you will be focusing 100 percent on you. At first glance, you may wonder how expanding your mind and gaining knowledge and wisdom will affect your relationship. As mentioned before, anything that you do to improve *you* will improve your marriage.

The power of your thoughts

How important are your thoughts? Aren't thoughts just small, intangible, harmless things? Napoleon Hill, in his book *Think and Grow Rich*, states that, "Every man is what he is because of the dominating thoughts which he permits to occupy his mind." A thought is the foundation upon which your life is built. A thought causes a chain reaction to occur in your life. When you have a disciplined mind, you have control over your thoughts and like any discipline, this control can be learned and perfected over time.

As mentioned several times before, you reap what you sow. If you plant a negative thought in your mind, you will experience negative results. If you plant a positive thought in your mind, you will experience positive results.

> *"Sow a thought, and you reap an act;*
> *Sow an act, and you reap a habit;*
> *Sow a habit, and you reap a character;*
> *Sow a character, and you reap a destiny."*
> *- Samuel Smiles -*

What is your destiny? What kind of a future life do you want to have? Your future starts today with your thoughts.

When it comes to your mind, the saying "garbage in, garbage out" holds a lot of truth. You must guard your mind as though your happiness and well-being depends on it, because they do. What goes into your mind comes from two primary sources:

1. Internal sources—self-talk and emotions
2. External sources—relationships and education

Internal

The power of your mind is incredible! Your internal thoughts control your life. They determine who you are and who you will become. Your thoughts can either be positive or negative. Very few people consider themselves to be pessimistic; they say that they are realistic. We have talked to thousands of people and in our opinion, many if not most of them are pessimists, they just don't realize it. Most people do not give themselves enough credit. They think that success is largely due to luck or circumstances. You don't have to be able to read minds to know this about people. All you have to do is listen to someone talk long enough and the person will tell you what he or she thinks and believes. What you think determines how you act and the choices that you make. And all of your choices have consequences, either good or bad.

Choose to be optimistic. It is the only way to achieve the Honeymoon Marriage. The more positive you become, the more negative others will seem to be. It isn't slightly noticeable, it stands out like a sore thumb. As you continue to expand your mind, you will even be able to pick out the comments that are holding others back from achieving what they want in life. More importantly, you will begin to notice that the thoughts that you have and the comments that you make are holding you back as well.

"No pessimist ever discovered the secrets
of the stars, or sailed to an uncharted land,
or opened a new heaven to the human spirit."
- Helen Keller -

Our future reality is whatever we think it is. If you think that it is impossible for you to have a "Honeymoon Marriage," then that is your reality. If you think you can and will become a multimillionaire, then it can be so. If you think that you will get cancer because your Mom had cancer, then that is a possibility. Whatever you think about and focus on becomes your reality. Even happiness is a choice. You can be happy if you choose to be. The choice is yours and it is within your control.

"A man cannot be comfortable
without his own approval."
- Mark Twain -

Let's take the positive alternative to the cancer scenario mentioned above. You know of someone who has cancer and you think to yourself, "I will remain healthy and free from disease." Those thoughts will lead you to discovering how to stay healthy and avoid diseases like cancer. You read everything that you can get your hands on regarding the avoidance of such diseases. Your subconscious mind will also be working on your behalf. Before you know it, you will have made major lifestyle changes that have been proven to reduce your risk of cancer. Disease and health can be rooted in your thoughts. A perfectly healthy person can get sick and even die due to the thoughts of fear and anxiety that occupy his or her mind. This is called a psychosomatic illness, and it is very real. So be very careful of your thoughts. Make sure that you think about only what you want to become.

"Finally, brothers, whatever is true, whatever is noble,
whatever is right, whatever is pure, whatever is lovely,
whatever is admirable—if anything is excellent or
praiseworthy—think about such things."
- Philippians 4:8 -

If you can take control of your internal thoughts, especially those that you may not be fully conscious of at the moment, you will be able to master anything that you desire.

Self-talk

Do you talk to yourself? There is a popular saying regarding talking to oneself that goes like this, "It is okay to talk to yourself. It is when you answer yourself that you need to be concerned." In reality, we talk to ourselves all day long. We may not talk out loud, however, we carry on conversations in our mind all the time. Unfortunately, we may not even realize that we are doing it. Some may think that you are a little crazy if you talk to yourself. That could not be further from the truth. What is crazy is not controlling this conversation. It is very important that you direct this conversation or self-talk because it will in turn direct your life.

"Wisdom is avoiding all thoughts that weaken you."
- Wayne Dyer -

It is amazing how some people would never allow someone to abuse them verbally, yet they abuse themselves verbally every day. This kind of self-inflicted abuse is known as negative self-talk. Is your self-talk positive or negative? Some examples of negative self-talk are as follows:

- "I will never have a great marriage."
- "It is too late to take advantage of that opportunity."
- "My husband or wife will never change."
- "There is no need for me to set goals because I will never reach them anyway."

"The tragedy of life doesn't lie in not reaching your goal.
The tragedy lies in having no goal to reach."
- Benjamin Mays -

- "I am not smart enough."
- "If only I had married someone else."
- "I can't make more money because I don't have a college education."

"The people who get on in this world are the people
who get up and look for the circumstances they want,
and if they can't find them, make them."
- George Bernard Shaw -

- "My spouse doesn't love me."
- "I always screw up."
- "I will always be overweight."
- "If only I had more time."
- "I'm too young."

- "I'm too old."
- "I'll never amount to anything."
- "I can't try that, what if I fail?"

> *"The only limit to our realization of tomorrow*
> *will be our doubts of today."*
> *- Franklin Delano Roosevelt -*

- "No other employer in the area will pay me what I am making here."
- "I'm a boring person."
- "What if the plane crashes?"
- "I'm not attractive."
- "If only I had more money."
- "You have to be lucky in order to become wealthy."

> *"Chance favors the prepared mind."*
> *- Louis Pasteur -*

- "I'll never find a close friend."
- "I am a clumsy person."
- "Uncle Joe tried that before and he failed."
- "You can't buy real estate with no money down."
- "I'll always be broke."
- "What will people think of me if I do that?"
- "I'll never be happy."
- "I never have enough energy and am always tired."

And the list goes on and on. It is amazing how effectively we can limit our success by allowing this negative self-talk to go on. We are great at thinking of why something won't work, but we fail to think of ways that we can make it work.

> *"Some men have thousands of reasons*
> *why they cannot do what they want to,*
> *when all they need is one reason why they can."*
> *- Mary Frances Berry -*

It is time to take control over your thoughts and purposely direct your self-talk. You are amazing and you can do anything that you believe you can do. In the words of Thomas Edison, the greatest inventor of his time, "If we did all the things we are capable of doing, we would literally astound ourselves." Start talking to yourself like you would want others to talk to you and don't settle for anything else. Be your own best friend by telling yourself only positive, encouraging and uplifting things. The thoughts that you have about yourself can even affect how others treat you. Respect yourself and others will begin showing you respect. Like yourself and it will be easier for others to like you. There is a Hasidic saying that states, "The man who has confidence in himself gains the confidence of others." Negative self-talk is nothing more than a bad habit and like all habits it can be eliminated.

"Most of our success in life will be determined
by our habits, either good or bad.
Good habits are hard to form, but easy to live with.
Bad habits are easy to form, but hard to live with."
- Brian Tracy -

As soon as a negative thought enters your mind, get rid of it and replace it with a positive one. This is not easy, but it can be done. You have had your negative mental habits for a long time. Likewise, it will take time to reverse these habits. Not only will it take time, but it will also take consistency. You have to constantly fill your mind with positive thoughts in order to overshadow the negative ones. Our mind is like a computer, and we need to reprogram it. Repetition is a way that we can rewrite our programming. We would suggest going on a daily diet of positive thoughts. Make sure to start your day off right by concentrating on the positive. At night just before you go to sleep, think thoughts that you would want played over and over again in your mind while you are asleep. Write a script, like the one to follow, and read it aloud as soon as you get up in the morning and just before you retire for the evening.

Today is a new day, full of new possibilities. I am full of energy and I can't wait to see what this day has in store for me. I am a very important person and many people want and need what I have to offer. I am an awesome husband/wife and I am always looking for ways that I can improve my relationships, my marriage and myself. I am in control of myself, my thoughts and my actions. I always take care of myself by watching what I eat, exercising, getting enough sleep, relaxing and thinking positive thoughts. I do not live under my circumstances, but instead I take the steps necessary to create a wonderful future. I love who I am and who I am becoming and so do others. I am excited about life and other people love to be around me. I am very thankful for everything that I have and I never complain about what I don't have. I am ambitious and always look for opportunities to improve my financial situation. I know that I have the ability to achieve anything that I desire and I will never give up trying until I have reached my goal. I read positive motivational books and/or listen to audio programs every day and apply what I have learned. I seek expert advice before making major decisions. I am organized and I get more organized every day. I continually look for ways to serve my wife/husband and in doing so my marriage keeps getting better and growing stronger. I am so blessed and I can't wait for the opportunity to bless others. I am a terrific person and I love life!

Repeat this to yourself twice a day every day for thirty days and see it transform your thinking. If you miss a day, you have to start all over. Remember that the key ingredient is consistency.

For a printable version of this daily affirmation, go to www.honeymoonmarriage.com and click on the keyword "affirmation."

Visualization

We have used visualization to achieve a greater level of success in many areas of our life. As a matter of fact, it is our vision to save one million marriages within the next ten years.

> *"Our imagination is the only limit to what we can hope to have in the future."*
> *- Charles F. Kettering -*

Visualization is nothing more than closing your eyes and imagining yourself doing whatever it is that you want to do. The trick is that you have to do it with emotion and believe that you are actually accomplishing the task at hand. Visualization not only works in athletics; it will work in any area of your life. Close your eyes and imagine your ideal life. See yourself walking through this life as though you were watching a movie. Go into as much detail as you possibly can. Feel how good it feels. Imagine all of the great things that will happen to you during the day. In time you will start to become that person.

Focus on the kind of person that you would like to become for thirty minutes a day. Keep doing this exercise until you start to see results. You will first notice that your thinking will begin to change. Then you will see your life starting to change ever so slightly. Be patient because it will be a gradual change. It is similar to looking at yourself in a mirror every day. You may not notice how much weight you are gaining until you look at a picture of yourself that was taken nine months earlier. Similarly, you will notice changes in someone whom you haven't seen for two years because you have an image of the person locked in your mind of how he or she looked two years prior. The person may not even recognize the change, but to you it is like the difference between night and day.

What you focus on the most will become your reality. What kind of a reality do you want?

The power of your emotions

What can be more powerful than your thoughts? The answer; your thoughts wrapped in emotions. We think that you would agree that your emotions influence many of the decisions that you make in life. Some of these emotions are relatively easy to recognize. You know when you are angry, sad, disappointed, hurt and happy. There are many other emotions that can determine the quality of your life, which are very powerful and take on many forms. Emotions, like thoughts, can be controlled, however, the process is more difficult. You may not be able to control everything that happens to you, but you *can* control how you react to what happens to you and how long you hold on to those emotions.

> *"That the birds of worry and care fly above your head,*
> *this you cannot change, but that they build nests*
> *in your hair, this you can prevent."*
> *- Chinese Proverb -*

Fear

One of those powerful emotions is fear. Fear is an emotion that can limit your success like no other. At best, fear can cause us to procrastinate, be indecisive, and be over conscious. At its worst, fear can be paralyzing. Overcoming fear can propel you to success in areas of your life that you have only dreamed of. A common acronym used to describe fear is "FEAR = False Evidence Appearing Real." In more cases than not, fear is caused by expecting something bad or undesirable to happen. That event may never take place, but there still remains the slightest possibility that it will. It is this small possibility that keeps us from doing the things that we want to do and becoming the person that we want to become. The following are some of the many forms of fear.

"We promise according to our hopes,
and perform according to our fears."
- Francois, Duc Dela Rochefoucauld -

The fear of failure. No one wants to fail at anything. What many don't realize is that if they never try, they have already failed. We like Anthony Robbins's take on failure. He says, "There is no such thing as failure, only results." If you discover enough things that don't work, you will eventually find the way that does work. If you never take on the risk of failing, you will never win.

"He who fears being conquered is sure of defeat."
- Napoleon Bonaparte -

Of course you are going to make some mistakes as you branch out and attempt something new. Everyone does. Remember that you are only after results. When you get good results, that's great. When you get negative results, don't worry about it, now you have learned what not to do.

"Failure is only the opportunity
to more intelligently begin again.
Failure is success if we learn from it."
- Malcolm Forbes -

The fear of success. The fear of success is not as easy to spot. This fear can be associated with comments like,

- "What will my friends think of me if I become extremely successful? Will they be jealous and no longer want to associate with me?"
- "I am concerned that success will change me."

"Money and success don't change people;
they merely amplify what was already there."
- Will Smith -

- "What if I am successful and then lose it all?"
- "I will have to give up a lot of things to become successful."

Oftentimes the fear of success is nothing more than the fear of failure in disguise. It is sometimes easier for us to tell ourselves or other people that we don't want success in a certain area because of what that success may bring, when in fact, we are just afraid to try and fail.

The fear of rejection and the fear of ridicule. These fears are oftentimes more paralyzing than the fear of failure. We are consumed with concerns of what others think of us. This is one of the earliest fears we learn in life. Remember playing ball in grade school? Two captains were picked and they took turns choosing their teams from all those who wanted to play. Perhaps you weren't very good or made a big mistake in a past game. From that day on you were picked last. You didn't like the rejected feeling that no one wanted you on his or her team. It was easier to not play ball at all than to be rejected. Perhaps you were not that person and you wanted to make sure that you never did anything that would blacklist you among your friends.

You may have been laughed at the first time that you made a mistake in front of your classmates at school. You became very embarrassed and you didn't like that feeling. Unfortunately, your first experience with ridicule was not your last. It is understandable to have this fear as a child; however, we give it way too much weight as adults. It is probably because of this that so many people have the fear of public speaking. According to *The Book of Lists*, a poll was conducted in the United States and showed that 41 percent of those asked to name their biggest fear listed the fear of public speaking as their number-one fear. The fear of death was several notches down the list at number seven. Taking a public speaking course will cure this fear. Not only will it cure your fear of public speaking, but it will also help you out in other areas of your life, including your relationships. It will make you feel more confident and in control.

Darren - the question man: Donna and I recently went to lunch with a couple that we had recently met. I'll call them Mary and Tom. We were making small talk and having a really great time. I tend to get bored easily when talking about what people do for a living unless it is something that they enjoy or are passionate about. It can even be an exciting career, but if I sense that it isn't something that they would "choose" to do, I can't help but ask them questions like, "If you could do anything for a living, what would you do?" You can learn a lot more about people by talking about their desires than you can by talking about their jobs.

Tom wasn't too clear about what his ideal job would be. He thought that a promotion at his current place of employment would be a great step in the right direction. Mary on the other hand was working in a job that wasn't even close to what she wanted to do. I knew that because she was talking about cutting back to part time so that she could spend more time doing the things that she enjoyed. So, I asked her what she would love to do. She said that she wanted to do training and hold seminars. She said that she loved to sell and be around people, but that she was scared to death to talk in front of people. I couldn't let that one go. The desire of her heart was to do seminars, yet she was afraid of people. To you and me, that may not make much sense, but to the person experiencing the fear, rational thought oftentimes goes out the window. Many people never even make the discovery that it is their fear that is causing them to miss out on many of the joys of life.

I asked Mary what it was that caused her to be afraid to speak in front of people. I pointed out to her that she had good people skills and that she even had the desire to speak in front of people. She had no idea but she was sincerely trying to figure it out. Several questions later, it hit her like a ton of bricks. A memory came to her that she had never thought of before. When she was in the fourth grade she had a teacher who was getting very angry with the class because no one understood the math assignment and everyone was coming up to her and asking her questions. Unfortunately, this teacher, like several of the ones I had in school, had no business being a teacher. She told the class that the next person who asked her a question would get a paddling.

Mary was the next person in line at the teacher's desk. I'm not sure if Mary wasn't paying attention or if she didn't think that her teacher was serious, but she was the next person to ask a question just the same. Believe it or not, the teacher paddled her. Mary almost started to cry after she told that story and said, "Oh my goodness; that is why I am afraid to ask questions."

Some psychologists may not like me for saying this, but you don't have to spend countless hours with a therapist in order to improve your life. You don't need to dig deep into your past and discover what significant event may be causing you to act or react the way that you do. The past events of your life are part of your mental programming. The current events of your life are also part of this programming. Mary could have solved her problem simply by doing the thing that she feared over and over again until the fear was gone. In doing so she would have overwritten her fourth grade programming. Besides, once you take control of your mind, you will be able to tap into the power of self-discovery and realize that something is wrong, very wrong, if you are not living the life that you think you should. All I did was ask her a series of questions. There is no reason why she couldn't ask herself those same questions. If you suffer from a destructive behavior, however, it may be best for you to seek professional advice.

The most important question to ask yourself is not *why* you do the things you do. The most important question to ask yourself is *what* you can do to improve the quality of your life and your marriage. You are a victim of your past only as long as you allow yourself to be.

In short, what others think of you is not as important as what you think of you. Besides, most people are too concerned with themselves to even notice what you are doing. If people do give you a hard time, brush it off. After all, they aren't the ones who are living your life. They won't pay your bills. They aren't the ones who will put your kids through college. They can't make your marriage better. They can't make you happy, only you can, so stop worrying so much about what other people think. It is your life so make it the best that you can.

The fear of intimacy and the fear of loss. These two fears can have a lot in common, and they can also be two different sides of the same coin. Intimacy is very important in a marriage, and the fear of intimacy can have a strong negative impact on your relationship. When you open up and give all of your love to someone, you become very vulnerable. You make it possible for that person to let you down or even hurt you. One who has been hurt before typically feels these feelings to one degree or another; however, they should not be long-term and should fade over time. Holding back some of your love or commitment may make you feel safer, like you won't be hurt as bad if the other person should let you down or even leave you. In this instance the fear of intimacy can be caused by the fear of loss. These feelings are not healthy and can push your spouse away from you, causing the thing that you fear to become a reality.

A person with this kind of fear will oftentimes have feelings toward others that run hot and cold. As soon as their feelings get too hot, they immediately cool them down. The other person can feel this coolness or cold shoulder and will ask what is wrong. Not being able to adequately explain the problem could cause frustration, an argument or even resentment. If the fear of intimacy is not addressed, it can lead to an eventual breakup, which is why the fear existed in the first place. Meeting someone halfway will not cut it. You have to give 100 percent in order to get 100 percent.

*"Intimacy is built on trust. If you don't trust someone
enough to be yourself, you can't be intimate,
and neither can he or she."*
- Mark Goulston -

The fear of loss can also be closely linked to the fear of failure. Let's say that a man just got downsized from a large corporation. He has marketable skills and could find another job in a month or two. He knows that getting a job would be the "safest" thing to do, however, he and his wife would prefer to start their own business. This has been a dream for them and they now have an opportunity to make it happen. Unfortunately, the fear of loss keeps them from pursuing their dreams. With a new job all of the bills will be covered, but with a new business, sacrifices may have to be made. They may have to move into a smaller house or an apartment, sell one of their cars, take more modest vacations, stop eating out at restaurants, etc. This couple is afraid of possibly losing some of the niceties of life, so the husband opts for the job. Now the couple will be comfortable in their discomfort. Not following your heart can be more painful than losing some of your things.

In the famous words of Franklin Delano Roosevelt, "The only thing to fear is fear itself." The best way to overcome fear is to take action. Action cures fear.

*"Do the thing you fear
and the death of fear is certain."*
- Emerson -

Once you have taken action, you will find that the thing you feared wasn't that bad after all. We once heard that success was being afraid and doing it anyway. Move out of your comfort zone and follow your gut feelings. If you desire more out of life, remember that those desires were put there for a reason, so act on them.

Remove and keep envy out of your life
Envy is not just wanting what someone else has, but it can be wishing that the other person didn't have it or will lose it. You can even resent someone for having success in a certain area of his or her life just because you don't. That resentment will push success further away from you. Envy and resentment can be caused by having a scarcity mentality. Marketers thrive on creating the illusion of urgency and scarcity. A marketer may tell the public that only 100,000 of their most popular toy will be available prior to Christmas. Parents will rush out and buy one as quick as they can.

After all, heaven forbid that little Johnny has to go through Christmas without the toy that is number one on his wish list. That type of scarcity isn't going to have a major negative impact on anyone's life. But a scarcity mentality directed toward success and successful people will. One of the reasons that successful people are envied is because they are thought to have attained what they have through luck or talents that less successful people can't or don't have.

The scarcity mentality is demonstrated by the Christmas toy example above. Let's say you go to your favorite toy store and you see one of the "scarce" toys on the shelf. Unfortunately, the lady in front of you grabs it before you can. She wins, but you and little Johnny lose. Another traditional example is that of the pie. We grew up thinking that if someone else gets a piece of the pie that there is less for us or worse, none at all. After all, there are only so many pieces of the pie and once they are gone, they are gone forever. So when someone gets a big slice of success, that you didn't get, you may envy or even despise him or her. Your subconscious mind somehow thinks that there is less success out there for you to have. With that attitude, success will avoid you. You see, you can never have what it is that you despise. Your subconscious mind will not allow it to happen. Instead you need to take on an abundance mentality. We like to use the following analogy to explain the abundance mentality:

"I am not concerned if you take a big piece of
the pie because I know the baker. He can make
me a pie whenever I want. If he is not open,
that is no problem because I know how
to bake my own pie."

The fact of the matter is, there is plenty of success to go around and if you believe that, then you open yourself up to a whole new world of opportunities. Learn how to bake and you will never be without a piece of the pie again.

Another great way to eliminate envy and the scarcity mentality is to spend time with those that you envy (or soon to be, used to envy). These are the people who have what you want. We truly enjoy spending time with successful people. What we discover from these meetings is that these people are regular people just like you and me. They all have their faults and weaknesses. They all have experienced failure and defeat yet continue to bounce back stronger than ever. When listening to their stories you will discover that their success was not due to luck or fate. They worked hard for what they have and they never gave up. The more time that you spend with them, the more you will realize that you can have everything that they have if you are willing to make the choices that they made. You will then begin to admire that person, and in the words of Mark Goulston, M.D., author of *Get Out Of Your Own Way*, "If you admire someone, you can let him or her have more without feeling you have less."

Stop living in the past

Put the past behind you. Glancing in the rearview mirror once in a while is a wise thing to do. But if while driving you only look in the rearview mirror, sooner or later you are going to crash. We all make mistakes. We all lose at times. We all have our setbacks and defeats. Continuing to focus on the past robs your chance of obtaining a successful future. A mistake that you can learn from is a very costly lesson; however, allowing a mistake to cause you to give up on your future is a tragedy. Just because things have gone wrong in the past doesn't mean that they will go wrong in the future. Today is a new day and yesterday is gone forever. Be the best that you can be today, and your tomorrow will be something to look forward to.

"It is difficult to say what is impossible,
for the dream of yesterday is the
hope of today and the reality of tomorrow."
- Robert H. Goddard -

Stop feeling sorry for yourself

It is easy to get caught up in the trap of feeling sorry for yourself. Self-pity can feel good for a while, but in time it will rob you of your joy in life. A great way to stop feeling sorry for yourself is to change your focus, to change your reference, your state of mind. Volunteering is a great way to take your focus off of yourself and to discover that things could be worse. Besides, helping others in need will bless your life in ways that you may not expect. Help out at a homeless shelter. If you are a woman, volunteer to work at a shelter for victims of domestic violence. Spend time visiting with people at nursing homes. Buy and drop off food to a food pantry. Help those who are less fortunate than you and your feelings of self-pity will be replaced with an attitude of appreciation.

"Never feel self-pity,
the most destructive emotion there is.
How awful to be caught up in the terrible squirrel cage of self."
- Millicent Fenwick -

Make eye contact with everyone you pass on the street. Say hello and offer a smile. Develop an attitude of gratitude. Focus on and be thankful for all that you do have. Make a list of all of the things that are great in your life. Ask yourself what you can do to make things better. Remember, whatever you focus on becomes your reality. Focus on the bad and bad things will be attracted to you. Focus on the good and good things will follow.

When you stop feeling sorry for yourself and develop a positive and thankful attitude, positive people will be drawn to you. Have you ever heard someone say, "She has such a magnetic personality?" What does that mean? It means that people are drawn to her like iron filings to a magnet. Why does this happen? It is because people see something in her that they want. She makes them feel comfortable and good about themselves. She may even give them hope. The opposite is also true. If you are angry, bitter, unforgiving, envious, feeling sorry for yourself, resentful, depressed or fearful, you repel the type of people that you need the most in life. Be the kind of person whom you would like to spend time with. Stop feeling sorry for yourself and look for ways to make yourself and your relationships better.

External

Our internal thoughts and emotions are very powerful, however, we cannot overlook the fact that much of who we are is developed through external sources. What we read and listen to and whom we spend time with often causes us to think differently. Expose yourself to positive influences and you get positive results. Conversely, expose yourself to negative influences and you get negative results. Your mind is like a valuable treasure locked in a vault to be guarded at all times. How many people have a key to your vault? Are these people going to make withdrawals or deposits? How easy is it to break into your vault? Or do you always leave the door wide open?

Relationships

The people that we surround ourselves with have a major impact on our lives.

> *"Tell me what company you keep,*
> *and I'll tell you what you are."*
> *- Miguel de Cervantes -*

We have all heard the saying, "birds of a feather flock together." Is that because we tend to hang around people whom we share common interests with or is it because we start to become like the people we hang out with? Both are true, but it is the latter that we need to be careful of. Peer pressure and the need to be accepted are not reserved for school age children. They are alive and well in our adult lives. Make a conscious effort to surround yourself with people that are positive, uplifting, encouraging, fun-loving, resourceful, big thinkers, moral and ethical, kind, good listeners and extremely optimistic. There is a Jewish proverb that says, "In choosing a friend, go up a step." Look for someone who has more of what you want. If you want to be wealthy, make wealthy friends. If you want to be healthy, join a health club and make friends there. If you want to become more creative, look for people who are artists, musicians, poets, actors, inventors and the like. If you want to become more spiritual, hang out with spiritual people or in spiritual places. If you want to have a great marriage, then spend time with happily married couples.

"Be careful the environment you choose
for it will shape you;
be careful the friends you choose
for you will become like them."
- W. Clement Stone -

Oftentimes you can tell whether or not someone has a good marriage just by listening to how the person talks about his or her mate. It is easy to get caught in a trap of spending time with unfulfilled married people. The "boys club" man will say that his wife, "the ball and chain", is always nagging him, won't let him convert part of the garage into a workshop, always makes him work overtime so she can spend his hard-earned money, etc. The "girls club" woman will say that her husband, "the armchair quarterback", would rather watch the game or read the paper than carry on a conversation, never listens, doesn't care how she feels, etc. While these may all be valid complaints, continuing to expose yourself to this environment is not healthy. It causes you to focus on the bad rather than on the good. Also there is peer pressure to join in on the spouse bashing.

"The pleasure of criticizing robs us of the pleasure of
being moved by some very fine things."
- Jean De La Bruyére -

A thought is powerful enough, but when you vocalize that thought, it takes on a force of its own. Once you say something out loud, that thought gets imbedded deep into your being. You believe it more than ever. It becomes real and the more you say it, the more real it becomes. Wouldn't it be refreshing to be in a group of men or women that have only great things to say about their husbands or wives? The conversation would go more like this: "It is so great to be married, my husband treats me so well, he is a great provider, he is my best friend, I don't know what I would do without him." Or, "My wife was made just for me, she knows how to make me relax, she helps me keep my other relationships strong, she works so hard for our family, I don't know what I would do without her." In short, spend time with the people you want to be like. Avoid spending time with negative, complaining, backbiting, gossiping, downgrading, discouraging, dull, small-minded, immoral and dishonest, mean-spirited, domineering, pessimistic people. Always remember that you will become like the person that you spend the most time with, and it is easier to pull someone down than to lift someone up.

"Be courteous to all, but intimate with few,
and let those few be well tried
before you give them your confidence."
- George Washington -

The wisdom of past generations
Have you ever heard kids or young adults talk to each other about a major problem that they are having? They talk as though their whole world will crumble if things don't work out the way that they had hoped. To them, their problems are very big and very real. You, on the other hand, may laugh to yourself and think that they are worrying over nothing, that their troubles are minor and can be easily handled. You see the answers very clearly, when they can't see them at all. Why is that? Is it because you are smarter than they are? That's not necessarily true. They may have a higher IQ and be better educated than you are. So what makes you so much "smarter" than they are? You have something that they lack. You have experience. Doesn't it make sense then that there may be people out there who may know the solution to your troubles, people who have more experience than you do? The answer to that question is obvious, but we often miss it. Perhaps it is because we think that we can figure out all of life's mysteries on our own, or maybe we don't think that the older generation can possibly have anything to offer us. If that is the way you think, then it is time to reevaluate your opinion. Otherwise you may miss out on one of life's most valuable treasures.

Your grandparents are the first place to look to find this treasure. If your grandparents are no longer living, then borrow someone else's, or seek the counsel of someone at least twenty years older than you. If you look up *grandparents* in the dictionary, they will be described as the parents to one's mother or father. That's it, nothing more and nothing less. Grandparents are much more than that. They are people who cannot be adequately described in the pages of a book. A grandparent is someone who can help shape your character and your destiny.

> *Just like Grandpa:* A week or so ago, Donna and I (Darren) were going for our daily walk when she said something to me that brought tears to my eyes. What she said was one of the most heartfelt compliments that anyone had ever given to me. She said that I was just like my Grandpa. I was speechless for several minutes as I thought about what she had said.
>
> I received a lot of gifts from my Grandpa. The gifts that he gave me were priceless and will last me a lifetime. They will live on well after I have breathed my last, as I will pass them on to all who want to learn some of these innermost secrets of life. The gifts that I am referring to include faith, wisdom, integrity, hope, contentment, peace, and joy. These are the gifts that I hope to pass along so that the legacy of a wise old man will be able to bless the lives of others as much as they did mine.
>
> Neither of my grandparents were ever short on words. They would oftentimes cut into each other's stories to add some of the missing details or even talk at the same time. It was as though they had so much life inside that they could not contain themselves. Donna would usually listen to Grandma while I listened to Grandpa so that they could both speak and be heard at the same time. Their stories were not just tales of old, but rather they were life itself. I sometimes hear their stories played in my mind when I am going through a challenging time. They bring me hope and increase my faith. Hope and faith are two ingredients that can help you to overcome any obstacle. Without them you can do nothing. With them you can do anything.
>
> The lost art of storytelling was alive and well with my grandparents. All my Grandpa would need was an ear that would listen. That is when he was in his element. He could talk nonstop for hours if you would let him, and I oftentimes did. I don't think that the art of storytelling is dead, it has just been suppressed by today's fast-paced, stressed-out lifestyle. We are always in a hurry. Urgency has become the normal state of affairs instead of a once-in-a-while occurrence.

> *"There is more to life than increasing its speed."*
> *- Mahatma Gandhi -*

Our work, home, and outside environments have been invaded with a high level of noise and distractions. Coworkers, bosses, customers, clients, patients, buzzers, bells, machinery, children, spouse, friends, television, radio, newspaper, Internet, telephone, traffic and construction all fight for our attention. Many homes in America have the TV on nonstop, whether or not someone is even watching it. We experience too much noise and have so many sources fighting for our attention. Quiet time? What's that? Reflection, isn't that something that you see when you look at yourself in the mirror? Many of us are so busy that we don't even have time to rest.

> *"Sometimes the most urgent and vital*
> *thing you can possibly do is take a complete rest."*
> *- Ashleigh Brilliant -*

It is very important that we take time every day to shut ourselves off from all of this noise and the many distractions in life. We need to slow down, breath, quiet ourselves, and concentrate on all of the beauty and blessings in our life.

Our conversations today tend to lean toward the negative. We talk about other people, events and the challenges of our day. We may even complain and feel stuck in our current circumstances. There tends to be more despair than hope, more stress than peace and more complaining than thankfulness.

Darren's Grandparents continued: That was not the case when speaking to my Grandma and Grandpa. There always seemed to be a moral to every story, a lesson to be learned. I didn't realize it at the time, but can see it very clearly today. Although my grandparents led a very difficult life, they never seemed to complain about their plight. They always seemed to have the joy of life.

My Grandpa worked on the farm during the day and worked at a factory at night. But Grandpa was one to do what had to be done. After all, he did have a total of eleven mouths to feed. My Grandma used to always say how rich she was because she had so many children. They always talked about everything working out for the best. An amazing thing happens when you believe that all things happen for a reason and that they will eventually work out in your favor.

My grandparents immigrated to America shortly after World War II. Because Grandpa lived through two World Wars, both of which were fought on his native soil, many of his life stories were war stories. They weren't stories of doom and gloom but rather stories of survival, hope and thanksgiving. When speaking with my grandparents, I could tell how thankful they were to be alive and living in America. They never thought that they would still be living past the age of eighty. Even though I have never been in a war and have never had to flee for my life, my grandparents' thankfulness for life still rubbed off on me. When you are thankful just to be alive, life's other problems seem much smaller. When you focus on what you have instead of what you don't have, life becomes a little brighter. When you believe that all things will work out for your benefit, life is filled with hope. And when you slow down, relax and reflect on life's many blessings, you live in peace.

My Grandma is no longer with us, but her memory will live on. On January 6, 2002, Grandpa celebrated his ninety-fifth birthday. That is a lot of years to be on this earth. He has seen and has experienced a lot. A ninety-five year old man sees things from a much different perspective than a twenty-five, thirty-five, forty-five, or even seventy-five year old man does. This perspective contains knowledge, insight and good judgment, otherwise known as wisdom.

In the western world we pride ourselves on how sophisticated we are. We have a level of accomplishment today that nobody one hundred years ago could have even dreamed of. Three- and four-year-olds are playing on computers. We have sent a man to the moon, developed the microchip and found the cure for many diseases. We have discovered innumerous ways to improve the quality of our life. But is the quality of our life really better? Have all of our modern advances made us happier?

Logically one would think so, but realistically this is not the case. We have the ability to live in extreme comfort compared to our forefathers, however, in many ways we are less happy, more stressed and less fulfilled than they were. Why is that? We believe it is because we have lost our perspective. When we talk to people who have gone through things a lot worse than we have and still have a positive attitude, it can cause us to rethink our attitude. They can listen to our stories and relate with what we are going through. They can offer encouragement and words of wisdom that can help carry us through the challenging times in our life. Because we know what they have gone through, we believe them when they say, "I understand what you are going through. It is tough, but don't lose hope. Everything will work out just fine."

It is wise to seek counsel prior to making any major decisions in life. Why not seek the counsel of someone who has been there and done that? Many times such a person can prevent you from going down the wrong path and can point you in the right direction.

Education

Many of us cannot think big enough on our own. We need to borrow the thoughts and experiences of others. Relationships are external sources of thought, however, it may be difficult to find people to become friends with that have all of the qualities that you desire for your own life. Books, tapes and seminars are great ways to stimulate your thoughts. These are excellent tools to accelerate your success and help you to miss some of the potholes and avoid many of the roadblocks in life. For less than $30 you can buy a book that describes in great detail the subject matter in which you would like more information. In many cases, the author will not only tell you what to do but what not to do. We can learn from their years of experience just by reading two hundred pages in a book. How awesome! There is not a more affordable way to get a practical education.

"The person who does not read is no better
off than the person who cannot read.
The person who does not continue to learn and grow
as a person is no better off than one who cannot."
- Earl Nightingale -

We prefer books to audio programs because they tend to give more detailed information. However, when it comes to motivational and some other types of self-help material, we prefer audio. This is especially true with dynamic and charismatic personalities. With audio, you can share in the presenter's enthusiasm and passion. Enthusiasm is contagious, and it may be just what you need in order for you to take action. A good example of an author that you need to hear is peak performance expert Anthony Robins. We have never read any of his works, however, we have listened to, studied, and implemented many of the principles outlined in his audio programs. They are great and are worth more than their weight in gold.

Anthony's "Personal Power" thirty-day audio program was instrumental in directing us down the path of personal achievement. Six years after taking on the thirty-day challenge our household income had tripled. Even though we have not listened to that program in years, several things that he said have stuck in our thoughts to this day. One was "the past does not equal the future."

You can achieve anything that you want to in life regardless of your past. Even if you have tried something in the past and it failed, that doesn't mean that you will always fail. It is almost impossible to achieve success in any area of your life without experiencing some kind of failure.

> *"You've got to believe that anything worth doing is worth doing well. But also, you have to understand that if you don't know how to do something, it is worth doing it badly until you learn to do it well. In other words, you have to think of failure as a part of the process not the end of the process."*
> *- Les Brown -*

We believe that if we can get one good idea from a book, tape or seminar, then it was well worth the time and money spent. This philosophy has served us well over the years.

> *"Nothing is a waste of time*
> *if you use the experience wisely."*
> *- Rodin -*

Another great advantage to audio programs is that you can listen to them while you are doing other activities. As long as these activities don't take a lot of thought, this multitasking can be very effective. It is not uncommon for us to be listening to an audio program while doing the dishes, working out, doing the laundry, driving, etc.

Become a success student. Study as much information as you can regarding the topic in which you desire to excel. Because in the words of Francis Bacon, "A man is but what he knoweth." You can never read too many books on a particular subject. Shortly after reading Suze Orman's book, *The 9 Steps to Financial Freedom*, we saw her new book entitled *The Courage to Be Rich*. Our first thought was that we had already read one of her other books on the same topic, and we are not going to learn much more from reading another one. But then we thought that we only needed to get one good idea from this new book. With an open mind, it is almost impossible not to get at least one good idea from a book, tape or seminar. In those 360 pages, we found our idea. That idea was to eliminate the clutter in our lives. We immediately went through all of our closets and boxes. We shredded all of the paperwork that we no longer needed. We gave away almost everything that we hadn't used in the last year. We had gathered so much "stuff" that we had to make several trips to the Salvation Army. When we were finished, the feeling that we both had was liberating. What life-changing idea could you get from reading that same book?

Even more powerful than a book or audio program is a live seminar. There is so much synergy that takes place at a live seminar. As mentioned earlier, synergism is the interaction of separate entities such that the total effect is greater than the sum of the individual effects. The ideas that are shared at a seminar are only the beginning. These ideas can spark an idea in your mind that you would never think of on your own. Add other people to the mix and the synergy grows. The presenter makes a point, which causes one of the students to comment. This comment causes another student to have an idea, which she shares. This idea causes the light bulb to go on in your head, and so forth. It is amazing what can happen when a group of like-minded people get together for a common purpose.

We prefer the weekend or week-long seminar to a one-day seminar primarily for networking reasons. You can talk to the presenter(s) after each session, ask questions, share ideas, and discover that this person is a regular person just like you and me. It is also a great way to meet other like-minded people. Make sure to talk to as many people as possible. The presenter isn't the only one in the room with good ideas and years of practical experience. Go to lunch and dinner with people at the seminar that you don't know. These seminars can be expensive, and you may need to take some time off of work, but remember, success isn't free.

> *"Success means accomplishments as the result*
> *of our efforts and activities. Proper preparation is the key*
> *to success. Our acts can be no wiser than our thoughts.*
> *Our thinking can be no wiser than our understanding."*
> *-George S. Clason -*

Of course all of this newfound knowledge isn't worth much unless we apply what we have learned. Ask yourself how these new ideas apply to your life. Practice what you have learned as soon as possible. Time has a way of slipping by without warning. The saying "Knowledge is power" is only one-third correct. More accurately the saying should be, "The correct knowledge, acted upon decisively and timely, is power."

> *"New knowledge is of little value if it doesn't change us,*
> *make us better individuals, and help us to be*
> *more productive, happy, and useful."*
> *- Hyrum W. Smith -*

No news is good news

Information is a good thing, however, it can also be a bad thing. Most of us look at the daily news as just information. We want to stay up with current events in our community, the country and around the world. It is good to be informed, but be aware of the negative consequences. You have probably noticed that most of the news you read, watch or listen to is negative. As a matter of fact, some of it can be downright depressing. This is because bad news sells. Let's face it, which of the following two headlines would cause more people to buy a newspaper?

1. Riverdale Mom Gives Birth to Healthy Triplet Boys
2. Area Robbers Hit Yet Another Suburban Home

The first headline may put a smile on your face as you walk on past the newsstand. The second causes you to be concerned. You buy the paper to find out all of the details. Since what we allow into our minds has an effect on the quality of our lives, doesn't it make sense to take a good hard look at how much news you want to subject yourself to? Do you really want to start and end every day filling your mind with such programming? We are not saying that you shouldn't listen to, read or watch the news. Just be aware of the fact that everything that enters your mind has either a positive or negative effect on you.

If you feel that you must listen to, read or watch the news, then we would suggest that you balance that potentially bad news with twice as much good news. If you watch the news for an hour every day, then make sure that you counteract the effects with two hours of positive, uplifting and/or motivational programming. If you don't have two hours every day that can be used for that purpose, then cut your news time down to a half-hour per day. Your mind, like your body, is yours to do with as you please. You can either feed it good things or you can feed it bad things. The choice is yours. But just remember, everything that you allow into your mind has an effect on your life.

Use it or lose it

You may have heard that our minds are like a muscle, you either use it or you lose it. There is something inside all of us that gives us the need to grow and expand our horizons. We need to be challenged in life or we lose some of life's excitement. Boredom can kill the human spirit. We can learn a lot from watching children. Ever notice how quickly they get bored? It doesn't take very long for them to say, "I'm bored, when can we . . . ," or "Are we there yet?" They seem to be very in tune with their feelings. They realize that what they are currently doing is not challenging enough and they want to make a change right away.

Kids are also very curious and ask a lot of questions. They need to either play or be intellectually stimulated. If they are not in one of these two camps, they get bored and even frustrated. They know when it is time for a change, and they act on that feeling immediately. Kids feel that they have to change or they will experience discomfort. They would never purposely live in an environment that did not challenge or stimulate them. We adults, on the other hand, choose to live that way often. We know what some of you are thinking. You are thinking, "Wait a minute, I don't choose to live like this. I would much rather live a more abundant life." We have no doubt that you would like to live a more abundant life, however, you *choose* not to do so. Our life is the sum total of all of the choices that we make.

> *"Choose well,*
> *your choice is brief,*
> *and yet endless."*
> *- Johann Wolfgang von Goethe -*

We adults typically go for entertainment when we get bored. A while back we heard a statistic that stated that the average American watched forty-two hours of television per week. That may seem extremely high, but we know several people who turn the television on right when they get home from work and it stays on until they go to bed. There are some who watch television most of the day on Saturday and/or most of the day on Sunday. How can you create the life of your dreams if much or most of your non-working time is spent trying to escape boredom through entertainment? Don't get us wrong, we have nothing against entertainment. We love a great show as much as the next person, but we don't live for entertainment. Studies have shown that the person who spends the weekend working on his or her deck is much more content than the person who watches television all weekend. Instead of spending so much of your time watching the tube, sit down, quiet yourself and think. Lorraine Hansberry said, "Never be afraid to sit a while and think." Many people do this because thinking can be hard work for the undisciplined mind.

> *"Thinking is the hardest work there is,*
> *which is probably the reason why so few engage in it."*
> *- Henry Ford -*

We realize that you may have no idea how much television you watch each week. And we know that if you are the kind of person who would read a book like this, then you are willing to make some positive changes in your life. We would suggest that you make a schedule for yourself and slot in a time for entertainment. That way you will know exactly how much time you spend each day on that activity. Take at least one hour each day that you used to spend watching television and take that time to think about how you would like your life to be. Less than 5 percent of the population does this. Is it any surprise than that 95 percent of the wealth in America is controlled by 5 percent of the people, or that only 5 percent of all businesses are still in existence after their first five years? Successful people think about success, while average people let someone else do their thinking for them.

Successful people think of possibilities. Average people spend their time and money without much thought at all. Successful people strive for knowledge, while average people look to be entertained. Successful people invest their time. Average people spend their time. Average people expect their spouse to do things for them, while successful people look for ways to please their lover. Average people give up when the going gets tough. Successful people persevere and know that they can have anything that their heart desires. Don't be average!

"The heights by great men reached and kept
Were not attained by sudden flight,
But they, while their companions slept,
Were toiling upward in the night."
- Henry Wadsworth Longfellow -

Like the saying goes, "The world is your oyster." However, in order to live the life that you desire, you must think about it, plan it and then work toward your goal. As David Sarnoff said, "A life without a definite plan is likely to become driftwood." Don't allow yourself to drift through life and just take what comes your way. Stay on focus and decide to live your life on purpose.

Something that may help you to stay on track would be to start a quote collection and even post your favorite quotes where you can see them every day. A quote is so powerful because it can sum up a paragraph of thought into a single sentence. They can even help motivate you when things get tough.

Never stop learning. It is true that no day is a complete waste if you have learned something. Discovery keeps us alive and vibrant and it makes life more exciting.

We need to look at learning as finding something valuable. There are so many treasures out there just waiting for you to discover them. Try to learn something new every day. Learn how to cook a new meal. Learn how to play chess. Learn a different language. Learn how to ice skate or snow ski. Learn a new word every day.

"To keep a lamp burning
we have to keep putting oil in it."
- Mother Teresa -

Allow your mind to grow and get stronger by allowing yourself to learn new things. If you do, your life will be much fuller, you will be happier, you won't get bored as easily, you will look forward to each and every day, and you will be a much more exciting person to live with.

CHAPTER 15

NURTURING YOUR SPIRIT—
THE ROAD TO INNER PEACE

"The body must be nourished physically,
emotionally, and spiritually.
We're spiritually starving in this culture—
not underfed but undernourished."
- Carol Hornig -

There is no doubt in our minds that we are all three-part beings. Those three parts consist of the body, mind and spirit. Their order of importance is spirit, mind and then body. In order to become the best person that you can be and achieve the best relationship possible, you must have a proper balance in all three areas. A good example of this would be that of a three-legged stool.

If one of the legs is missing, sitting on the stool will be a balancing act. This balancing act is very challenging and it takes a lot of effort. It would be very easy for someone to push you over. Any little outside force can knock you down. After a while you will get tired and fall.

This describes someone like Kim. She is an energetic career woman who eats well, exercises and manages her stress. She thinks positive thoughts, is continually learning, and she has control over her emotions. Unfortunately, her spiritual life is nonexistent. When hard times come she can handle them for a while, but in time this stress becomes overwhelming.

If one of the legs is broken or weak, you may sit on the stool and not notice that anything is wrong. Every time you sit down the stool is getting weaker. You have no idea that it could break at any time. The stool might last for several more years or it might fall apart tomorrow. What do you think would happen if your spouse came and sat on your lap while you were sitting on the stool? That's right, it would break under the additional pressure.

The second example describes Eugene, who is in tune with his inner self and is growing spiritually. He is expanding his mind and is very balanced emotionally. But he is not taking care of his body. He feels tired all of the time and doesn't have the energy to run and play with his kids. He gets sick at least once per year, which knocks him out for a week. He doesn't know it, but his body is slowly deteriorating. This deterioration is affecting every other area of his life, including his marriage. His spouse wants to go out and have some fun every once in a while, but he is too tired and just wants to stay at home and take it easy. Instead of exercising, he watches several hours of television. His poor eating habits and lack of exercise are causing him to gain a lot of weight. Because of this he thinks less of himself, and his spouse doesn't like it very much either. The whole situation is causing arguments and fights between them. Then one day he breaks, he has a heart attack. Fortunately he is one of the lucky ones. He doesn't die and is given a second chance at life.

If all three legs are strong, the stool is solid and it can take a lot of pressure before it breaks. If you know that the stool is strong and solid, you will sit on it with full confidence, knowing that it will support you. Outside forces cannot easily knock you down. The pressure from carrying extra weight will not cause it to break.

The third example describes Jake. Jake is a soft-spoken pillar of strength. He takes excellent care of himself and reads every day. He controls his emotions instead of letting his emotions control him. When negative things happen in his life he has a peace about them. He knows that God is in control of his life and that everything will work out in his favor.

Our lives are like a three-legged stool. Our three legs, spirit-mind-body, must all be strong to handle the outside forces and pressures that life throws our way.

We have already discussed the importance of nourishing your body and expanding your mind. Now we will discuss the third and most important leg of the stool—nurturing your spirit. This chapter is by far the most important. It is the glue that binds all of the other sections together. Some of the ideas may be hard for you to believe at first, and that's OK. Perhaps this is the first time that you have ever considered that there may be more to us humans than what we see before us. New ideas can be hard to grasp or believe the first time that we hear them. But if you keep an open mind and a receptive attitude, you may learn something extremely valuable about yourself, something that could change your life and your marriage forever.

It is oftentimes difficult to believe or fully understand things that we cannot smell, touch, hear, taste or see. Over three hundred years ago Sir Isaac Newton developed his theory of gravitation. You can't see gravity, but it exists and you can see and feel its effects. Over one hundred years ago Louis Pasteur developed his germ theory, which recognized the existence of microorganisms and their role in contagious diseases. You can't look into the air and see these germs, but they do exist and you can see and feel their effects. The belief that there is a spiritual side to humans has been around for thousands of years. You can't see this spirit world, but it exists and you can see and feel its effects on your life.

Have you ever had a feeling that something was going to happen, and then it did? There may not have been any outward signs that led you to that conclusion, but for some reason you just knew it was going to happen. Were you ever in a conversation with someone and you knew what he or she was going to say before the person said it? Have you ever gone someplace and felt very uncomfortable? Nothing was out of the ordinary as far as your five senses were concerned, but yet something just didn't feel right. Have you ever met someone for the first time and you felt very uncomfortable about him or her? Perhaps you knew something wasn't right before the person even opened his or her mouth. If you have experienced these things, you are not alone. Many people experience these "gut" feelings. Some call it intuition, while others call it their sixth sense. Some people don't even notice it at all.

Donna and the bad man: Several years ago I (Donna) briefly met a man who was a friend of a friend. He was married and seemed to have a nice family. When I got home I told Darren about my brief encounter. I told Darren that there was something very dark about him that repulsed me. I said that I didn't trust him and that he wasn't a good man. Darren asked me why I thought that, because he thought that man might have tried to hit on me or something. I said that there weren't any outward signs—I just sensed that something wasn't right. Several months later we discovered that he was having an affair with a married woman. I didn't see anything nor could I explain my feelings, but my inner voice, my spirit, was telling me to stay far away from this one.

Darren and corporate America: Earlier I (Darren) had mentioned that I was downsized from corporate America. I also promised to tell you how I was able to handle it so well and even be excited about it. The following are the details of what transpired in my life just five short months ago.

We have been big believers in exercise, self-improvement, positive thinking and faith in God our whole married life. We practiced nourishing our bodies, expanding our minds and nurturing our spirit; however, we didn't have the consistency that we thought was needed in order to experience the full and abundant life that God had intended for us. Donna thought that it would be a good idea for us to print up a calendar and write down all of the things that we wanted to do each and every day. She printed up a calendar for each of us, which included the following:

- One half-hour of gaining knowledge
- One half-hour of spiritual learning/growth
- Listening to the positive self-talk tapes that we made for each other
- Reading our affirmation/projected expectation cards
- Prayer
- One half-hour exercise

Each time we did one of these activities we would put a mark next to it on our calendar. If we exercised for an hour, we would put two marks next to exercise. This may sound like a lot of work, but it really isn't. We would often listen to our self-help tapes while exercising or listen to our self-talk tapes while getting ready in the morning. Our goal was to do this for thirty consecutive days. If we missed any of these activities, with the exception of exercise (it is good to give your body one day's rest after a really hard workout), we would have to start all over. As I write this sentence, I am on day one hundred fifty. All of the experts say that if you do something for thirty consecutive days that it becomes a habit or that something really big will happen around day thirty.

We also made it a point to listen to our inner voice and act on these thoughts as soon as they happened. If we weren't able to act at that time, we would write the thought down. We began to listen to and trust our gut feelings. We prayed for God's guidance through every situation. As we were going through this program, things started to happen that cannot be explained logically. We became much more aware of our surroundings. We could see life much clearer than before, almost as though a hazy film had been removed from our eyes, a film that we didn't even know was there before.

Three weeks before I was downsized, we started to talk about the possibility of me being let go. We both felt that it was a strong possibility. There were no outward signs that this could happen. As we walked together we would joke about me getting fired. We even did a little dreaming, thinking that it would be neat if they let me go and then gave me a six-month severance package so that we could focus all of our time finishing Honeymoon Marriage. We also thought that it would be great if they would let us keep the office furniture the company had purchased for my home office just ten months earlier. Those thoughts pretty much left our minds until one Monday morning three weeks later.

At the start of our thirty-day program it became very clear to both Donna and I that I shouldn't be working for someone else and that we should both dedicate our lives to helping other people. To that end I wrote the following goal stated in the present tense on my affirmation/ projected expectation cards:

"It is the fourth of July, 2002. I no longer work for
ABC Company or anyone else."

This was only the first sentence of the card. I would read the card every morning and every night. After the first week, something didn't feel right about what I saying. I couldn't read the card as it was written so I crossed out the first part so that it read:

"I no longer work for ABC Company or anyone else."

I read the revised card for about another week until I just couldn't do it any more. Something wasn't right. I couldn't bear the thought of working there for much longer. Those thoughts didn't make any sense. I liked my job, my boss, and the company I worked for. They always treated me well and I never had any problems with anyone I worked with. But for some reason I had to get out of there, so I prayed "God, please get me out of there today."

The following morning I was taking a shower when a thought came to me. I thought that I should give one of my coworkers a call and tell him that one of us was going to be let go. That is pretty specific considering that the company had over sixty thousand employees.

About a month earlier, I had set up an appointment for my boss, his boss and myself to visit one of my customers. Later that Tuesday morning a notice went out over the E-mail system that my boss's boss was let go. Now it was going to be just my boss and I who would visit my customer that Friday. I called my coworker friend and told him that I felt that I should tell him something and that it might sound a little crazy. I told him that I thought that either he or I was going to be let go relatively soon. I told him that if it was me then no problem. But if it was him, he should call me before signing anything because I would be willing to take his place. Of course he didn't believe me and told me that we didn't have anything to worry about.

On Wednesday, Donna and I knew that I was going to get fired and that my boss was going to give me the proverbial pink slip when we met on Thursday. We even started to feel sorry for my boss knowing that he would be driving for six hours and thinking about having to fire one of his friends. Thursday came and sure enough our expectations became a reality. I didn't get a six-month severance, but I did get to keep the furniture, and for that we are grateful.

How did we know that this was going to happen? It could have been a complete shock followed by the feelings of betrayal, bitterness, anger or even depression. Instead it became an expectation and it was greeted with a peace that passes all understanding. We believe that our experience was spiritual—that God was preparing us for what was about to take place.

We believe that our spiritual beliefs have made a greater positive impact on our marriage than anything else in our lives. We aren't alone. Thousands of people have experienced a more abundant life through nurturing their spirit. They have moved away from a life of comparison, worry, anxiety, tension, fear and negativity and toward a life filled with hope, peace, joy, forgiveness, connectedness and purpose. All you need is the desire to have a more abundant life and the faith to believe in something you can't see.

Faith is a belief without doubt or question. When you first start your spiritual journey your faith or belief may be small or even nonexistent. Don't worry about that for now. Your faith will increase as you apply spirit principles. Your faith will grow as you continue to practice the truths mentioned in this chapter. When you start to see results, your faith will be confirmed and you will believe without a doubt that these principles were meant to be part of your every day life.

Your marriage will improve greatly by applying everything that you have learned so far; however, some situations and circumstances can only be fixed by seeking the help of a greater power. This power is available to all that seek and ask for it.

We all have a void in our lives. Perhaps you can sense that void. You know that something is missing in your life, but you can't put your finger on it. You may have thought that this void could be filled through a successful career, but when success came you wondered if that was all that life had to offer. Some look for it in relationships only to end up emptyhanded. You may have thought that starting a family would fill this void only to find that your life had improved, but there was still something missing. Some will search their whole lives and never find it. What is life all about? Why are we here? Is there more to life than what we now have? We all have within us a desire to have this empty spot filled. There is a void deep within us, and God is the only one who can fill it. We will never be complete until we allow God to be an integral part of our lives. You will learn how this is possible as you read through the rest of this chapter.

We realize that some consider it taboo to talk about politics and religion. But we aren't at a dinner party; we are discussing how you can have more peace, joy, love, harmony, passion and fulfillment in your life. And besides, we are not talking about organized religion. We are all for organized religion, and of course our country was founded on the free expression of religious beliefs. However, there are a lot of "religious" people in this world who do not have peace in their life. There are a lot of people who attend a local gathering of their faith, but do not know what they are supposed to be doing on this planet. Many of them are lost and seeking for the answers as well. What we are suggesting is that you allow your spirit to be open to the truth so that you can live a life filled with hope and thanksgiving.

Something very amazing happens when you take your focus off of yourself and your circumstances and rely on the wisdom and guidance of a greater power. When you sense that you are hearing the voice of God, doubt and worry disappear. Knowing that there is a divine purpose for your life and that you are on a spiritual journey allows you to be more tolerant with others since you know that you are not perfect nor have you "arrived." The egocentric person is in essence spiritually bankrupt. The "holier-than-thou" person has not gained spiritual completeness. When you are humbled by the vastness of the universe, you no longer think that you are better than others are or that you always have to be right. When you realize that when you judge others you are in turn heaping judgment on yourself, you become more loving and accepting.

As you experience spiritual enlightenment, you will become less selfish. You will be more aware of your vocabulary, and you will make the decision to change from overusing the pronoun "I" and substituting it with "we," "you" and "your." As you grow spiritually, your outlook on life will completely change. You will start to see things in a whole new light. Your marriage will improve because your life will be filled with purpose and meaning. When you are living your life on purpose, everything seems a little brighter.

"When I look into the future,
it's so bright it burns my eyes."
- Oprah Winfrey -

A good friend of ours is the owner operator of a business that solves many of the production problems in various industries. He has been able to solve complex problems that complete engineering departments of very large companies can't figure out, and he doesn't even have an engineering degree. When asked how he figures these things out, he says that God gave him the solution. His sales increased by 25 percent in 2001, right in the middle of an extremely bad recession. When asked if he has any salesmen he says, "God is my salesman." He will admit that when he looks at a problem, he oftentimes has no idea how he is going to pull it off and then God gives him the solution. Most importantly, he gives the credit and thanks to his spiritual partner.

We recently read a book that told the stories of twenty extremely successful men and women, including some of our nation's top CEOs, who rely on spiritual guidance for their accomplishments, happiness and peace of mind. The name of the book is *God is my CEO* by Larry Julian. It is an excellent and inspirational read that gives real-world examples of the importance of living one's life directed by spirit principles. It is encouraging to know that there are many people out there like you and me who realize that they cannot figure everything out all on their own and don't consider it a weakness to call for help. As a matter of fact, it is a sign of strength and wisdom to call on the guidance of this higher power. When you know that there is a spiritual solution to your problems, you begin to look for it, and when you earnestly look for it, you will find it.

Back to our roots

America was founded on the principles of freedom. Freedom of religion and freedom of speech are two of the cornerstones that make this country great. The forefathers of this great nation trusted in the divine wisdom and guidance of a higher power. Even today we can see printed on our money the words, "In God We Trust." Notice that it doesn't say, "In God We Believe." There is a big difference between believing and trusting. It is one thing to believe that there is a higher power, but to trust your life to that higher power is a completely different story—a life-changing one at that.

Something very amazing happened shortly after September 11, 2001. In the wake of the horrific terrorist attacks, our country almost in unison turned to God for comfort. Our President led by example by holding a nationally televised prayer service. People who were never part of an organized religion started attending places of worship. People who hadn't been to a place of worship in years, even decades, were drawn there once again. Our country, which banned school prayer and the assembly of religious groups on school grounds, now printed flags with the title *In God We Trust* printed on them. Billboards, store marquees and bumper stickers proudly displayed the words *United We Stand—In God We Trust*. Candle vigils and prayer groups sprung up all over this great nation. It appeared that we were once again one nation under God.

The country came together in a spirit of compassion and brotherhood. Families started to do more things together and set higher priorities. People expressed more love for the important people in their lives. Men and women began to question whether or not their goals, ambitions and fast-paced lifestyle were leading them down the right path.

"What is the use of running
when we are not on the right road?"
- German Proverb -

People started to bond with each other and develop closer relationships as they took their focus off of themselves and placed it on God and others. Your marriage can be affected in the same way by taking your focus off of yourself and placing it on God and your spouse.

There is something very attractive about living with someone who is traveling down the road to spiritual enlightenment. We are attracted to the outward signs of the person's spiritual growth. These virtues are love, joy, peace, patience, kindness, goodness, faithfulness, gentleness and self-control. Do you think that possessing these attributes would improve your marriage? You bet they would, and you can have and grow in all of them. The following is a list of the things that you can do to improve your marriage and nurture your spirit:

1. Have quiet time

We all need time alone, time when we can block out all of the noise and distractions that are all around us. For most Americans, the only quiet time that they get is when they are asleep or taking a shower. Most people don't think that quiet time is something that they need. Many believe in the importance of hard work, exercise, education and recreation, but think that quiet time is a waste of time.

Quiet time is an opportunity for you to recharge your spiritual batteries. What happens when your television remote has weak batteries? The signal that it sends becomes sporadic, not giving you the results that you want. And if the batteries are dead, it won't send a signal at all. In order for you to be a spiritual receptor of God's signal, you need to make sure that your batteries are charged and that there is nothing blocking the signal.

Quiet time is the opportunity to clear your mind of all of the thoughts that are racing through your head. Lie back, close your eyes, and relax. Take deep slow breaths through your nose. Think of calming, tranquil thoughts. Picture a sunset, a meadow, a mountain lake, a blue cloudy sky, or any peaceful setting that makes you happy and relaxed. Keep thinking these thoughts until your mind becomes clear and you feel calm and relaxed. Stay quiet and listen.

Listen to that still small voice inside of you. That voice that is always right. Follow its direction and it will lead you down the right path.

"Be still, and know that I am God."
- Psalm 46:10 -

It is from this place that we are able to tap into our true self and understand our purpose in life. It is a time of introspection and self-awareness. Reflect on your life and determine if the things you are doing bring fulfillment and happiness. What do you value most in your life? Are your actions bringing you closer to or further away from your ideal life? Ask yourself what you can do to become a better husband or wife. What do you need to work on to become a more loving and kind person? Meditate on these thoughts until an answer comes to you. Your answers will most likely not come to you right away. The more you practice the art of quiet relaxation and introspection, the more in tune you will become to your inner voice.

2. Pray

The power of prayer is awesome. It is a life-changing force. Prayer is spiritual communication. It is what links us with the Creator. Prayer opens up doors of opportunity for you to walk through. It can give you peace of mind and an excitement about the future.

In the last chapter we discussed how positive thinking and self-talk can change you. Prayer reaches even deeper in that it can change our surroundings and other people as well. Perhaps you think that it would take a miracle for you to have a Honeymoon Marriage. You may be right, and that is where prayer comes in. We have heard hundreds of examples that demonstrate the power of prayer. Since the scope of this book is very diverse, we will only take the time to share just a few.

Prayer during the war—the story of Darren's Grandpa. During World War II my Grandpa was given orders to retrieve documents that were left behind in a village that was under attack. He and two other men went to retrieve these documents. When they arrived they found that the building that they had to enter was on fire. My Grandpa told one of the men to come with him and the other to stay downstairs so that he could throw the briefcase to him out of the window. Before my Grandpa entered the building, he told the man with him to wait outside the door, and if he didn't come right out, the man was to come in and get him.

My Grandpa entered the burning building, retrieved the briefcase and when he got to the window, he noticed that the man on the ground was nowhere to be seen. Both men had taken off in fear because airplanes were flying overhead and they started to drop bombs on the village. My Grandpa threw the briefcase out the window and quickly ran out of the building. By that time the air attack was in full force. The only thing my Grandpa could think to do was to close his eyes and pray. As he was praying, he could hear bricks whirling by his head like shrapnel. He said that he could feel the breeze from the bricks as they continued to fly by his head.

When the attack had stopped he opened his eyes and attempted to walk, but he couldn't. He looked down and found that he was buried knee-deep in bricks. The village was leveled, yet he was still standing. He walked out of there without even a scratch on him. The other two men were casualties of war.

Prayer for protection

Our friend Paul from Minneapolis, Minnesota, told of an event that happened to him at midnight while he was driving through the mountains in Washington State. The temperature was below freezing and it started to rain. The wet roads quickly turned to ice. A horseshoe turn was coming up, and as he started to turn he began to slide sideways toward the edge of the road. There were no guardrails between him and a two-hundred-foot drop-off. He knew that he was going to die that night.

He is a believer in the power of prayer, but as he recalls the event, he said that everything happened so quickly that he didn't have time to pray. All of the sudden his car stopped at the edge of the road as though he had hit a brick wall. His heart was beating like crazy as he got out of the car to take a look at what had stopped him. There was nothing there that could have stopped him. He had no idea why his car stopped.

When he returned to Minneapolis, he received a call from two friends of his who said that it was urgent that they speak with him. When they met; this husband and wife team told Paul their story. At 2:00 A.M. on Tuesday they were both awakened from their sleep and felt that they needed to pray. They had no idea what they were supposed to pray about, they just knew that they should pray. The next morning the husband said that he felt like he was praying for their friend Paul. His wife said that she felt the same thing.

They then asked Paul what he was doing at 2:00 A.M. on Tuesday morning—midnight Washington time!. Paul was the recipient of someone else's prayers. Prayers that just may have saved his life.

Prayer for the job—Donna's story. Several years ago I (Donna) accepted a job in downtown Chicago. They offered me 41 percent more than I was previously making working five hours per week less. Everything looked great, that is until my first day of work.

My first day of work was terrible. I hated it. I felt very uncomfortable and knew that I had made the wrong decision. The atmosphere was very cold and everyone had a bad attitude. There seemed to be no respect, and the language that was being used was far from appropriate for a professional office or for anywhere for that matter.

After two days, I was ready to quit. Instead of giving my notice, we decided to pray about it. The next day it was as though I had entered a different building. The language that was used around me had completely changed. On the occasion that someone would use inappropriate language, they would immediately apologize to me. The atmosphere stayed pleasant for the year and a half that I was there.

How to pray.
Pray expecting to see results. Faith is the key ingredient to effective prayer. You have to believe in order to receive. Pray with a thankful attitude. Be thankful for the things that you have and for the things that you are about to receive. Pray for wisdom that you will make the right decisions. Pray that the right doors will be opened and the wrong doors will be closed. Pray that God will show you the areas of your life that need improvement and ask for His help in making those changes. Pray that God will use you to bless the lives of others. Give all of your concerns to God, trusting that He will take care of them and that everything will work out according to His divine plan. Be patient. Only God knows the future, and only He knows what is best for us. God's timing isn't always the same as our timing, but it is always the right timing.

3. Learn and grow
As we discussed in the last chapter, what we put into our minds has an effect on us. The same holds true regarding nurturing our spirit. It is very important that you fill your mind with positive, uplifting spiritual readings every day. The ancient texts are filled with guidance on how to become a spiritually balanced person.

The most important books that we have in our library are spiritual books. Our favorite is the Bible. We have learned more from this one book than all of our other books combined. We read at least one half-hour every day. It is one of the few books that can be read every year and still have an impact on our lives. Every time that we read it, we learn something new. That is because we are at a different stage in our lives from one year to the next. One of our favorite books is Proverbs. We also enjoy reading the proverbs from all over the world. A proverb has the unique ability to sum up years of wisdom and thought into a few sentences.

There are a lot of other spiritual books available that are fantastic reads. Shop around, read the chapter titles and pick out a book that seems to offer something that interests you. You will also want to check out specialty bookstores because they will carry spiritual titles not found in the larger mainstream bookstores. A recent spiritual bestseller is *The Prayer of Jabez* by Bruce Wilkinson. It is an excellent book that we have recommended and given to several of our friends.

4. Find a spiritual mentor

It is good to have mentors in your life. We have a wealth mentor, a health mentor, a relationship mentor and a spiritual mentor. We recommend that you do the same. A mentor doesn't have to be someone that you know. That is the ideal case; however, you can still learn a lot from the books, tapes, seminars, speeches, television programs, and/or newsletters that various speakers produce.

Your spiritual mentor can be clergy or a friend of like spirit. The main thing to look for when selecting a mentor is to choose someone who has something that you want, or someone who is the kind of person that you would like to become. They will become your counselor, coach and/or guide. Be careful not to put your mentors on a pedestal. They are human and prone to all of same mistakes that you and we make. A mentor should be looked up to and respected, but should never be worshipped. Put your trust in God and not in your mentor or anyone else for that matter. Consult with your mentor every week if he or she is someone you know. Try and make sure that you are also contributing to the relationship. A "give and no take" relationship can grow stale quickly. Always be very grateful and ask what you can do for your mentor. A good mentor is worth his or her weight in gold. A good spiritual mentor is priceless.

5. Associate with spiritual people

As mentioned earlier, the company that you keep is very important. It is a very enriching experience to hang out with people who have similar spiritual views to your own. They will understand you, encourage you and pray for you. When times get rough, it is always good to know that you have a person or group of people who will lift you up and agree with you in faith.

When good advice is not enough

Your marriage will greatly improve by applying everything that you have and will learn in all of the other sections of this book; however, some situations and circumstances can only be fixed by seeking the help of a greater power. You may need healing in your life before your relationship can be all that it is meant to be. God, the creator of all things, is the only one who can give you this kind of healing.

A new beginning

Have you ever wanted to start your whole life over again or erase some of the mistakes or stupid things that you have done? That is impossible in the physical world; however, it is very possible in the spiritual world. God gives everyone the ability to start all over in His eyes. This new start begins with forgiveness.

The freeing power of forgiveness

We covered forgiveness in the chapter entitled "Bedtime harmony—an oasis of love"; however, we need to dig a little deeper into this all-important area. The Honeymoon Marriage is not possible as long as there is unforgiveness in your life. Allowing forgiveness to flow in and out of your life will enable you to live a free and abundant life.

Forgive others. An excellent example of forgiveness can be found in the last thirteen chapters of Genesis, the first book of the Bible. In this account, Joseph's brother had so much envy and hatred toward him that they plotted to kill him and tell their father Jacob that a ferocious animal had killed and devoured him. Joseph's oldest brother Reuben stepped in and told his brothers not to kill him but to just throw him into one of the empty reservoirs in the desert. He had planned on showing up later to rescue him. The brothers stripped Joseph of his clothes and threw him into the reservoir. Then Joseph's brother Judah had a great idea as he saw a caravan of Ishmaelites coming toward them. He suggested that they sell Joseph to the Ishmaelites, who were headed to Egypt. Joseph was sold as a slave for twenty shekels of silver. The brothers then tore Joseph's robe, dipped it in goat's blood and told their father their original story.

While in Egypt Joseph was purchased by Potiphar, an Egyptian who was Pharaoh's captain of the guard. Several twists and turns occurred until Pharaoh placed Joseph in charge of the whole land of Egypt. By that time a severe famine had swept the land and Joseph was in charge of selling Egypt's grain to many countries. As it turns out, Joseph's brothers were sent by their father to go to Egypt to buy grain. You guessed it; they had to buy grain from the brother that they had betrayed. When the brothers came before Joseph, he recognized them, but they didn't recognize him. The story takes some more twists and turns until Joseph finally reveals himself to his brothers. They were terrified because they knew how much power he had. Then Joseph said, "I am your brother Joseph, the one you sold into Egypt! And now, do not be distressed and do not be angry with yourselves for selling me here." (Genesis 45:4, 5)

He then asked for his whole family to move near him in the region of Goshen so that he could take care of them during the famine. When his family had arrived, he threw his arms around his youngest brother Benjamin and wept. Joseph also kissed all of his brothers, wept over them and talked with them.

He was wronged, rejected, hurt and betrayed by his brothers. He could have thrown them into prison for life, had them tortured or put to death. Instead he chose to forgive them. A great healing took place and they became a family again. Have you been wronged, rejected, hurt and/or betrayed by someone you cared about, possibly even your spouse? If so, forgiving the offender will release the weight that you have been carrying around with you. It will allow you to feel like a whole person again, light and free.

You may not feel like forgiving your spouse or others. You may think that they don't deserve forgiveness because what they did was wrong and inexcusable. Forgiveness doesn't take away the wrongness of their actions; it just releases you from your bondage. After all, your unforgiveness, bitterness and anger doesn't hurt them, it hurts you. Holding on to these emotions allows them to continue to hurt you long after the initial act was committed. Don't give them that much power and control over your life. Take your power back by letting go of the negative emotional ties you have with them. We must forgive everyone with no exceptions. It is the only way to true peace, joy and spiritual growth.

Forgive yourself. We all mess up and do the things that we shouldn't. We do things that we wish that we could take back, but we cannot. We can't go back in history and undo our wrongs. We only have control over what we do today. If you have wronged someone, ask him or her for forgiveness and ask God for forgiveness, then you should also forgive yourself.

Final thought

We believe that doing mutually enjoyable activities together as a couple is a great way to strengthen your bond and improve your relationship. The most important of these are spiritual activities. We feel that it is our spiritual beliefs and spiritual growth that has united us together more than anything else has. It is a feeling that cannot be explained. We pray for each other, we pray together and we pray separately. We learn spiritual truths and we share them with each other. We attend a place of worship every week and we associate with like-minded people.

If you would like more information regarding the application of spirituality in your life and marriage, go to www.honeymoonmarriage.com and click on the keyword "spirituality."

In these last three chapters we have discussed the importance of nourishing your body, expanding your mind and nurturing your spirit. The body, mind and spirit connection is very important to recognize, appreciate and develop. This is an ongoing process that will last the rest of your life. Being the best that you can be will make a huge difference in how you feel about life, and it will make a huge difference in your marriage. Continue to reach for new heights and remember,

"A little knowledge that acts is worth infinitely more than much knowledge that is idle."
- Kahlil Gibran -

SECTION 6

MONEY
MATTERS

CHAPTER 16

THE 5 SIMPLE STEPS
TO FINANCIAL ABUNDANCE

Pressure and stress seem to be the norm in America today. These pressures can come at us from all directions. There are job pressures, health concerns, family challenges and relationship struggles. Even the ride to work can be a stressful experience. We have been run off the road by a semi, rear-ended, sideswiped, followed by a nut case, tailgated by people who never learned the "one car distance for every ten miles per hour" rule and chased down by someone who didn't like the fact that we merged in front of him (one car length distance) while passing. Some of these pressures are so great that people just explode.

Many of life's pressures are difficult to avoid. How we react to and handle these pressures is within our control. That is easier said than done. We like the easy way out. Instead of learning how to handle every pressure that is in our lives, we would rather eliminate them altogether. Learn to live with a particular pressure or live without that pressure--which would you rather do? Now we're not talking about avoidance. You can avoid getting into a fight with your mate by simply not talking to him or her, but that is not healthy. We could have avoided all of the abovementioned road incidents by never leaving the house, but that isn't practical. What we are talking about is facing your problems, dealing with them and eliminating them.

So far you have been given many tips on how to eliminate or at least greatly reduce many of the potential stresses of life by:

- Developing a closer relationship with your lover.
- Forgiving each other.
- Discovering and appreciating your spouse's uniqueness.
- Communicating more effectively and eliminating potentially harmful fights.
- Becoming more committed to your relationship and each other.

- Discovering your spouse's desires and treating his or her needs as equal to your own.
- Doing the small things that make a big difference.
- Improving your health.
- Harnessing the power of your thoughts.
- Leaning on God for guidance, strength, joy and peace of mind.

Now it is time to address one of the biggest causes of stress in many marriages.

As you know, too many marriages end up in divorce. The number one reason stated for these break-ups is *money*. Financial pressures add to the other pressures of life. Many of these pressures, when taken separately, are no problem to handle. But add them all together and throw money problems into the mix for good measure and you have a formula for disaster.

Financial pressures can put a huge strain on a marriage. They can even cause illnesses. According to a Lou Harris Poll, 96 percent of people lying awake at night are worrying about finances or health. We have already addressed the health concern in the chapter entitled "Nourishing your body--experience better health, more energy and greater self-confidence." Now it is time to talk about money--one of the least discussed and greatest causes of stress in a marriage.

If we can address and handle the number-one cause of divorce, then our chances of having a Honeymoon Marriage greatly increase. We have boiled down the formula into five simple steps. But before we jump right into these five steps, we must first address your thoughts and attitudes toward money.

Your thoughts and attitudes determine how much money you have.

Your thoughts and attitudes toward money control how much of it you have and how much of it you keep. Earlier we discussed how powerful our thoughts are. Our thoughts, what we focus on and our beliefs will either hold us back or propel us forward. What are the first thoughts that come to your mind when you think of money? Write them down, because they will tell you a lot about your attitude toward it.

Perhaps you have a belief that money is the root of all evil. If you are referring to a quote from an ancient text of wisdom, then you need to look up the quote for yourself because that is not what it says. The quote is, "The love of money is the root of all kinds of evil." In other words, greed, selfishness and valuing money more than people will cause all kinds of problems. Money is not evil--greed is evil. Money puts food on the table, clothes on your back and a roof over your head. Money plows the roads in the winter and mows the grass in the summer. Money funded the research that found the cures for many of the world's diseases.

Would you like to have more money or less money? That may sound like a crazy question, but we often wonder when we hear people talk and watch what they do. When you see someone who has a lot more than you do, what are your thoughts toward them? If you are driving a $20,000 car and someone pulls up next to you at a restaurant, at school, at church or at a stoplight in a $60,000 car, what is the first thought that comes to your mind?

The reason we ask these questions is because of a thing called *class envy*. The envy that we are talking about is not seeing someone in a nice car and thinking that you would like one just like it. We are talking about an extremely bad attitude that one has toward wealthy people. Class envy is very prevalent in America. We have seen firsthand how vicious this prejudice can be. We have seen it more often than racial, gender, religious and age discrimination. That is probably because it crosses the boundaries of every race, sex, religion and age. In some cases wealthy people are looked at as being evil or corrupt. And the poor are looked at as being righteous and pure. It can even be a "them versus us" mentality as if we were at war and the rich were winning. It is almost as though these people despise the affluent and then try to justify these wrong emotions by saying things like:

- "They must have stepped on a lot of people to get where they are."
- "All they care about is money."
- "They have a lot of money, but I'll bet they're not happy."
- "You have to be dishonest or take advantage of people in order to be rich."
- "Rich people are greedy and selfish."

- "The wealthy sacrifice time with their family."

Unfortunately, you can never have what you despise. Your subconscious mind will not allow you to have a great deal of money while simultaneously thinking negatively toward money or the people who have it.

Sure there are rich people who are crooks, but there are also broke people who are crooks. Of course there are wealthy people who are unhappy, but that is also true of the poor and middle class. Some affluent people spend more time making money than they do with their family, but that is not a problem reserved only for the rich. Some of the nicest, most caring, generous, optimistic, happy people whom we have ever met were wealthy. Some of the rudest, selfish, pessimistic, depressing people whom we have ever met were broke. If you have even the slightest ill feelings toward people who have more than you do, it is time to let go of those limiting thoughts and start to experience abundance in every area of your life, including money.

How do you treat your money?
The unfortunate thing about money is that it is a lot easier to spend than it is to earn. Most people enjoy spending it, but they don't enjoy making it. Many people work hard for their money and then throw it away instead of letting it work for them. Some people spend $40 per month on cable or satellite television, but they don't invest anything into their future.

The rich treat their money differently. They make every effort to ensure that their money grows. They respect their money and treat it well. Respect money? Respecting people I understand, but how do I respect my money? How long would you remain friends with someone who treated you as though you weren't worth much? With someone who felt as though he or she could blow you off at any time because you would always come back? What if the person always tried to hold you back and keep you from growing? Is that how you treat your money? If so, it will leave you the first chance it gets.

We enjoy the phone commercial that talks about the value of a dollar. If you watch television at all, you will have seen it. Someone receives a dollar and has a bad attitude thinking that it isn't worth much. Then the celebrities rush to the scene and inform the person that he is gravely mistaken and explain what that dollar can buy him. We like that commercial because it stresses the importance and value of a dollar. A dollar is very valuable, and it should be treated with respect and not just given away as though it was worthless. When we are walking through a parking lot and spot a penny on the ground, we always bend down and pick it up. It is not about the penny; after all we can live without it. It is about valuing money. Money is a fickle friend. If it is not treated well it won't stick around for long. If you value and respect money it will be drawn to you like iron filings to a magnet. If you don't, it will slip through your fingers like water.

The parable of the talents

We love to read ancient sayings and stories. They are so deep and full of wisdom and insight. There is a story in the Bible that teaches what we should do with our money.

There was a man who was about to go on a long journey. Before he left he called for his servants so that they could see to his money while he was away. He divided his money among them according to each one's abilities. He gave the first servant $5,000, the second $2,000 and the third $1,000. The man who was given the $5,000 quickly went and put his money to work and gained an additional $5,000. The man who was given $2,000 did the same and gained $2,000 more. The man who was given $1,000 went and dug a hole in the ground and hid the money.

When the master returned he called for his servants to see what each had done with his money. The first servant brought his master the $10,000. His master replied, "Well done, good and faithful servant! You have been faithful with a few things; I will put you in charge of many things. Come and share your master's happiness!" The second servant brought his master the $4,000. His master replied, "Well done, good and faithful servant! You have been faithful with a few things; I will put you in charge of many things. Come and share your master's happiness!" The third servant came and explained that he was afraid so he hid the $1,000 in the ground. His master replied, "You wicked, lazy servant! . . . You should have put my money on deposit with the bankers, so that when I returned I would have received it back with interest." That servant's $1,000 was then given to the one who had $10,000, and he was evicted from his master's presence.

If this story was told today, it might have included a fourth servant. This fourth servant would have been given only $500 because he wasn't as good with his money as the other three. As soon as he received the money he started looking in the sales flyers to see what he could buy for $500. Wow, how lucky can you get? XYZ Mart is having their semiannual clearance sale. All merchandise is 30 percent off. He quickly goes to the store before all of the good stuff is gone. After about an hour of shopping, he finds the perfect purchase. He can't wait to show his master how much money he saved.

The first servant receives his praise and the fourth servant thinks, "Of course you can make a lot of money if you have a lot, but I only had $500." The second servant receives his praise and the fourth servant thinks, "I wish someone would just give me $2,000. If only I could be that lucky. Some people get all of the breaks." The third servant gets slammed for putting his portion in a hole in the ground and the fourth servant thinks, "What an idiot. Who would put his money in a hole in the ground? No wonder the master is upset. At least I did something with my money. The first two servants made a 100 percent return on their money, but I can't afford to invest. After all, I only have $500. Besides, wait until I show my master how much money I saved him." When the master saw what the fourth servant had done with his hard-earned money, he could hardly contain himself, he was so angry. "You did *what* with my money? I didn't need one of those, I bought one three years ago and it still works fine. You are worse than the one who buried my money! And he threw the man in debtor's prison until he could pay back the $500.

Think your way to riches.

There is a reason why the rich keep getting richer, and it has nothing to do with luck. It has very little if anything to do with upbringing, race, religion, formal education, age or experience. The reason they are rich and getting richer every day is because they think differently about money. The following table lists a few examples:

What the average person thinks	What the rich person thinks
My $3,000 bonus will buy an awesome big screen TV.	My $3,000 bonus can be used as a down payment on a rental property.
I always look for bargains.	I always look for opportunities.
If it sounds too good to be true, it's probably a scam.	Sounds interesting, please tell me more.
95% of all new business start-ups fail within the first 5 years.	I better make sure to do my homework so that I can have a successful business.
The grass is always greener on the other side of the fence.	The world is full of opportunities just waiting for me to discover them.
It takes money to make money.	It takes a great idea to make money.
I don't have the time to add anything else to my plate.	I may have to rearrange my priorities in order to take advantage of this opportunity.

What the average person thinks	What the rich person thinks
I'll never be rich.	Everything that I touch turns to gold.
I tried that before and it didn't work.	What can I do differently this time to ensure my success?
I don't have a college degree.	I can learn the skills necessary to be successful at anything that I choose.
I can't afford it.	How can I make more money so that I will be able to afford it?
How awesome! I got a $2,500 tax refund.	OOPS! I overpaid my taxes by $2,500. I hate to think of the things I could have done with that money instead of giving Uncle Sam an interest-free loan.

Now do you have a better idea why the rich get richer and why the poor and middle class can never get ahead? They look at money differently, they value it differently and they treat it differently. All you have to do is look at money differently, value it differently and treat it differently and you too can become wealthy. Now let's take a look at the five steps necessary to accomplish just that.

Step 1--Know where you are and get out of debt.

Identify the problem areas

Before you can fix any problem you have to first realize that you have a problem. Before you can improve a situation you have to first know where you are. This is very straightforward when it comes to money. To best analyze the situation, you must revisit the past. What did your past spending habits look like? Where did you spend your money and on what? Go back through every credit card statement, receipt, and checking account ledger for the last year. Divide all of your expenditures per month into the following categories:

- Restaurant charges
- Grocery bills (food)
- Utilities (oil, gas, electric, water)
- Phone bills
- Insurance
- Entertainment
- Gasoline
- Merchandise
- Household & personal care supplies
- Charitable giving
- Education
- Clothes
- Mortgage
- Property tax
- Car payment
- Student loans

Take out thirteen pieces of paper, one for each month and one for the yearly total. Write down all of your expenses for each of the sixteen categories in the appropriate space. You may need to add a couple of categories to suit your particular situation, but *do not* put down a miscellaneous category. Each piece of paper will be an extended version of the following:

August 2002 Spending		
Category	Amount Spent	Total
Restaurant charges	$10.94, $32.14, $5.83, $12.79, $21.31, $3.93, $27.83	$114.77
Phone bills	Home--$63.73, Cell--$37.93	$101.66
Grocery bills	$123.91, $28.86, $85.74, $11.83	$250.34
Merchandise	$108.74, $74.84, $210.19	$393.77
Mortgage	$893.83	$893.83
Monthly Total	$1,754.37	$1754.37

Now take a look at the annual dollar amounts in each category. Out of all of these categories, which of them can you control? For now, do not focus on your fixed expenses like the mortgage, car payments, insurance, property tax and student loans. Which categories seem to be out of line? Those are the categories that you will be focusing on over the course of the next year. Notice that you spent a lot more in certain categories during one month than you did in another. Notice where you are spending too much and where you are not spending enough. Perhaps you spent $6,849 on restaurant charges but only $189 on education. Take each controllable spending category and trim it down as low as you can possibly live with. Write those numbers down next to each category. These are your new spending goals. Add them all up and subtract that number from your net monthly income. The amount that is left over will be used to develop a debt reduction plan.

Monthly Net Income - Monthly Net Expenses = Monthly Debt Reduction Amount (MDRA)

Post a chart like the one above on your refrigerator door and keep it up-to-date daily. Sure you can keep your running totals on an accounting software program and you should, however, we think that it is important to have these numbers in front of you where you can see them throughout the day. You know the saying, "Out of sight, out of mind." This exercise will take some time to get used to, but it is well worth it.

What, no budget? That's right, we are not big fans of budgets. They tend to have a zero balance. Your goal is to spend as little as possible and save as much as possible, then use that amount to pay down your debt. Budgets are kind of like diets. They work, but they are rarely permanent. Once you reach your goals and go off your budget, you tend to gradually get right back in trouble again. What we are suggesting is a lifestyle change--a change where you think about money differently; where you become concerned with your financial health. Be creative. Look for ways to cut costs. The first time we did this exercise we went through the whole house and took back everything that we had recently purchased. We took that money and applied it toward our debt.

Pay off your debt

Now let's take care of that ugly thing called debt. The debt that we are referring to here is primarily consumer debt, the worst kind. This debt would include credit cards, car payments, personal loans, store credit, etc. Write each debt down in descending order based on the interest rate charged. Your 19 percent store card should be listed above your 15 percent Visa card followed by your 8.5 percent car loan and so forth. Don't worry about paying off your mortgage. It is the cheapest money that you will ever be able to borrow since the interest portion of your mortgage payments is a tax writeoff. Next to each debt write down the interest rate, monthly payment and balance.

Now is where you take control of your financial life. You will be paying off one debt at a time, starting with the highest interest rate. Write down today's date and starting balance. Now subtract the MDRA calculated above and calculate a new starting balance for the next month. Keep doing this for every month until that debt is paid off. Then move to the next highest interest rate debt and continue the cycle until all of your debt is paid in full. This exercise will tell you exactly when you will be out of debt. Keep monitoring your expense matrix on a daily basis so that you don't drift back into old habits. The following table gives an example of how you can calculate exactly when you will be out of debt given an MDRA of $450.

Debt Reduction Schedule

Debt	Interest Rate	Monthly Pymt	Start Bal.	August Bal.	Sept. Bal.	Oct. Bal.	Nov. Bal.
Store	18.9%	$85	$3,200	$2,750	$2,300	$1,850	$1,400
Visa	15.9%	$65	$1,278	$1,278	$1,278	$1,278	$1,278
School	9%	$190	$28,846	$28,846	$28,846	$28,846	$28,846
Car	8.5%	$220	$12,837	$12,837	$12,837	$12,837	$12,837
Total			$46,161	$45,711	$45,261	$44,811	$44,361

Debt	Interest Rate	Monthly Pymt	Dec. Bal.	Jan. Bal.	Feb.* Bal.	March** Bal.	April Bal.
Store	18.9%	$85	$950	$500	$0	$0	$0
Visa	15.9%	$65	$1,278	$1,278	$0	$0	$0
School	9%	$190	$28,846	$28,846	$27,674	$27,074	$26,474
Car	8.5%	$220	$12,837	$12,837	$12,837	$12,837	$12,837
Total			$43,911	$43,461	$40,511	$39,911	$39,311

* You expect a $2,500 bonus on Feb. 15, which will pay off the store and Visa cards.

** Your MDRA has increased to $600 since the store and Visa cards are paid off.

(For planning purposes only, we will assume that the minimum monthly payment will not pay down the principle.)

Continue filling out this chart until your total is zero. This may seem like a lot of work when all you have to do is divide your MDRA into your total debt to figure out approximately how long it will take you to get out of debt. The point of this exercise is to develop a detailed written action plan. As discussed earlier, something very powerful happens when you write down your goals. It will also keep you on track. If your store credit card balance is $1,600 in November instead of $1,400, you will need to tighten the belt a little. Your MDRA is just your best guess. If you end up with more than that amount at the end of the month, pay it directly toward your debt. To accelerate this payment schedule, you can get a temporary part-time job or add an additional profit center to your life as will be described in step number five.

Celebrate each time you pay off one of the categories. Nothing expensive, of course, but make a big deal out of it. You have earned the right to pat yourself on the back. When all of your debt is paid in full then treat yourself to something really special. We would recommend a nice trip somewhere. Pick out the place today, find a picture of it and tape it on your refrigerator next to your charts.

Congratulations! You have taken control of your financial future and you will soon feel like a huge weight has been lifted off of your shoulders. In order to keep from falling back into your old habits, you must apply the principles taught in step number two.

Step 2--Live below your means
Now let's take a look at what got you in debt in the first place. We live in a land of instant gratification. We see something, we want it, so we buy it. It happens that quickly. We pay no regard to whether or not we can afford it or if we really need it. Buying things today is so

easy. All we have to do is give the nice man behind the cash register our credit card, sign on the dotted line and the "stuff" is ours. If you don't have your credit card with you or if it is maxed out, no problem, the store will give you 10 percent off of your purchase if you apply for their card. It doesn't matter that the card has a 21 percent interest rate because you plan on paying it off when the statement arrives (or will you?).

But wait--what about the 10 percent savings? It sure would be a shame not to take advantage of a deal like that. After all, the store is filled with really nice "stuff" that you can't live without. Retailers know that a customer will buy approximately 30 percent more when using a credit card versus paying with cash. So what should that tell you as a consumer? Leave your credit card at home and pay for everything with cash. But that makes things more difficult, you say. That's the point. We need to start making spending more difficult. So you have to go to the ATM machine every time you go to the store--big deal, there is one on just about every corner. You want to make buying "stuff" as inconvenient as possible.

When you pay with cash you have to take the money out of your purse or wallet, count it and then watch it leave your hands. Parting with your cash should be a hard thing to do. You worked hard for it. Credit cards are funny money. It's not real, that is, until your statement arrives. When you go to the ATM, take out as little money as possible. You can always go back if you need more. Try to make spending money at least as difficult as it is to make it.

Forget about keeping up with the Jones'. Thriftiness and delayed gratification need to be your new principles. A book that wonderfully illustrates the benefits of living below one's means is *The Millionaire Next Door* by Thomas Stanley and William Danko. In this book, the authors describe the average American millionaire. In most cases they didn't come from affluent families (as a matter of fact, they point out how many spoiled rich kids or ones who expect to get an inheritance don't do as well financially). More than 80 percent of them are ordinary self-made people who have accumulated their wealth in one generation. They typically don't drive expensive cars, wear designer clothing or live in huge houses. Both husband and wife are conservative with their money, however, the wife is the most conservative. They have a great money consciousness. They respect and value their money and save at least 15 percent of their earned income. Financial independence is more important to them than displaying high social status. And this is the part that we really liked--most of them have been married once and remain married. Could it be that relieving one's financial pressures makes for a happier marriage?

Living below your means is absolutely necessary, however, don't take it too far and fall into the trap of extreme frugality or miserly living. Living below one's means is not the same as living without many of the comforts of life even though you can afford them. An example of living below your means is purchasing a $200,000 home when you are approved for a $350,000 home. If you are not careful, frugality can lead to the love of money, where the accumulation of money is more important than meeting the needs and desires of your loved ones. As in everything in life, you must strike a healthy balance. Having a lot of money is not wrong, but holding on to it too tightly can be. You are free to have when you are free enough to give it away. Being too tight with your money can also limit the amount of financial abundance you will have. This is true because extremely frugal people can miss moneymaking opportunities because of their fear of losing what they have accumulated. Some of these opportunities will be discussed later in this chapter.

"No gain is so certain as that which proceeds from the economical use of what you already have."
- Latin Proverb -

Step 2 may not seem very appealing. In fact, most people will skip it altogether. But please keep in mind that this is the step that gets most people into financial trouble in the first place. If you really want to improve your marriage, get out of debt. Remember, the number-one stated reason for divorce is money. Do Steps 1 and 2 for one year and your life and your relationship will greatly improve.

There is light at the end of the tunnel if you are willing to discover exactly where you are and what problem areas you have, start paying off your debt, and let go of your strong desire for instant gratification. Once you have developed the habit of living below your means, you can then focus on increasing your means. Step 5 will show you how to increase your means.

It is very important for you to understand that making more money is not the answer to your money problems. As a matter of fact, making more money can actually increase your money pressures if you have not mastered Steps 1 and 2 above. A higher income will allow you to acquire more debt. And this level of debt can make you feel trapped. It can literally make you its slave. If you are not willing to do the first two steps then you will never be free of your money pressures.

Step 3--Build your nest egg

Ben Franklin was an extremely ingenious and wise man. We are all familiar with his saying, "A penny saved is a penny earned." This saying is the bargain shopper's creed, and it gets a lot of people in trouble. Lets say that you buy an item that you don't really need. The item regularly costs $50, but it is on sale for $30. How much money have you saved? If you answered $20, then you are wrong. You haven't saved anything. You have spent $30. However, Mr. Franklin's saying is true when purchasing something that you truly need and were going to have to buy anyway, like bread for example. It is also true for the first day that you invest that penny. After that, a penny saved is more that a penny earned thanks to the magic of compound interest.

The investment value of a dollar

How do you treat a one-dollar bill? Is it important to you or do you think nothing of just throwing it away? What about a five-dollar bill? A ten? A twenty? How about a one-hundred-dollar bill? Surely buying a little something for $100 is harmless enough? Just remember that all of those little $100 purchases add up over time. And don't forget the opportunity cost of buying those little items. An opportunity cost is simply what you are giving up due to your financial decision (return on one investment minus the return on another).

What is the opportunity cost of buying that $100 item? Let's say that you can sell that $100 item at any time during the next year for $40. Instead of buying that item, you decided to put it in an investment that pays 25 percent interest. You may think that you can't make a 25 percent return on your money. The wealthy do, and you will see how later in this chapter. In one year, your investment would have grown to $125 and your $100 item can be sold for $40. The difference in return between these two purchases/investments is $85. So by buying that item, you not only lose $25 in potential interest, but you also lost $60 due to its depreciation. If you made the investment, great, now you can spend the $25 and never have to touch the original $100.

But wait, that would rob us of taking advantage of the time value of money. Let's look at this scenario twenty years down the road. For argument's sake, let's assume that you will still be able to sell your trinket for $40 and that you receive 25 percent interest compounded monthly on your investment. Your investment would have grown to $14,098 and your purchase would be worth only $40. Which would you rather have, a $100 trinket or a $14,098 investment?

*"Every gold piece you save is a slave to work for you. Every copper it
earns is its child that also can earn for you. If you would
become wealthy, then what you save must earn, and its children must
earn, that all may help to give to you the abundance you crave."*
- George S. Clason, The Richest Man in Babylon -

If you really want to have a wealthy mindset, you will need to
look at least twenty years down the road. If you were to invest that
$100 every month instead of spending it, you would have $75,937 in
twenty years.

Once your high-interest debt is paid off and you are
accustomed to living below your means, let's make wise use of the
money that is left over. Take the money that was going directly
toward paying off your debt and invest it. You will start out rather
small and conservative at first. Your goal is to build a solid
foundation. We will touch on some higher growth areas later in this
chapter.

Start an emergency fund.

Life can be very unpredictable; therefore it is wise to save for a rainy
day. This fund should be approximately three months' living
expenses. The money should be placed where you can gain access to
it without much difficulty. When this new account reaches one
month's living expenses, roll it into a 30-day certificate of deposit
(CD). A CD will pay a higher interest rate than a passbook account.
Continue to save until you have your second months worth of living
expenses invested. Roll your 30-day CD into a 60-day CD and place
your new savings into a 30-day CD. Continue this process until you
have a 30-day, 60-day and 90-day CD. Keep upgrading until you have
three 90-day CDs that expire 30 days from each other. These CDs
will ensure that you will be covered for three months should an
unforeseen financial setback occur. Three months of living expenses
may not sound like a lot, but believe us it can make a world of
difference. The peace of mind that this strategy buys is priceless.

Max out your company's 401(k) and/or invest in an IRA.

A 401(k) is a great place to diversify your investment portfolio and
receive a relatively high rate of return given the fact that your money
is deposited pre-tax. The other obvious benefit is the fact that your
pre-tax dollars will grow taxed-deferred for as long as the money
remains in your account. You win twice. You have a larger dollar
amount to invest since you didn't have to pay taxes on it, and you are
not taxed on the interest that grows over time. Your money and its

interest are allowed to grow and get quite large over time. The time value of money is a wonderful thing.

Some people will say that they cannot afford to invest in their company's 401(k). The fact of the matter is that you cannot afford not to. This is especially true if your company matches a percentage of your contribution. You wouldn't want to walk away from $1,000,000 would you? Let's take a look at an example: *If you were to invest a total of $562.50 per month into a 401(k) at 12 percent interest, you would be a millionaire in twenty-five years.*

If you do not have a 401(k), you can choose between two other options. The traditional IRA (Individual Retirement Account) and the Roth IRA. Each of these investment vehicles allows you to contribute up to $3,000 per year per spouse with certain income limitations. There are two main differences between the two. The traditional IRA allows you to contribute pre-tax dollars, whereas you invest post-tax dollars into the Roth IRA. When you withdrawal your money at age fifty-nine and a half or later, you are taxed on the full amount taken out of the traditional IRA, whereas the money withdrawn from the Roth IRA is free and clear of additional taxes (that is, unless the government changes its mind sometime in the future). Again, let's take a look at a couple of examples.

IRA Investment	$3,000 Investment	$6,000 Married Investment
Monthly Contribution	$250	$500
Interest Rate	10%	10%
Duration	25 years	25 years
Ending Balance	$331,708	$663,417

You *can* afford to invest.

Again, we would like to stress the fact that you can afford to invest in a 401(k) and/or IRA. We know of several couples who said that they couldn't afford to invest any money because they could barely make it as it was. Most of these couples had dual incomes. Years down the road a significant event happened in their lives. Either the husband or the wife stopped working. One retired, one decided to be a stay-at-home caregiver, and the other was downsized. Guess what? They didn't starve. They all made adjustments to their lifestyle and were able to do just fine. What if they had been investing their spouse's income for all of those years instead of spending it? One couple would be millionaires right now. Today--none of them are even close.

The secret to investing when things are tight is to pay *yourself* first. If your paycheck is $1,000, take $100 of that and invest it right away before it is spent. Then learn how to live on the rest. You are a very resourceful person--you will figure out how to make it work.

The next step

We'll admit, paying off your debt and living frugally isn't much fun. But it is necessary to build a solid financial foundation to build on. Living below your means can be kind of a drag--that is, unless you have a lot of means. We're sure that you wouldn't be too upset if you could only spend $200,000 of the $350,000 you brought in every year. Of course, $350,000 won't just fall into your lap. You have to plan for it.

Step 4--Plan on becoming wealthy

You may not realize it, but today you woke up with a plan to either become wealthy or to be broke. Plan to be broke? Who would plan to be broke? Well, if you are broke, then the answer is you. We don't become who we are in life because of chance. Our life is made up of a series of decisions. These decisions mold us into the person we see in the mirror every day. Sure there are many things that happen to us that are out of our control, but how we act and react to those events makes all the difference in the world. We don't want to go into a deep philosophical discussion; however, we do want to point out some practical insights that will enable you to have the wealth that you desire.

What do you expect?

We have all heard that life is a journey. You can choose to wander through life aimlessly, or you can set out a course that will lead you to where you want to go. Let's say that you want to take the family to Disney World. You have decided that you are going to drive. You look at a map in order to determine the best way to get there. What are the two most important points on the map? Where you are and where you are going. It is a sad fact that many people spend more time planning out their vacation than they do planning their lives. Step 1 identified where you are. Now you have to lay out a course that will take you to where you want to go. Most people call them goals; we like to call them expectations. If you set a goal and miss it, no big deal, you can just set another one. But not meeting your "expectations" can cause enough discomfort to make you want to try harder. Which sounds more definite?

A. I plan to be a millionaire by June 15, 2010, or
B. I expect to be a millionaire by June 15, 2010.

There are many great books that have been written on the topic of goal setting. For the scope of this book we will only be touching the surface of this very important topic. One of the most powerful examples of the effectiveness of goal setting that we have heard is a study that was done in 1953 at Yale University. They interviewed the graduating class and asked them if they had written goals with an action plan detailing how they would achieve their goals. Less than 3 percent had written goals and an action plan. Twenty years later, they interviewed the class members to find that the 3 percent that had written goals with a plan on how to achieve those goals were worth more financially than the other 97 percent combined! Becoming wealthy--is it luck or could it be a well-defined and well-executed plan?

The following exercise will help you design a road map to success. Post your expectations where you will see them every day. Have fun with this exercise. Dream a little. After all, as we discussed earlier in this book, one person's dream is another's reality. With that in mind plan big and expect these things to happen.

Expectation Sheet

Prepared by: _____

Date: _____

Signature: _____

Annual household income 20 years from now: _____

Annual household income 15 years from now: _____

Annual household income 10 years from now: _____

Annual household income 7 years from now: _____

Annual household income 5 years from now: _____

Annual household income 3 years from now: _____

Annual household income 1 year from now: _____

Net worth 20 years from now: _____

Net worth 15 years from now: _____

Net worth 10 years from now: _____

Net worth 7 years from now: _____

Net worth 5 years from now: _____

Net worth 3 years from now: _____

Net worth 1 year from now: _____

Imagine your dream life.

Now close your eyes and imagine your life as a multimillionaire. Be as specific as you can. What do you see? What do you smell? Who are you with? What kind of a house do you live in? What kind of a car do you drive? Where do you vacation? How many people are you helping? How much money are you giving away? How many people are being blessed by your generosity? Write the screenplay of your new millionaire life on the walls of your mind. Rehearse it over and over again. Go someplace quiet and visit that place every day. Before long this picture will become so real that your subconscious mind will make it a reality.

Now that you have set some goals, how do you plan on achieving them? Goals without a plan for their achievement are little more that just dreams. Step 5 will give some guidance as to making your goals become a reality.

Step 5--Become wealthy

Before you can become wealthy you first need to believe that you can become wealthy, and then you need to decide to become wealthy. A decision is a very powerful thing. As mentioned before, the word *decide* is derived from the Latin word *decidere*, which literally means "to cut off." In other words, when you decide to become wealthy, you cut off from all other possibilities. There is no turning back.

Step 2 gave you a new mindset that will keep you living financially responsible. With that new mindset you are now ready to make more money--a lot more money. As stated earlier, making more money will not solve your financial problems. As a matter of fact, it may make matters worse. That is unless you have mastered Steps 1 and 2 and have started building the firm foundation described in Step 3. Step 4 is where you want to be and Step 5 will give you some practical steps toward becoming wealthy.

What is wealth? Webster's dictionary defines wealth as an abundance of valuable material, possessions or resources. Kind of vague, isn't it? You can ask one hundred people for their definition of wealth and you will get one hundred different answers. What is your definition of being wealthy? We like Robert Kiyosaki's definition of wealth as stated in his New York Times #1 Best Selling book *Rich Dad Poor Dad*. He basically defines wealth as the length of time that one can support oneself if one stops working. High-income earners such as lawyers and doctors are not necessarily wealthy. They may make a lot of money, but if they were to lose their primary source of income, they would be just as bad off as most Americans. Maybe even worse. High-income earners, such as the ones mentioned above, oftentimes have a greater desire to keep up with the Joneses than middle-class Americans do. They spend as much or more than they earn. The rich are not immune to financial pressures. We have seen $650,000 homes go into foreclosure. During the stock market crash in the 1930s it wasn't the poor that were jumping off the rooftops of buildings.

Now that you are financially responsible and have a new respect for your money, you are ready to start creating wealth. There are many ways to make money, however, some are much better than others at creating wealth. Prior to choosing a wealth-building strategy, you must first ask yourself five very important questions.

1. Which is more important to you?
   a. Being wealthy (living for several years or even indefinitely should your primary source of income stop).
   b. Having the illusion of wealth (having a lot of "stuff" but living paycheck to paycheck just to pay the monthly payments).
2. Do you want to work hard for your money or do you want your money to work hard for you?
3. Do you need to show up in order to get paid?
4. Do you want to get paid once, or would you like to get paid over and over again for your efforts?
5. What are your hobbies, interests and passions? How can you turn your hobbies, interests or passions into money?

In the beginning, you will have to work hard for your money; however, your goal is to have that money in turn work hard for you. You also want to derive a large portion of your income from a source that will continue to work for you long after you stop working for it. The $100 *item* mentioned earlier demonstrates how you can work hard for your money and then have little to show for it. The $100 *investment* shows how you can have your money work hard for you. Do you have to be there for that $100 to have earned $25? No, that $100 will grow to $125 in a year regardless of where you are or what you are doing. And as long as you keep your money in that investment, it will continue to make more money for you over and over again.

That is one of the secrets of the wealthy--they put their money and/or time to work for them so that they don't have to be there to receive the profits. This is known as reoccurring, passive or residual income. Another example of residual income comes in the form of royalties. Each time one of a musician's songs is played or recordings is sold; she gets a little piece of the action. Residual income is money that will come to you while you are riding your bike, vacationing in Hawaii, doing the laundry or even sleeping. How would you like to make money while basking in the sun on Waikiki beach? Do you think that this kind of income would help you become wealthy more quickly?

What are you passionate about?
There are thousands of ways to make money, but which ones are right for you? Which income vehicles will make the most money and which will make you the happiest? We used to think that making a lot of money and being extremely happy doing what we were doing for a living were two unrelated things. We kept hearing the same kind of thing from dozens of sources. Sayings like:

- "Love what you do and you'll never work another day of your life."
- "Do what you are passionate about and the money will follow."
- "Follow your heart and it will lead you to riches."
- "Listen to your gut feeling because it is always right."

For us, it sounded too good to be true. We didn't believe it. We thought it was pie in the sky, warm and fuzzy babble designed to sell books and seminars. We thought that fun was what you did after work. We knew that money could increase one's enjoyment in life, but we didn't think that doing what we enjoyed, what we were passionate about, would bring us the most cash.

Boy were we wrong. The big money is made by people who are passionate about what they do. They are following their heart, not just their head. We came to this conclusion after talking with many very successful multimillionaires. They all had such passion. You could tell it by the look on their face and the tone of their voice. There was no doubt that there was nothing that they would rather be doing for a living, and they were making a lot of money doing it. It makes sense, really. If you dislike or even hate your job, you will probably only do what is expected of you, nothing more, nothing less. If you don't love what you are doing, you will most likely not give it everything that you have. Consequently, you can never reach your full potential unless you pour your heart and soul into something.

People who are passionate about what they do often don't even need an alarm clock to get them out of bed in the morning. Many of them can't wait to get up in the morning to begin a new day.

If you are the type who hits the snooze several times in the morning, then you are probably not passionate about your work and you might be better suited doing something else. If you still don't believe us, we understand. We used to feel the same way. We didn't have a hard time getting up in the morning; however, we did sleep in until the last minute. We rarely looked forward to going to work. It took a while to get into the flow of things on Monday morning, and Friday afternoons were something to look forward to. The weekends always went by too fast. Even though each day was slightly different than the day before, it seemed as though every day was the same.

Things are not like that for us anymore. Sleeping in for us now is 6:30 A.M. on a Sunday morning. Last Saturday we woke up very early. In the past we would have rolled over and gone back to sleep. That is not the case anymore. We got out of bed fixed ourselves something to eat and started writing another section in *Honeymoon Marriage*.

The best and oftentimes quickest way to become wealthy is to discover what you are or could become passionate about and then pursue that thing with everything within you. What are your interests? What do you think you would like to do for a living? When you were a child, what was it that you wanted to do or be? Have you done any part time work or volunteer activities in the past that you thoroughly enjoyed?

Darren and the JA kids: I (Darren) volunteered to teach a Junior Achievement course twelve years ago. I taught basic economics to troubled sixth graders. I had a blast! I looked forward to the class every week and so did the kids. Is it any surprise then that I should be a teacher?

I once asked a corporate vice president what he would like to do for a living. The reason I asked is because I could see that he was very stressed out and wasn't enjoying his job. I asked him if he could be doing anything for a living, what would it be? He said that he would like to teach. Come to find out, he taught college night school courses several years ago and loved it. When I asked him why he didn't go into teaching, he said that it didn't pay enough. How sad it is to miss out on your life's calling because of money. When the amount and caliber of your "stuff" becomes more important than your happiness and peace of mind, it is time to sit down and take a good hard look at your life. And besides, he could have had them both. He could have made say $55,000 as a teacher and also had a part-time home-based business that supplied enough money for him and his family to have the "stuff" as well.

What about you? What would you love to do for a living? You can have your cake *and* eat it too. You can love what you are doing even if it doesn't pay very much *and* become wealthy. This can be accomplished by adding multiple profit centers to your life. Most people derive at least 80 percent of their income from one source. In a dual-income household, most if not all income comes from those two sources alone. One or two sources of income are not enough. It isn't safe and it just doesn't make sense to the serious wealth builder.

What would happen to you and your family if your primary source of income should stop? How long could you be without this source of income before you received a letter from your financial lender stating that foreclosure proceedings were about to begin? Not long if you are like most Americans. Of course you will be different since you will have at least three months of living expenses saved up, won't you? But the average American couple would be in jeopardy of losing their house in less than three months. According to Dorcuc Hardy, former Commissioner for the Social Security Administration, the average fifty-year-old has less than $2,300 in savings.

If you inherited $100,000, would you invest it all in one company's stock, or would you diversify that money and limit your risk exposure by investing in several companies in several markets or possibly investing in a mutual fund? You have probably heard the saying, ""Don't put all of your eggs in one basket," yet that is exactly what we are doing when we live off of one or two sources of income.

There are dozens of ways that you can make money, why limit yourself to just your job? In today's day and age, you need to have what *New York Times* #1 Best Selling Author Robert Allen calls *Multiple Streams of Income*.

The vice president in the example above could have his cake and eat it to. He could love his job as a teacher, and have the income and lifestyle of a Fortune 500 vice president. If he had only discovered the power of multiple streams of income, he could be living a much fuller life, but instead, he is trapped. Perhaps you feel like you are trapped. Maybe you think that you can't afford to follow your heart. Don't lose hope. All you have to do is increase your income by starting up another profit center. Fortunately, there are several profit centers that you can start part-time while still keeping your day job. The scope of this chapter is to get you thinking in the right direction. You will need to do further investigation into wealth creation in order to get the step-by-step details. Become a student of success. We have read dozens of financial books and have found at least one nugget of gold in every one of them. The following are some profit center examples that you may want to consider:

Real estate

There is no doubt that many people have made a lot of money in real estate. Real estate is a relatively stable investment. In a down economy, people may stop buying new cars, television sets, furniture and microwave ovens, but they will always need a place to live. As a matter of fact, you can get some of your best real estate deals when the economy is slow. There are always deals to be had regardless of current economic conditions. There are basically three ways to make money in real estate.

1. Rent. Buy a property and rent it out. This is a great way to create a residual stream of income, while simultaneously building your net worth. We purchased a rental property four years ago for $145,000. Our total out-of–pocket expenses, including the down payment, escrow and closing costs was $8,500. Our positive cash flow is $250 per month, which is an annual return on investment of 35 percent. This ROI is great, but it could have been much better had we met Bob Allen two years earlier and learned that we could have purchased the property using none of our own money. But wait, it gets even better.

The home is currently worth $170,000 and the mortgage balance is $128,000, $9,750 of which was paid down by our renters. We could sell the property today and pocket a cool $34,750 profit. Add that to the $12,000 positive cash flow that it has generated during the last four years and you get a $46,750 return on an $8,500 investment. That's equivalent to a 47.7 percent interest rate. Remember earlier when we said that it was possible to get a 25 percent return on your money? Best of all, this money was generated without us having to "work" for it or be there to collect it.

Uncle Sam also allows us to depreciate the property over 27½ years. Tax rules treat investment real estate as though it was a piece of capital equipment that decreases in value every year, when in fact, it increases in value every year. Therefore, each year we get an additional income tax deduction of approximately $5,009. So according to the government, we are losing $2,009 every year ($5,009 deduction minus the $3,000 positive cash flow). We realize that this is a unique example and each property's results vary greatly, however, it should give you an idea of what is possible.

Now assume that you have done your homework and have purchased ten properties each with a $125 per month positive cash flow. That will give you a passive cash flow of $1,250 per month. If you were at the 20 percent income tax bracket and invested that money at 9 percent interest, you will have over $1,000,000 in twenty-five years and nine months. This is how you get rich off of other people's money.

2. Resell. Buy a property and resell it for a profit. This is known as flipping a property. If you don't want to wait years to cash in on the profits, you can buy a property at 20 percent below fair market value, clean it up, possibly do some painting and then sell it at market value for an instant profit. This kind of property will take a little longer to find than the rental example above because you need to make your profit when you buy rather than when you sell. In other words, if you buy a property for $60,000 and it is appraised at $73,000, then you have already made $13,000 because your net worth has increased by $13,000. You turn this net worth into cash at the time of sale. Flip seven or eight properties per year and you will have created a six-figure profit center.

Who would sell a property for 15 to 20 percent below fair market value? They are known as motivated sellers. They need to sell the property quickly for one reason or another. They may have already moved and are paying two mortgage payments. Perhaps they just got downsized, realize that they can't make their mortgage payments, and want to move to a smaller house before they miss too many payments and ruin their credit rating. The house may be in foreclosure or the bank may already own it. You will also be able to save at least 6 percent by buying a home that is for sale by owner. This is true because you don't have to pay the Realtor's commission and you can also negotiate directly with the decision-maker (the seller). A Realtor by law represents the seller, not you the buyer. Realtors are obligated to get the best deal possible for their client. That doesn't mean that you shouldn't use Realtors. A good assertive Realtor can be a very valuable asset. Realtors can save you a lot of time and effort, and they are well connected. And as the saying goes, "Time is money."

3. Rehab. If you are skilled in the trades, are good with your hands, and/or love a project, then this could be your pot of gold. Most people only see what is before their eyes. They can't look past the things that are wrong and see the potential. You may be the kind of person who sees an old rusty 1932 Ford coupe in someone's back yard and says, "Wow, nice car." The person with you may think you are nuts because he or she only sees a broken-down rust bucket. You on the other hand see the finished product, an awesome street rod. The owner of the car may even pay you to take it off his hands.

Make sure to do your homework and go through the property with a fine-toothed comb so that you don't get burned. This is where a building inspector comes in handy. You should always get a property inspected by a professional anytime you make a purchase, especially with an older building or house. The last thing you want is a money pit.

Investments

We feel that everyone should invest at least 10 percent of his or her gross income somewhere. If real estate is not your cup of tea, then consider placing this money in the stock market. Some people get really freaked out when considering investing in the stock market. Don't be afraid of this awesome moneymaking tool, just make sure you know what you are doing.

> *"Knowledge is the antidote of fear."*
> *- Ralph Waldo Emerson -*

Stock market investing in and of itself doesn't have to be risky. Not being properly educated on how best to invest is what is risky. A great way to start your education is to read investment books. Your local bookstore is loaded with them. Take classes, go to seminars, and talk with a Certified Financial Planner. Not Uncle Bob, your best friend Sally, or your high-income-earning brother. Listen only to the experts and make sure that you interview several prior to investing any of your hard-earned cash. The time and money that you invest in your stock market education is not only beneficial, it is absolutely necessary. Take it from someone who lost over $40,000 in three months, ignorance is expensive. Don't kid yourself, all investments carry with them some level of risk. Investments with a higher risk associated with them typically pay higher returns.

The first thing that you have to do after you have become educated is to determine your risk tolerance. If you can't stand the thought of possibly losing money, even if it is only a short-term loss, then you should not invest in aggressive stocks. For your own peace of mind, you may be better off placing your money in bank CDs. If you can only handle a very small loss, then a conservative mutual fund or money market account may be to your liking. However, if you can afford to lose half of your money and it won't stress you out, then the world of stock market investing may be your ticket to financial independence. If you decide that a more aggressive strategy is for you and you have taken the time to become educated, practice investing on paper for several months before you do it for real. You can start investing for real once you are consistently making money on paper.

Dispelling one of the biggest investment myths.

Is your home your best investment? If you look at your house as being your largest and/or best investment then you are in trouble. You are not alone in this belief. It was the way we were brought up to think. We were taught to think of our house as our best asset. While it is true that your house can be a relatively safe place to put your money, it makes for a very poor investment/asset. The definition of your net worth may be your assets minus your liabilities, however, if your assets are not making you money, you may have your money in the wrong place. Is your house putting money into your pocket every month or taking it out? An asset should put money into your pocket.

The money (equity) in your house is not paying you back any return on your investment. As a matter of fact, if your house is appreciating in value at a slower rate than the rate of inflation, then your hard-earned money is dwindling away before your very eyes. Let's say that your house is worth $100,000 and it is appreciating in value at a rate of 5 percent each year. At the end of five years, your house will be worth $127,628. How much will your house be worth after five years if you paid a $40,000 down payment? The answer is $127,628. How much will your house be worth after five years if you paid a $2,000 down payment? That's right, it is still worth $127,628. Which sounds better to you, a $27,628 profit from a $40,000 investment (down payment) or a $27,628 profit from a $2,000 investment? Look at it this way, if you could only sell the house for $100,000, how much money has your $40,000 made you? That's right--zero.

"Yes, but if I put down a large down payment my monthly payments will be lower and I won't have to pay mortgage insurance (PMI) ," you say. True, your payments will be a lot lower, but you won't have $38,000 ($40,000 - $2,000) hard at work for you either. The following chart shows what that extra $38,000 could be doing for you if it wasn't stuck between the four walls of a house. We will also consider the investment of the difference between the lower and higher monthly payment.

	Scenario 1	Scenario 2
Down Payment	$40,000	$2,000
Loan Amount	$60,000	$98,000
Interest Rate	7%	7%
Loan Duration	30 years	30 years
Total Interest Paid	$83,863	$136,972
Interest Difference		+ $53,109
Monthly Payment (Principle & Interest)	$399	$652
Monthly PMI	0	$50
Total Monthly Payment	$399	$702
Monthly Savings	$303 ($702 - $399)	N/A
Investment Option	$303 per month	$38,000
Investment Interest Rate	13%	13%
Investment Period	30 years	30 years
Final Investment Balance	$1,325,101	$1,838,329
Investment Difference		+ $513,228
Investment Balance - Mortgage Interest + Down Payment	$1,281,238	$1,703,357
Total Monetary Difference		**+ $422,119**

As you can see, putting down a large down payment isn't the best move financially. Of course that is assuming that you invest the money that isn't going toward paying off the house.

In our opinion, the monetary advantage of not putting your money between the four walls of your house is not the most important reason for not doing it. If all or most of your money is "invested" or trapped between the four walls of your house, how do you get it out when you need it? Let's say that you just lost your job. The money that you have in the bank is enough to keep you afloat for one month (you haven't worked up to the three months living expenses as laid out in Step 2 yet). Month number two comes and you still haven't found a job. You have $40,000 equity in your house, but how can you get it out? You have two choices--you could sell your house, or you could get a home equity loan. A home equity loan is your best bet, but who is going to give you a loan if you are unemployed? We have seen dozens of homes in foreclosure that had equity built up in them, but the owners couldn't get it out. Choice number two is to sell your house. That is a tough position to be in. It would be a lot easier on you to liquidate your $38,000 investment in the above example than it would be to sell your house. After all, you need a place to live.

Also, get the longest-term mortgage that you can and never pay it off. Okay, now we know we have lost some of you. You may have been shown how you could save thousands of dollars in interest if you have a fifteen-year loan versus a thirty-year loan. We have seen the numbers too and they are quite large. Don't let these large interest figures scare you. First, remember that your interest is a tax write-off. Secondly, don't forget that you will be investing the difference between the fifteen-year and the thirty-year payments. The following chart shows why a thirty-year loan is the better investment.

	Scenario 1	Scenario 2
Loan Amount	$100,000	$100,000
Interest Rate	7%	6.67%
Loan Duration	30 year	15 year
Total Interest Paid	$139,772	$58,522
Interest Difference	+ $81,250	
Monthly Payment (Principle & Interest)	$665	$880
Monthly Payment Saving	$215 ($880 - $665)	
Monthly Investment amount	$215	0
Investment total after 30 years at 13%	$940,253	$483,759*
Investment difference	+ $456,494	
Investment difference - Interest Difference	**+ $375,244**	

* After year fifteen, the fifteen-year loan will be paid for and the whole amount of $880 can be invested every month for the next fifteen years at 13% interest.

Perhaps you would feel safer if you owned your house outright in the event that you should lose your job. At least you wouldn't have to worry about making a mortgage payment. That is true as long as you still have enough money coming in to pay your other living expenses including your property tax. You may think that you own your house and the property that it sits on, but stop paying your property taxes and see who really owns it. We have been to the county court house and have seen several people who were in jeopardy of losing their home if they didn't pay their past due property taxes.

As an investor, you can help your local county government and make a healthy return on your investment by helping them solve the cash flow problem that has been caused by people not paying their property taxes. You can buy what is known as a tax lien or tax deed certificate. These certificates can earn up to 25 percent interest and are backed by the local government. The government isn't doing this out of the kindness of its heart. The county charges the homeowner a late penalty (interest charges) and passes this charge on to you. Just call your county courthouse and ask for the appropriate personnel. You can even purchase these certificates from another state. Texas offers 25 percent even if the homeowner pays up the following month.

Note: If your house is currently paid for, we are not suggesting that you take out a mortgage and go out and invest that money in the stock market or anywhere else for that matter. The purpose of the above example was to tell you the truth about money so that you can make educated decisions. It is always best to seek the advice of a trained financial advisor prior to making any investment decisions.

Coin operated businesses

A coin operated business can be a great source of income assuming you do your homework. Talk to as many owners as you can and don't listen to all of the hype that the distributors and manufacturers give you. To put it bluntly--they lie. A coin operated business is a quasi-residual income. It makes money without you having to be there, however, you still need to show up to collect the cash and in the case of product, fill your machines. Coin operated business can range anywhere from a Laundromat or car wash to a gumball machine. Have you ever passed by a gumball machine and wondered how anyone could make any serious money selling gumballs for 25¢? Consider that the owner has one hundred machines, each machine holds two hundred gumballs, and she buys the gumballs for 2¢ apiece. Do the math and you can see that this would make for a nice part-time business.

Intellectual property

You have most likely heard that it takes money to make money. That is not always true. It takes an idea to make money. We all have ideas floating around in our head. Some of these ideas can make you a lot of money. The ideas that we would like to cover in this chapter are in the form of information that you can sell to others for a profit. Information is where the big bucks are. The following are just a few examples:

Author. You could write a book. Everyone has at least one book in them. Your book can either be fiction or nonfiction depending upon your interests and talents. If you have a great idea for a book, we would encourage you to start putting your thoughts down on paper today. Don't worry about *how* you will write it for now, just start writing. All too often we spend too much time thinking about the *how*. Develop a strong enough *why* and the how will take care of itself. Come up with a strong enough reason *why* you want to accomplish something and you will figure out *how* to make it happen.

Perhaps you have a great idea for a children's book. You may have a great imagination and can think of fictional stories that you would love to tell. Your own personal story can sell as well. You don't have to be a famous person in order for people to want to read your story. Your life is uniquely yours and you do have a story to tell. People are very interested in the life stories of others.

"How to" books are also big sellers. Your knowledge and past experience can be exchanged for money. Your "How to . . ." or "The 101 Best Ways to . . ." or "The 10 Steps to . . ." can be in either a book or pamphlet format. You could even sell it as an E-book over the Internet.

You may have heard that only one out of every ten thousand books will ever get published. Don't worry about that. If you want it badly enough, you will get published. Publishers need authors. Without them, there is nothing to sell. After all, publishers don't write books, people like you and I do. Think of your book today. If nothing comes to you right away, keep thinking about it until something does. This process may take a couple of days or it could take several months. Just remember: you have at least one good book in you. Let it out and share it with the world.

Writer. Perhaps you are a gifted writer but never thought that you could sell your talents. We all have marketable talents whether we know it or not. The following are just a sampling of some possibilities:

- Write music
- Write lyrics
- Write plays
- Write movie scripts
- Write articles
- Write a recipe book
- Write instructional manuals
- Write speeches
- Ghost writer for other authors

Inventor. Maybe you have a great invention in mind or perhaps you know how to greatly improve an existing product. You could sell your idea for a fixed amount of money, market the product yourself or license it. Licensing allows you to create a residual income like that of an author or music artist. You get a piece of the action for every unit sold. Even actors are now taking less money up front in exchange for a percentage of the box office take. The better the movie does, the better they do. It is also a lower risk for the studio in case the movie is a bust.

Consultant

You may be selling yourself short if you have specialized knowledge and are working for someone else. It is not uncommon for a consultant to earn $100 or more per hour. They are also treated with a higher level of respect than many employees are. Consulting can be done on a part time basis while you keep your current job (assuming there isn't a conflict of interest) or you can branch off on your own. You can also diversify your income by doing work for several companies. That way your income will only decrease somewhat if one company decides that it no longer needs your services.

A consultant who does work for five separate companies and only lives off of the income from three of them is much better off than an employee who is living at his or her means. That may sound like an unfair example, yet it holds true in real life. The person who knows exactly how much money he or she will make from week to week, month to month, year after year, will typically spend exactly that much money. The person whose income varies from month to month is less likely to spend everything. We were once told that if you knew how much money you were going to make next year within 10 percent, then you were already broke.

Teacher

There will always be a high demand for teachers. Those who can teach their knowledge to others in an easy-to-understand manner are worth a lot of money. We are not referring to teachers who are employees of a school or university. The type of teacher we are referring to is an independent contractor much like a consultant. They are known as public speakers, lecturers and trainers. They inform, instruct, motivate, and encourage audiences all over the country.

Business Ownership

If you are an employee, do your employers pay you what you are worth? Of course not, they can't afford to. If they paid you exactly what you were worth, there would be no profit left for them. And the only reason for being in business in the first place is to make a profit. If you want to get ahead of the game, you will need to start making what you are worth. And that my friend is a lot!

The key ingredient to becoming wealthy in America is business ownership. It is no coincidence that self-employed people make up only 20 percent of the American workforce yet they account for 67 percent of the millionaires. That means that there are approximately 2,345,000 self-employed millionaires in America. And there is no valid reason why you can't become one of them. If you are already a millionaire and would like to increase your cash flow, then stay tuned. We will discuss an excellent profit center that you can add to your portfolio in the next segment of this chapter.

Why would a millionaire want or need to increase cash flow? Well, being a millionaire may sound glamorous, but it doesn't mean that the person makes a lot of money. It just means that he or she has a net worth of at least one million dollars. Here are a couple of examples:

- Teresa is a small business owner and estimates that her business is worth $2.5 million. She doesn't want to sell the business because she wants to keep it in the family. Her business has been manufacturing products for the automotive industry for fifteen years. Business is great; however, profits have been eroding for years due to an increase in competition. Although she works seventy hours per week, her company's profit, half of which she takes in the form of a paycheck, is only $130,000.

- Jerry is fifty-seven years old and is looking to retire. He is a high-income earner, but only has $250,000 invested. He purchased his house twenty-five years ago for $75,000 and it is currently worth $450,000. He also owns a six-flat that is worth $325,000. The cash flow that he receives from his investments and rental property isn't enough to afford him the lifestyle that he is accustomed to.

Business ownership is a must these days. You simply cannot afford not to own a business.

There is another reason why the rich get richer and the poor and middle class barely stay afloat. The rich pay less in taxes. That is of course if they are business owners. The reason for this is simple. As an employee, you buy everything that you need after you have already paid taxes. Uncle Sam takes his cut before you even see your paycheck. You buy your home computer with after-tax money. You go to Hawaii with after-tax money. You pay your car payment with after-tax money. You pay your taxes first and then buy what you need with what is left over. Business owners, on the other hand, buy what they need (expenses) and then pay taxes on what is left over. They win in two ways.

1. Buying with pre-tax dollars is like getting everything at a discount. Your savings is whatever your current tax rate is. An employee who claims a business write-off will receive his or her discount (tax credit or deduction) when filing his or her income taxes. The self-employed business owner receives his or hers up front.

2. The self-employed business owner saves money by lowering his or her taxable income. Let's say that a business owner and an employee both "make" $75,000 per year. They are both married filing jointly. Since they both have two children, give to charities, and can write off the interest on their home, we will not include these items in our calculations. The employee will pay $14,982 in federal income tax. The business owner has $15,000 in business expenses, lowering his taxable income to $60,000. He pays $10,857 in federal income taxes. That's a difference of $4,125. Not owning your own business would be like throwing that $4,125 in your fireplace.

If you want to pay off your debt faster than your projected payoff schedule, then you need to start your own business. If you want to build up a net worth of over one million dollars sometime before the next thirty years, then you need to start your own business. If you want to increase your cash flow and/or be able to afford some of the nicer things in life, then you need to start your own business.

You may be thinking that you can't start a traditional business because you don't have any great ideas for a product to make or service to sell. Or you may think that you can't afford the start-up costs of a turnkey franchise. Don't let that stop you from starting up a home-based business. There are thousands of home-based business opportunities available, many of which cost less than $2,000 to start.

A million dollar business on a shoe string

The following is what Robert Allen, the author of the New York Times Bestsellers *Multiple Streams of Income*, *Nothing Down*, and *Creating Wealth* has to say about his business experiences:

"I've owned restaurants, clothing stores, a chocolate factory, apartment buildings, commercial buildings, seminar companies, newsletter businesses, and direct-mail, multimedia, and software businesses. I've invested in Broadway plays. I've even owned a piece of a professional basketball team, the Utah Jazz. Network marketing beats them all. My overhead is minuscule compared to my former company that had 250 employees. Just the thought of going back to managing employees makes me cringe. I no longer need to pay salaries, benefits, social security taxes, workers' comp, health care, retirement plans. To an ex-employer like myself, it seems like a miracle." From *Multiple Streams of Income*

Network marketing
Millionaires-R-Us. More millionaires are created on a yearly basis through network marketing than in any other industry. During the last decade, approximately 20 percent of all self-made millionaires made their fortune through network marketing. That is one out of every five! The company that we represent paid out over one million dollars each to twenty-two individuals during its first nine years in business. Twenty-two millionaires in just nine years, now that's a track record worth bragging about.

So what makes network marketing so different than a traditional business? Almost everything-- the following is a sampling:

- Turn-key operation at a fraction of the cost of a typical franchise
- No need to stock product
- Low or no overhead
- You are your own boss
- You set your hours and workplace (the commute to our office is twelve seconds)
- Your income potential is unlimited
- Your income is residual rather than linear. Residual income is like working one hour and getting paid over and over again for your efforts. An example of linear income is the typical job where you work an hour and get paid for an hour.
- Self-improvement
- Takes advantage of the law of the harvest principle. You become successful by helping other people become successful.

Network marketing has come of age and it is a profit center that everyone should consider adding to his or her income portfolio.

Many of today's leading success coaches and authors are either in or promote network marketing as a great way to increase one's income or even create financial independence.

"I think network marketing has come of age.
It's become undeniable that it's a viable way to
entrepreneurship and independence for millions of people."
- Dr. Stephen Covey,
interview with Network Marketing Lifestyles, April 1999.
Author of the #1 National Bestseller, The 7 Habits of Highly Effective People -

In its simplest form network marketing is a distribution channel that supplies a product or service directly to the end user. It pays its associates or distributors a commission for their word-of-mouth advertising, the promotion of the product or service, and for building a successful business. Word-of-mouth advertising is one of the most powerful sources of advertising available. That is why network marketing is such an effective distribution channel.

Everyone is a network marketer. Your network is your circle of influence. Your circle of influence is everyone whom you know and will come in contact with during your day. Every time you make a recommendation to someone, you are network marketing. Examples would include recommending a restaurant to a coworker, recommending a movie to a family member, recommending a mortgage broker to your neighbor, and recommending a doctor to a friend. Network marketing is word-of-mouth advertising and marketing that you get paid for. For a great non-biased education on the network marketing industry, read Richard Poe's book entitled *Wave 4 Network Marketing in the 21st Century*.

Network marketing is a very misunderstood industry, even among those who have had network marketing experience. We believe that life is all about managing expectations. Misdirected expectations have led to a lot of mistruths being circulated regarding this method of distribution. People accept the fact that if they open a traditional business, they will have to work fifty to seventy hours per week in order to turn a profit in the second or third year. The traditional business owner knows that he or she will have to work extremely hard to be successful since over 90 percent of all businesses fail within their first five years. But for some reason, people can join a network marketing company, work their new business for five to ten hours per week, become discouraged and quit after four months because they are not bringing in $10,000 per month. People who need to have instant gratification will never make it in network marketing. As a matter of fact, they will never make it in any business.

Network marketing is a slow build that picks up momentum as more and more people join your network. It is very simple, but it isn't easy. It won't work without belief, patience, persistence, enthusiasm, the willingness to follow instructions and good old-fashioned hard work. If you are expecting something for nothing, then keep playing the lottery. If, however, you are willing to put forth some effort, then network marketing may be just what you have been looking for. If you would like more information regarding this wonderful business, go to www.honeymoonmarriage.com and click on the keyword "network marketing."

"I do not think there is any other quality so essential
to success of any kind as the quality of perseverance.
It overcomes almost everything, even nature."
- John D. Rockefeller -

Building a business together as a couple can be a great way to improve your relationship. That is of course if you are both passionate about what you are doing. If one of you loves the business and the other one hates it, then it would be best if you didn't built it together. Network marketing may not be your cup of tea--it isn't for everyone. But if it is something that you would like to consider or reconsider, then it may be a business that you can build together as a couple. We have heard of many couples whose marriages improved by building a network marketing business together. The following are several reasons why:

Change of focus. Happiness is a choice and it is largely dependent upon what you focus on. If you only focus on the bad things in your life, then you will be unhappy, even depressed. If you choose to always see the "silver lining" and focus on all of the blessings in your life, then you will become happier, healthier and more fun to be around.

Darren's focus changing experiment: Years ago we were eating at a restaurant with friends of ours who had two children. The youngest was about two years old, and was not happy being strapped in a highchair at the restaurant. He was crying and wanted everything that he didn't have. He wanted our food, our attention, and to get out of the highchair. No matter what his parents said he kept on crying. After a couple of minutes, his parents almost became immune to his acting up. It started to get under our skin, so when his parents weren't looking, I (Darren) dipped my fingers in my glass of water and flicked the water on his face. The two-year-old was shocked and became quiet immediately. He then began to laugh. As he looked at me I started laughing as well. He was a perfect little boy for the rest of the evening. I knew that my harmless act would change his focus. His parents only told him what he shouldn't do. I took him down a completely different path. I took his focus off of all of the things he didn't have.

Network marketing has a wonderful way of taking your focus off of what you don't have and placing it on the things that you can have.

1. **Hope**--Hope is one of the best gifts that you can give someone. Many couples are stuck in a rut with no hope of escape.

   > *"The only difference between a rut and*
   > *a grave are the dimensions."*
   > *- Patricia Swerda -*

   These couples have lost sight that they are in control of their destiny. They wake up at 6:30 a.m., get ready for work, put in an eight- to twelve-hour day, drive home, eat, watch a little TV, go to bed and then repeat the cycle the next day. After a while, they begin to think that there is no other alternative. Life can become stale and predictable when you don't have hope for a brighter tomorrow.

   If that describes you, be careful because that kind of lackluster existence can spill over into your marital relationship as well. Network marketing can give you hope for a better future. A hope for a future that you didn't think was possible for your family. This hope turns into excitement and anticipation of a better life. Hope that things will get better has a side effect of improving your relationship.

2. **Relieving financial pressure**--Concern, worry and stress can take its toll on a marriage. Financial pressure can amplify other problems in a relationship, blowing them out of proportion. An extra $1,000 per month can make all of the difference in the world to many couples. An extra $1,000 per month has the ability to decrease the number of arguments that take place between couples. Now all of a sudden that $100 phone bill doesn't cause a

fight. Little Johnny can now get braces without concerns of where the money will come from. That trip to Disney World is no longer a problem. That old car that is on its last leg can now be replaced with a new one. There are a lot of pressures in life; money doesn't have to be one of them. Network marketing can relieve these money pressures.

3. **Personal development**--This is one of the most important aspects of building a successful network marketing business. Building a network marketing business requires that you move out of your comfort zone and grow as a person. Many of the skills that one learns while building this kind of business will be beneficial in other areas of life as well.

4. **Helping others**--Helping others is one of the most rewarding things that we can do in life. Through network marketing, you have the ability to make a major impact in people's lives. In network marketing you become successful by helping others become successful. It is a perfect example of a win-win relationship. All of the benefits mentioned earlier can be passed on to others. If you represent a company who distributes nutritional products, you can even give them the gift of better health.

Final thoughts on starting you own business

As you can probably tell, network marketing is one of our favorite profit centers. It is one of the easiest and least expensive ways to start a home-based business. If network marketing doesn't interest you, make sure to start some kind of business. We have only listed a few possibilities, but there are many more that are available. Use your imagination and start writing down your ideas today. Every day that you wait is a day that you are robbing from your future. Make today a day of new beginnings. We wish you massive success! Now let's discuss life's greatest wealth secret.

Giving--life's greatest wealth secret

So far we have discussed:

- How your thoughts and attitudes determine how much money you have
- How to treat your money
- How to identify your spending problem areas

- How to get out of debt
- How to stay out of debt by living below your means
- The investment value of a dollar
- How to start an emergency fund
- The importance of investing in your company's 401(k) and/or an IRA
- That you must put together a wealth-building game plan
- Several ways that you can add additional profit centers to your life.

Now that you know how to save, invest and earn money, we will talk about giving it away.

We believe that giving away a portion of your money will enable you to receive even more in return. Remember the *Law of the Harvest* discussed earlier? If you give money, you will get money. Give more and you will receive more. We know that doesn't make sense logically. How can you make $100, give $10 away and then end up with more than your original $100? It is possible because your mind and spirit make it so.

The mental, emotional and spiritual levels of giving

Mental

As stated earlier in the chapter entitled "Expanding your mind--the pursuit of knowledge and wisdom," our minds are extremely powerful. One of the things that hold people back from making a lot of money is fear. The fear of losing your money can keep you from making profitable investments. Fear can keep you from buying an investment property because you are worried that you may get bad tenants. The fear of failure can hold you back from starting your own business. The fear of rejection can keep you from building a successful network marketing business. These fears may never come true yet they can hold you back just the same.

When you give money, you meet fear head-on. By giving you are saying to yourself, "I am not afraid of losing my money, and I am proving it by giving it away." When you give you know that there is more out there to get. You know that giving is not losing, it is only planting seeds for your future harvest. If you are afraid to give because you think that your money will be lost forever, then you deny yourself the ability to receive abundance.

Emotional

It feels good to give. Knowing that you have helped someone who was in need can bring you heartfelt satisfaction and an enormous sense of self-worth. Giving will bring joy into your life. We believe that deep down we all have the desire to be needed. That desire is met the moment that you give. Giving can make you feel like you are part of something much bigger than yourself. It can make you emotionally wealthy.

Spiritual

Look at your money like this. Hold out your hand--palm facing up. Now close your hand into a tight fist. If we poured sand on top of your fist, how much sand would you receive? Now open up your hand and form a slight cup. If we poured sand into your hand now, how much would you receive? If you hold on to your money so tightly that you can't let go of it, then more money cannot be poured into your hands. But if you open your hands to give, your hands remain open to receive.

When you give you become an attracting force. Opportunities and money are attracted to you. Just like in an earlier example, you become like a magnet and money acts like iron filings. The only difference is that the reaction is not necessarily instantaneous. If you give today, that doesn't mean that you will receive tomorrow. When you give to someone or something, that doesn't mean that you will get your return from that same source. If you plant in the spring, you may have to wait until fall for your harvest.

Giving money is a spiritual experience. The Bible says, "Give, and it will be given to you. A good measure, pressed down, shaken together and running over, will be poured into your lap. For with the measure you use, it will be measured to you." We believe that when we give to others, we give to God.

Most, if not all, of our millionaire friends give away at least 10 percent of their money. They know that it is one of the principles of wealth creation. John D. Rockefeller gave 10 percent of his income from the time he was a little boy until the day he died. A tenth of one's income is known as a tithe. Mr. J. C. Penny, founder of one of the largest chain stores in the world, started tithing 10 percent and continued to increase that amount until he was giving away 90 percent of his income and keeping 10 percent. It was on this 10 percent that he became a multimillionaire.

Perhaps you were one of the people who said that you didn't think that you could afford to invest any money. If so, you probably think that it would be impossible for you to tithe. As in the investment example--you cannot afford *not* to tithe. Earlier we mentioned that you should pay yourself first. We suggested that you invest 10 percent of your income and learn to live off of the rest. If you really want to have great abundance, pay your tithe first, pay yourself next, and then live off of the rest. Do this and you will be amazed at how well your financial house comes into order.

Where to give

If you attend a place of worship, then start there. If not, then find a charity that you believe in and give there. There are also a lot of sponsorship programs where you can feed hungry people all over the world. Give and you will get much more in return.

We have partnered with Children's Hunger Fund giving $1.00 for every book and $3.00 for every audio program of Honeymoon Marriage purchased. These funds will go to feed, clothe and shelter those in need. For more information regarding Children's Hunger Fund, go to www.honeymoonmarriage.com and click on the keyword "Children's Hunger Fund". Thank you for helping us help those in need.

Final thoughts

Congratulations! You made it through the money chapter of this book. We know that you may not have expected the topic of money to be discussed in a relationship book, however, money touches every area of our lives. If our money situation is out of control, then odds are good that other areas of our life are hurting because of it. Eliminate the financial pressures in your life and you will be free to experience the Honeymoon Marriage.

As a follow up to this chapter, we highly recommend that you buy a copy of The One Minute Millionaire written by our friends and best selling authors, Mark Victor Hansen and Robert G. Allen. They are on a mission to create one million enlightened millionaires within the next ten years and there is no reason why you can't be one of them.

CHAPTER 17

GROW TOGETHER BY DREAMING TOGETHER

When was the last time you dreamed? We're not talking about the dreams that you have when you are sleeping; we are talking about the dreams that you have when you are awake.

As children, we would dream all of the time. We would imagine ourselves as some superhero able to accomplish anything that our minds could conceive or dream of, the things that we would rather be doing or places that we would rather be. Pretend, make-believe and dreaming of something exciting was part of our everyday lives. It was fun. Can you remember what you used to dream about as a child? As we progressed through grade school our dreams started to become a little fuzzy. We were taught to color within the lines, to cooperate, not to make waves and to never question authority. Our original thoughts and dreams were slowly being replaced by the thoughts of the collective. We were being programmed to lose some of our identity and not to think on our own.

When we entered middle school we were exposed to more of the same. As if that wasn't bad enough, we also became more self-aware and peer pressure started to raise its ugly head. Not only did our teachers demand that we fit in, but we also wanted to fit in with our peers. If you were different, you were teased. As you know, kids can be so cruel. Our individuality started to fade even more. Sure we thought we were different, we thought we were doing what we wanted to do, but unconsciously we were falling prey to social conditioning. These can be the toughest years for most kids. A part of them is crying out to be themselves and another part of them longs to belong.

This sense of belonging is very powerful. We all want to fit in and feel like we belong. This feeling can be so strong that we will give up our desires (and stifle our dreams) to be like everyone else. Our friend Trev told us a story of when he was serving lunch to middle school students. As the kids were going through the line he would ask them if they wanted french fries. As you know, kids love french fries. One of the kids was goofing around and didn't hear the question, so he said no. The next kid in line saw that the kid in front of him said no so he also declined. About fifteen kids in a row said no even though they loved french fries. That cycle continued until one kid didn't notice that the one in front of him said no so he said yes. The first thought that came to us when we heard this story was "Maybe that is why 5 percent of Americans own 95 percent of the wealth. Maybe we are robbing from our potential success by wanting to go with the flow. After all, if you strive to become extremely successful, you won't be doing what most people are doing."

We had never thought of it like that before. The desire to want to fit in and belong goes hand-in-hand with the fear of rejection and ridicule. Unfortunately, many of us carry these middle school feelings into our adult lives.

As we progressed through high school, we started to regain some of our own uniqueness. We were still being taught to think within the box, however, we started to dream again. These dreams came in all different sizes and colors. Perhaps you dreamed of making the team, dating Joe Cool or Ms. Popular, becoming President of your class, becoming valedictorian, passing history class or just getting out of school.

As graduation from high school or college was drawing closer, perhaps you started to dream of the good life. No more teachers, no more school and no more books. Freedom at last! Now you could get a good job, buy the new car and wear the nice clothes. You dreamed of a very bright future, one filled with possibilities. Then as you grew up and took on responsibilities your dreams began to fade. Now instead of dreaming of life's possibilities, you started to become more practical. Slowly but surely our dreams were no longer part of your life. And if you were to dream again, your friends, family and peers would only ridicule you calling you a crazy dreamer or something to that effect. Who is really the crazy one--the "dreamer" or the "realist"? The one who is excited about his or her future life or the one who is stuck in a rut with no hope of getting out?

Do you remember the moral of the story of the *Wizard of Oz*? The Tin Man wanted a heart, the Scarecrow wanted a brain and the Lion wanted courage. At the end of the story they realized that they had already possessed what they wanted. They just needed to believe. Dreaming is believing.

A dream is nothing more than a compilation of our imagined thoughts. Our imagination is a very important part of our being. As mentioned earlier, psychologists have determined that our subconscious mind cannot differentiate between an actual event and one that is vividly imagined. That is an extremely important fact to consider because our thoughts can control who we become. Every great moneymaking idea, every invention, every improvement in every aspect of life begins as a thought. A thought is the spark that starts the imagination on fire. If we allow our imagination to run free it will ignite our creativity, become a desire and then a dream, which in time can become an expectation. Our expectations will then become our reality. As mentioned in Chapter 14, you can if you think you can. This is so very true; unfortunately the converse is also true. You can't if you think you can't. Unfortunately, the latter is where many people live their lives, unable to even imagine a better way of life for themselves. We have asked many people what they would do with their lives if time and money were no object. Most of them really didn't know. They stopped dreaming a long time ago. Life had beaten them up and they felt that there was no way out.

The good news is that we can control our thoughts and that our dreams can come true. Dreaming is not child's play. It is a vital part of success in every aspect of life. Dream big and dream often. Write down your dreams. Post them where you can see them every day. Read them out loud to yourself when you first awake and before you go to sleep. Another powerful exercise is to write down your dream life in a movie script format.

The following is an example that Darren wrote years ago:
"It is Tuesday night October 12, 2004. I am excited about tomorrow, but before I can retire for the evening, there is something that I must find. I open the French doors to the storage closet hoping that it is still there. I remember putting it in here years ago, but for some reason I can't find it. While continuing to look, memories flash into my mind. Memories of long ago, a time when I used this missing item often. The memories are so faint today. It is as if they belong to someone else. A smile comes to my face and then a chuckle. Most people

would not have any problem finding theirs; however, my lifestyle is no longer like that of the masses. I now call my own shots.

There it is, I have finally found it. Wow, I almost forgot what it looked like. It is covered with dust and I'm not sure if it still works. I haven't had to use it in so long. Today it's very name makes me cringe. Alarm clock. To think that I allowed someone so much control over my life that they dictated when I had to get up almost every day. Those days will never come again. I am now in control of my own destiny. I go to sleep whenever I want and for as long as I want. I eat whenever I want and wherever I want. I work whenever I want and for as long as I want. I play whenever I want. I work out when I want to. I am no longer tied to a limited amount of vacation time. I can travel to any destination at any time and stay for as long as I wish.

So why am I looking for my alarm clock? *Money Magazine* invited Donna and me to their corporate office to do a feature article on us. Our flight leaves O'Hare at 9:00 a.m. and I don't want to be late. Apparently there aren't very many couples that have amassed a net worth of $10 million in their thirties and are teaching others how to do the same. Not very many people are impressed by the professional athlete or movie star that is rolling in the dough, but for the 'average' person to have arrived, now that is a story that sells.

The morning has arrived. What do you know--we woke up before the piercing sound of the alarm clock could scare us out of our peaceful slumber. I look at the clock and say, 'well, it looks like it is back to the closet for you.' Our bags are already packed, the house is locked and the alarm is set. Now for the next big decision, which car do we take? As we walk into our four-car garage we take inventory of the mood that we are in. Do we take the Ferrari F355 Spider, or the BMW X5 4.4i Sports Activity Vehicle? It is a gorgeous summer day so we opt for the Ferrari.

The wind blows in our faces as we wind down our cobblestone driveway and head for the road. There is something therapeutic about driving a convertible. Everyone should own one. Donna and I look at each other and just smile. No words are necessary; we can read each other's mind. This is the life. It has been worth all of the hard work, persistence, determination and willpower. Looking back, the effort that it took to get here wasn't really all that difficult. Life is grand!"

*"Yes, you can be a dreamer and a doer too, if you will
remove one word from your vocabulary: impossible."*
- H. Robert Schuller -

A dream is a very powerful thing. The above dream was focused toward money and work and today we are both self-employed and rarely wake up to an alarm clock. Our dream movie script today is quite different as its primary focus is directed toward improving people's lives.

Your "daydream" can be about anything that you would like. You can picture the perfect vacation, your dream house, helping others, reaching new levels of success, or even the Honeymoon Marriage. Make sure that your dreams are not just one-sided. When dreaming about the perfect marriage, picture in your mind what *you* are doing to make it so. Then picture how your spouse responds. Make your dream as real as you can and pack it full of emotion. Don't just see it but feel it. How does having the ideal relationship feel to you?

This dreaming stuff may seem like a bunch of pie in the sky mumbo jumbo to you. If that is true, then a lot of the other suggestions we have made may seem a little hard for you to believe as well. You weren't taught these kinds of things in school. Your parents may have never told you to dream big dreams. Your friends may consist of a group of people who never dream together. We understand how you feel. If this is the first time that you have been exposed to these kinds of thoughts, then you may have to take a giant leap of faith. All we can say is that dreaming works. You have God-given talents and abilities. A dream may be all that you need in order to access them.

Dream together as a couple. There is something very powerful that happens when two like-minded people come together united in a single cause. When you begin to believe that your dreams can come true, hope starts to fill the part of your life where despair used to live. Hope is a very powerful thing. Hope can turn depression into anticipation, boredom into excitement and a strained relationship into an awesome one.

*"Love does not consist in gazing at each other,
but in looking outward together
in the same direction."*
- Antoine de Saint-Exupéry -

You may still think that dreaming is not being realistic. What is realistic? What is reality? As discussed earlier, your reality is whatever you focus on. You have the choice to focus on the bad, the past and how things will only get worse. Or you can focus on the good, the future and how things will only get better. The latter is where dream building comes in. Get together as a couple and determine where you want to be. Where do you want to live? What kind of a house do you want to live in? What kind of cars do you want to drive? Where do you want to send your kids to college? What kind of a relationship do you want to have together? Make dream building a part of your daily activities. Magic starts to happen when husband and wife dream together. How can your relationship get stale when you are excited about the future? How can you *grow* apart when you are *planning* together? How can you fall out of love when you love sharing ideas and life with each other? Keep the honeymoon alive by looking forward to your future life together. Look forward to a future filled with passion, enthusiasm and hope (it can't hurt to throw a little romance in there either).

Dreaming together, thinking of life's possibilities and working together toward your common goals will keep your marriage fresh and exciting. Find other like-minded, fun-loving couples to hang out with. Look for mentors who will cause you to dream even bigger dreams. We are amazed when we hear extremely successful people talk about their mentors. These are the people who cause them to think bigger thoughts and dream bigger dreams. Our mentors have mentors. Their mentors have mentors and so forth. Sometimes in order for us to dream big enough, we need to borrow the dreams of others. One of our mentors, Robert Allen, once said that if you believe that you can obtain your goals, then you haven't dreamed big enough. He said that you need to set goals that are so incredible that you have no idea how you are going to reach them. Then get to work and make them happen.

Perhaps having a Honeymoon Marriage is too big of a dream for you. Don't let that stop you from doing everything that you can to make it happen. Many couples have a Honeymoon Marriage and so can you. It won't happen overnight, but if you do your part and never give up, it will happen. The following steps can help you in your dream building exercises:

1. Decide what it is that you want to have.
2. Believe that it is possible for you to have it.
3. Go somewhere quiet, close your eyes, and envision yourself having what it is that you want. Do this for at least fifteen minutes every day.

4. Imagine how good it feels. Experience all of the emotions that go along with having what you want. Make it seem real.

5. Write a movie script, in the present tense, of your perfect day like the example above. Give as much detail as you can.

6. Read this script out loud every day when you first awake and again before you go to bed. Memorize your script so that you can say it to yourself whenever you want.

7. Believe that you will have your dream life.

8. Anytime during the day that you have some free time, recite your script (out loud if you are alone and to yourself if there are people around).

9. Know that this reality is on its way to you.

10. Be thankful.

Think and talk about your possibilities as a couple instead of always thinking and talking about your limitations. Dream big dreams and believe that they can become a reality. Rely on each other for support and never let yourself or your spouse lose hope. Life is a wonderful journey and together you are unstoppable!

CHAPTER 18

TURNING EACH OTHER'S
TALENTS INTO $$$

The greatest team that has ever been assembled is that of husband and wife. United, you are unstoppable. Divided, you will come up short. While it has been said that there is a woman behind every successful man, the same can be said about the successful woman. A marriage is a partnership in every sense of the word. One's success is the other's success. One's failures are the other's failures. You need the help of your spouse and he or she needs your help for both of you to reach your full potential.

> *"No man is an island, entire of itself;*
> *every man is a piece of the continent, a part of the main."*
> *- John Donne -*

Within your marriage is the key to financial success. You have the ability to do more good or more damage to your spouse's success than anyone else. You can build your spouse up or you can tear him or her down. You can be your partner's best supporter or you can be a thorn in his or her side. Both are very easy to do, but only one will increase your wealth while giving you the piece of mind to enjoy it.

Maximizing your financial success as a couple will be largely dependent upon the following two areas:

1. Discovering your spouse's talents and desires.
2. Encouraging and supporting each other.

One way to increase your wealth-building capacity is to recognize and utilize each other's talents. The first step is discovering what your spouse's talents and interests are. This can be done by following the guidance laid out in the chapters entitled "Discovering who your spouse is" and "Discovering your spouse's desires." Once you have discovered what your spouse is good at, what he or she wants to do, and more importantly, what he or she is passionate about, then find a way to turn that talent into money.

> *"Find out what you like best and then get*
> *someone to pay you for doing it."*
> *- Katherine Whitehorn -*

Remember, just because you are good at doing something doesn't mean that that is what you should be doing. Ask your spouse what he or she would love to do if given the chance. What kind of a job or career does your mate think would be fun, exciting and rewarding? What would your spouse like to change about his or her current job? Don't worry about your experience or education. Only focus on what you want.

> *"The question should be, is it worth trying to do,*
> *not can it be done?"*
> *- Allard Lowenstein -*

If you could do anything for a living, what would it be? Ask each other this question often. What was fun and exciting yesterday may be monotonous and unchallenging today. There is no doubt that you will be more successful doing the things that you enjoy. And your marriage will also improve when you and your spouse are doing something that you are each passionate about. Being passionate about your career can spill over into your relationship.

The second thing that you can do as a couple to maximize your success is to encourage each other. We live in a very negative world and there are more than just a few people out their that would love to rain on your parade and steal your dreams. We need the encouragement and support of our spouse to stay the course and never give up on our dreams. The following words and phrases should be added to your daily conversation with your spouse:

- You are awesome!
- I believe in you.
- You can do it.
- You can make your dreams come true.
- What can I do to help?

- You are my hero!
- I love you.
- I'm so proud of you.
- You are extremely talented.
- All of your hard work will pay off big time.
- Hang in there. These obstacles are only stepping-stones on your way to success.
- Tomorrow is a new day.

Do everything that you can to encourage, support and help your spouse achieve his or her dreams. The only way that your mate can give you all that he or she has to give is if your mate becomes all that he or she can become.

The number one cause of stress in a marriage
We feel that it is very important to end this chapter by reemphasizing how important it is to come to agreement as a couple regarding your money. As mentioned earlier, the number-one reason stated for marital break-ups is money. As many as 90 percent of divorced couples say that it was money issues that drove them apart. Those numbers are way too high for us to treat this subject lightly.

Oftentimes disagreements regarding how money is spent or invested cause more strain on a marriage than not making enough of it. Money can be a tool to help you build upon a great marriage or it can be a weapon that can destroy your marriage. That's right, destroy your marriage. We know of several couples who are either on the verge of a nervous breakdown or are moving one giant step closer to divorce court because of money issues. When money pressures are high, something has to give. Ignoring it won't make it go away. Trying to "keep the peace" by not talking about it won't make things better. These two options will only make matters worse. And don't fall into the trap of "his money", "her money." That may sound like a great compromise, but it won't draw you closer together as a couple.

Honest, open, and frequent conversation about your money is the relief valve that keeps the pressure in check. Without it, you run the very probable risk of an explosion, one that can cause your world to collapse.

How often do you sit down with your spouse and talk about your money? Do you do it every day, every month, once a year or never? This is very important. If you want to have a Honeymoon Marriage, you need to talk about your money often. If you want to avoid being a statistic, you need to stop avoiding money

TURN EACH OTHER'S TALENTS INTO $$$

conversations and meet this potential threat head-on. We know we sound like a broken record, but we wouldn't be writing this book if we didn't sincerely want to help you to improve your marriage.

Schedule a time this week when the two of you can get together for several hours to talk about money. Talk about the following:

- How much money is spent every month and on what.
- Itemize your debts and tally a grand total.
- Put together a debt reduction plan.
- Talk about what you think your money should and should not be spent on. When it comes to your money, it is time to act like a responsible adult and not like a kid in a candy store.

*"No matter what age we happen to be today,
most of us are still acting like five year old children
when it comes to our money."*
- Suze Orman -
Author of the #1 New York Times Bestseller,
The 9 Steps to Financial Freedom

- Talk about where you think your money should and should not be invested.
- Discover what each other would like to be doing for a living and then support each other in finding a way to make it happen.
- Decide which profit centers you will add to your income portfolio.
- Be your partner's biggest fan. Support and encourage him or her every step of the way.

Separately, you can accomplish a lot. Together, the sky is the limit. Make your marriage partnership as fruitful as possible. Support, encourage, and love each other and know that you can accomplish anything that you wish.

INCREASE THE FUN FACTOR IN YOUR RELATIONSHIP

PLAY WITH ME—BRINGING OUT YOUR INNER CHILD

Have you ever seen someone who looked twenty years older than he or she really was? The person might have seemed down and looked like he or she was having a really bad day. When commenting on that fact you might get feedback from someone who knows the person saying, "Yeah, he's had a pretty tough life." Stress and the pressures of life can age people beyond their years. Conversely, a light heart and a playful spirit can cause people to look and feel much younger than their biological age. Inside all of us is our very own fountain of youth, and we can tap into this resource at any time. All you have to do is play and become a little more childlike.

"A light heart lives long."
- William Shakespeare -

Perhaps you feel like your marriage has grown stale. Maybe it doesn't have the same spark that it used to when you first got married. You may even feel like you have been married twenty years longer than you have (and we don't mean that in a good way). How would you like to find the marital fountain of youth? The fountain that can give your relationship the excitement that it used to have? The fountain that will give you the Honeymoon Marriage? That resource is available to you and you can tap into it today if you would like.

You have probably heard the saying, "The only difference between men and boys is the price of their toys." In a way, this is absolutely true for both men and women. Deep down within all of us is that little boy or little girl who never grew up. There is a part of us that still wants to run and play. That part of us that is saying, "Look at me. Look at me." We may have stopped saying, "Can Johnny come out to play?" however, we have not stopped wanting to play. We still want to have fun. We still want to experience that childlike fun and excitement.

Tapping into the marital fountain of youth is as simple as bringing out your inner child by playing and having fun with your spouse. That's right, play with your spouse. Joke around together. Do crazy things that make you both laugh. Have fun. Not just once in a while, but try to have fun together often. Schedule fun events. Have fun at home, at the park, everywhere you go. Having fun causes you to change your focus from the current pressures of life and places it on the fun-filled activity. Increasing the fun factor in your relationship will keep it fresh and exciting.

Hopefully it hasn't been that long since you have had a really fun time. If it has, then try and remember back to how much fun you used to have as a child. Close your eyes and relive those past experiences. Make the memories so vivid and real that they put a smile on your face. Imagine what it would feel like to have those feelings back again. Who says that you can't? Who says that just because you are a grownup you can't have fun anymore? You can and you should.

As a child, your imagination and desire to have fun ruled the day. Then you grew up, got a job and took on other responsibilities. It didn't take long for the fun to start to fade. You still had fun from time to time, but it wasn't the same as when you were a kid. You became very serious. You started to take life and yourself more seriously, oftentimes to the point of squelching the child that still lives within you.

Life can become very stale and boring when we stop having fun. As the stresses of life grow, it becomes even more important to play and have fun. So how can you have more fun in your life? How can you bring out your inner child?

Learn by example

One of the best ways to learn how to do something well is to find someone else who is doing it and then do what they do. They say that imitation is the greatest form of flattery. It is also one of the quickest ways to success in any area of your life. If you have an interest in real estate, buy real estate books, go to real estate seminars, and talk to as many people as you can who are successful in real estate. Having a mentor or role model to follow is the quickest and least painful way to success. So whom do we turn to in order to learn how to bring out our inner child? You guessed it. Study an expert. Learn from a child.

This holds true for all people in every stage of their life. Whether you have no children of your own, have young ones, teenagers, or your children are grown and on their own, the study of children is a subject that you need to visit or revisit. Of course it isn't good enough to just watch children, you need to play with them, talk to them, listen to them and treat them like a little friend. When you can get to the point where you are having a blast with your little friend, you have unlocked the magic that rests inside of you.

You should look forward to spending time with children as much as they look forward to spending time with you. Grandparents have the advantage. They have a relationship that is already set up to take advantage of this great learning experience. Even if you are not a grandparent, you can still experience life through the eyes of a child. You will most likely fit into one of four categories. The following categories show how you can learn from a child expert regardless of your current position in life.

No children. Not having children of your own will not deter you from gaining this wonderful and necessary educational experience. In some cases you may be able to benefit the most because you are not dealing with some of the day-to-day challenges that parents of young children are faced with. You have the ability to experience the joy of being childlike from a different perspective. Since you don't have children, you will need to borrow other people's children. This is the perfect win-win-win scenario in three very important ways.

1. You can give parents an oftentimes much-needed break from their child/children. Remember the chapter on dating your spouse? Well, a couple cannot have a proper date if they bring the kids along, and your free-of-charge baby-sitting service will be a welcomed suggestion. Every couple needs to have time away as husband and wife even if they don't think that they do.
2. Kids also need a break from their parents. And what kid doesn't like to spend time with a fun-loving adult? It means a lot to

children to know that an adult takes an interest in them and in their life. It makes them feel special that you want to spend time with them, and in turn they want to spend time with you. Kids need good adult role models in their lives.

3. You come out the big winner. Your selfless involvement in the life of a child makes a difference in the world. When you give of yourself, you end up getting even more in return. Your life will become richer, more meaningful and productive, and you have the opportunity to have fun like a kid again.

If you have nieces or nephews that live near by, make it a point to spend time with them often. Awesome memories of their childhood experiences with their aunt and uncle will be created.

Young children. You have the greatest opportunity to participate in the teach-learn cycle with young children. Every day you have the opportunity to take advantage of the gift that God has given to you. Your family has built-in examples of how to take life and yourself less seriously and how to have fun and dream like a child. Your learning curve can be a little more challenging than that of the person with no children. You have the responsibility to provide for your family, are pulled in several directions at the same time and have to balance the roles of friend-parent-disciplinarian. Your first and foremost responsibility is to be your child's parent, not necessarily his or her best friend, however, you can still have fun, dream and play make-believe with the best of them.

The scope of this book is not to discuss parenting skills, however, it is important to follow some basic guidelines that will improve your learning experience.

1. **Listen.** Everyone wants to know that he or she has been heard, and children are no exception. Listen to them as though they have something very important to say, because they do. Children can teach us so many things if we only give them the chance. They can also increase your fun factor tenfold.

We had planned a trip to Chuck E. Cheese's to celebrate our nephew Zac's seventh birthday. We were in the front seat while Zac was in the back singing to the CD we were playing (his parents had the same CD at home). Then out of the blue he asks, "Do you think that cats have dreams? They do, just like dogs." We all had a great laugh including Zac. He didn't know what we were laughing about, but he knew that whatever it was that he said, we liked it. When they have a question or want to tell you something make sure to stop, look at them, and listen. They are your most valuable assets.

2. **Answer their questions.** Avoid using the phrase, "because I told you so." The question "why" is not necessarily a challenge of your parental authority. As you know, kids are very curious and they are always in learning mode. When you tell them something and they ask why, your response of "because I told you so" will not teach them anything about life and it will not improve your relationship with them either. As a matter of fact, it will most likely frustrate them or perhaps make them think that you enjoy being a dictator. We used to hate hearing "because I told you so," and there is no way we would accept that kind of an answer as an adult.

How would you feel if you found yourself in the same situation? Your boss tells you to change something that you were doing, but it doesn't make any sense to you. You think about it for a minute and then you ask her why she wanted it to be done in that manner. She tells you, "because I told you so" with a look in her eye that says, "and don't ask me again." How would that make you feel? Do you really think that your child feels any different when told the same thing? We are not saying that children should be treated like adults, however, we should use every question as an opportunity to teach them a lesson.

3. **Play with them.** This is the easy part, however, it is oftentimes not scheduled into our busy lifestyle. If you do not have the time or energy to play with your kids every day, then it is time for a priority check. Why are you so busy that you can't play with your kids? If your answer is because you are working hard to provide a good life for them, then you are missing the point. Your kids need you; not necessarily what you think is a better life. They want and need your time, your attention, and your love. It is much better to make $30,000 per year and spend a lot of time enjoying life with your family than it is to make $130,000 per year and miss the most valuable time of your life and theirs. Of course, we believe that you can have both as discussed in the chapter entitled "The 5 simple steps to financial abundance."

If you want to have a close relationship with your children when they are grown, then you have to bond with them when they are young. Spending time with them is great, but nothing can replace how they feel when you play with them. Playing is also an excellent stress reliever and it can give you a healthier perspective on life. Don't miss this opportunity and don't let your kids miss out on it either.

Many studies have shown that one of the most bonding experiences that you can have with your children is to go camping as a family. This will create loving memories that will last the rest of your life and theirs.

Teenage or grown children. This is the time in your life where you may be the most reluctant to spend time with children. After all, you just spent the better part of your life raising yours. This is very understandable, and a brief break from children is perfectly acceptable. However, don't keep children out of your life for long, otherwise you may grow old quicker than you would like.

You are now in your forties or fifties and there is a strong tendency for the mid-life crisis to creep in. You may even start to feel like you are getting old. You don't have to think this way. You are just now starting to enter your most productive years. You have lived life, experienced many things, and have a lot to offer society. One of the best ways to feel young again is to change your state of mind. Think of yourself as being young and full of energy with a lot to offer the world. As a matter of fact, write those words down on a note card and repeat it out loud to yourself every morning and night. Repeat the following statement to yourself on that schedule every day until you believe and feel it:

> *"I am young and full of energy. I wake up every morning excited and ready to make a major impact in my environment. People like and respect me. They look at me as someone with knowledge and experience beyond my years. I love life and life loves me back. I will always feel young, fit and full of life. Today will be one of the best days of my life!"*

Repeat that day and night for thirty straight days and see for yourself what a difference a few words can make. It doesn't matter if you believe it at first, do it anyway. What do you have to lose besides the feeling that you are getting old?

Keep children in your life and enjoy life just as they do. Since many couples are waiting longer these days to start a family, it may be a while before you are playing with your grandchildren. Just like the no children example, you have the opportunity to really bless a young couple's life by offering to watch their kids for a night every month. This will also set a good example for your older kids who may still be living at home. Any time you do a good deed that goes above and beyond the call of duty, you set a good example for your children.

Grandchildren. You are never too old to act and feel young. Sure your body may not be what it used to be, but you live your life primarily in your mind through your thoughts, and what you think about can affect how you feel. Your daily affirmation may be as follows:

> *"I feel vibrant and alive. Today I have the opportunity to enrich my life by enriching the lives of others. My opinions, thoughts and feelings are very important. People need and want what I have to offer them. They appreciate me for my kindness and willingness to share with them my golden nuggets of wisdom. I feel as young and productive as I did twenty years ago and I look forward to the next twenty years. Today will be a day to remember, a day that will bring me much joy. I love life and everyone knows it!"*

As a grandparent, you have built in youth machines. They are called your grandchildren. As the saying goes, "If I knew how great it was to have grandchildren, I would have had them first." Spend time with your grandchildren. If they live close, spend time with them at least once a month. If they live far away, try to see them on every holiday and once or twice during their summer break.

Don't just exist

When you stop having fun, you stop living and start existing. When you take the fun out of your marriage, you lose more than just the fun experience itself. You also lose the potential closeness that can only be gained by playing with your spouse. Joke around, laugh, tickle each other once and a while, plan fun events, chase your mate around the house, etc. When you have fun with your spouse it makes him or her feel special and wanted. In a way it reaffirms your loyalty and commitment to your mate. That may sound strange, but whom did you play with when you were young? Who were your best friends? Your best friends were the kids that you spent the most time and did the most things with.

Play with your spouse

Take out a piece of paper and start writing down all of your fond childhood memories. What made you the happiest? What did you love so much that you could do it every day? We don't change as much as we think we do as we get older. If you are a woman reading this chapter, it is very important for you to realize that just because your husband is no longer a kid, it doesn't mean that he no longer likes to play. For the most part, men like to play and if they cannot be playing, they like to watch other people play (i.e., sporting events.)

Not only does your husband still like to play; he also still wants a playmate. He may not admit it or even realize it, but he wants you to be his playmate. When you take an interest in his interests, it makes him feel closer to you. This bonding experience is to him like meaningful communication is to you. Remember in the chapter entitled "Discover who you are and who your spouse is," we discussed how little boys and girls play differently? Little girls tend to talk with their girl friends, whereas little boys tend to play and roughneck with their boy friends. Things don't change that much when we get older.

> ***Our bike rides:*** Even though Darren is no longer a little boy, he still loves to ride his bike. As for me (Donna), I could take it or leave it, but I ride with him because he needs me to be his playmate. He will even thank me afterwards and tell me what a great time he had. Likewise, he will do the things that I like to do even though he would prefer doing something else. Neither one of us feels slighted and we both always have a great time doing what the other likes to do the most. It isn't the enjoyment of the activity that matters the most; it is the enjoyment of each other and knowing that we are doing something that makes our partner happy. You see, we don't look at our marriage as a give and take relationship. We consider our marriage to be a give and receive relationship. There is a big difference between the two.

Be careful not to fall into the trap of "his activities/her activities." We're not saying that you have to do everything together, just be aware of the fact that the more things that you do together the lower your odds of "growing apart" will be. If he likes to watch the football game, then watch the football game with him. If she likes to go shopping, then go shopping with her. It won't kill you to spend time doing the things that your spouse enjoys. You may even find that the activity doesn't matter that much, what's important is that you are spending time with your lover. Look at it as enjoying your spouse, not just enjoying the activity.

The best-case scenario is to find activities that you both enjoy doing. Both of you should make a list of the twenty to thirty things that you enjoy doing the most. Trade lists with each other and put a checkmark next to all of the things that you like to do as well. Compare notes and start spending time doing the things that you both enjoy. Don't limit your activities to only the ones on your list. Discovery and variety can be the spice of life. Learn new things together. Learn how to golf, play tennis, play chess, scuba dive, cross country ski, draw and paint together, go to sporting events, learn new card games, go hiking or backpacking, bike together, go fishing, go to concerts, etc. You may even consider writing a book together. We can tell you from personal experience that writing this book together has been an awesome bonding experience for us.

Be best friends

Is your spouse your best friend? Do you like to spend more time with your mate than with anyone else? We believe that the closest couples are also the best of friends. It is hard to spend time away from your best friend without missing him or her. It is difficult to stay mad at your best friend. Time flies when you are spending it with your best friend. Your best friend may not be perfect, may irritate you at times, may let you down, but you love him or her just the same. After all, he or she is your best friend.

If you and your spouse are not currently the best of friends, then apply the truths that you have learned so far in this book, and remember to have fun and play with your mate often.

CHAPTER 20

BEING
SPONTANEOUS

The world that we live in is very fast paced and structured. We go from event to event without giving ourselves time to relax and enjoy the moment. If it isn't planned, it oftentimes doesn't get done. We live our lives as slaves to the clock. Time controls us instead of us controlling it. Planning and structure are important. They help us to be stable, efficient and productive. However, if your life is too structured and too fast paced, you can become somewhat insensitive to the needs of others and out of step with nature. In order for us to be more in tune with our surroundings, we need to have some unscheduled time and be more receptive and flexible when we are in our scheduled time. It is OK to be very focused, but not at the expense of missing an opportunity to make a positive impact in someone else's life.

Everyone could use a little more spontaneity in his or her life and marriage. We all have the ability to be more spontaneous. Contrary to popular belief, being spontaneous is a matter of choice. You can choose to be more spontaneous just like you can choose to become more organized. The word spontaneous is derived from the Latin word *sponte*, which means of "one's free will, voluntarily." Spontaneity doesn't have to be an action based on an impulse or thought that just popped into your head. It doesn't mean reacting without thinking. On the contrary, you may put a lot of thought into being spontaneous. Let's say that you have a thought to do something special for your spouse. The first thought that comes into your mind can be handled as follows:

1. You dismiss the thought as not being practical, rationalize it away or second guess whether or not you should follow though with it. You may even be concerned with what *others* may think.
2. You act on the thought right away.
3. You think about it, add to it and make it even better than the original thought.

We all have spontaneous thoughts. Some of us choose to act on them, others do not. Being spontaneous does not mean throwing caution to the wind. It just means listening to your gut feelings and acting on them. If you move through life at too fast a pace, always concerned with beating the clock, you may not be able to hear that still small voice inside of you. Slow down and quiet your mind. Relax and live in the moment. Listen to what your heart tells you to do and then act on it.

Every marriage could use a little more spontaneity. The Honeymoon Marriage is not complete without it. Plan on being more spontaneous. Put aside your busy schedule every once in a while and exercise your free will to follow your natural tendencies to do what you know your spouse would appreciate. The following are just a few examples of spontaneity at work:

- Give flowers for no particular occasion.
- Go to the store and pick out the perfect card that describes your feelings for your spouse.
- Write each other little love notes and love letters.
- Surprise your spouse with a weekend getaway.
- Hug and kiss whenever you get the urge.

Bonus romantic tip
This Valentine's Day we decided to do something spontaneous. Instead of the typical Valentine's Day dinner that most people enjoy, we decided to spend half of the day together. We would work until noon and then take the rest of the day off. That was our initial thought as described in option two above. The more we thought about it the more we wanted to make a whole day of it and that was what we did (option three).

We woke up when we were done sleeping and went to Blueberry Hill, an excellent breakfast restaurant in town. We then went home and played games with each other for about forty-five minutes prior to going for an hour walk. After we came home and took a shower we headed to "bd's mongolian barbeque" for an early dinner. Then it was off to see a movie followed by refreshments at

Starbucks. We sat, talked and enjoyed each other's company at Starbucks for well over an hour. We then headed home, sat on the couch, snuggled up close and watched a video.

The best part about spending the whole day together was that fact that we could enjoy all of the above activities at off-peak hours. We ate breakfast when most people had already gone to work. We ate dinner right in between the lunch and dinner hours. We went to the twilight movie while most people were still at work. And we enjoyed a quiet evening at Starbucks while most couples were fighting the crowds for dinner. All of this contributed to the best Valentine's Day we have ever spent with each other.

We would highly recommend that you make a day of it every Valentine's Day. It may just be one of the most romantic days of your year. Have your kids spend the night at a friend's house the night before so that they can hitch a ride to school with their friend's parents. Have a sitter pick your kids up from school and watch them at your place the following day. Now you have the whole day, not to mention the night before, all to yourselves. Enjoy!

Be spontaneous and do things for each other that you normally wouldn't do. All the little things that you can do for or say to your spouse add to your overall sense of appreciation and belonging to each other. Remember that it is the small things that make all of the difference in the world.

CHAPTER 21

SMILING LOUDLY—THE HEALING POWER OF LAUGHTER

"Humor is the great thing, the saving thing. The minute it crops up,
all our irritations and resentments slip away,
and a sunny spirit takes their place."
- Mark Twain -

Lighten up
The many pressures of life can weigh us down and even crush our spirit if we are not careful. So far you have been given many tips on how to decrease the amount of pressure that is in your life as well as how to better handle the stress that is left over. Doing all of those things may still not be enough.

You may still need something to take the edge off of your challenges and bring a little more joy into your life. Maybe what you need is as simple as not taking life so seriously. We tend to treat too many things as if they are "life and death" concerns. For some, life is like a war, where you either win or get killed. We have seen parents get into huge fights with their kids over the color and/or length of their hair. Husbands and wives fight over many things that really don't matter in the overall scheme of things. While there are many things worth fighting for, many of the fights that take place in a marital relationship are just plain silly.

Lighten up! Stop being so hard on your spouse and yourself. Stop trying to be perfect and expecting others to do the same. Thank goodness perfection is not a prerequisite for success, happiness and the Honeymoon Marriage. If you want to be truly happy in your marriage, then you are going to have to learn when to let go and let live. Before engaging your partner (or yourself for that matter) in a negative conversation, ask yourself if what you are so worked up about really matters in your journey through life. Will it bring harm to yourself, someone else, or your relationship? If not, ask yourself if it is really worth getting all worked up about.

If you are the kind of person who thinks that life is a war, battle, conflict, etc., then it is time for you to lighten up. Let go of the self-induced pressures that you are placing on yourself, your spouse and ultimately your marriage. Instead of thinking of life as a war, think of it as a gift. Instead of always going into battle, decide that some things aren't worth getting all worked up about. Life is not about conflict it is about enjoyment.

Lighten up and focus on enjoying life more. You don't always have to be right, perfect or even accepted to be happy. As a matter of fact, knowing that you won't always be right, that you can't be perfect and that people will sometimes reject your ideas will relieve much of your pressure and enable you to live a more balanced and happy life. You don't have to prove anything to anybody. All you are responsible for is living the life that you were meant to live and helping others along the way. And as mentioned earlier, happiness is a choice.

"Most people are about as happy
as they make up their minds to be."
- Abraham Lincoln -

A great way to help you lighten up is to put on a happy face.

Smiling loudly
A smile can brighten up a whole room. It can also be very contagious. Have you ever noticed that when you smile at someone he or she typically smiles back? It is amazing to think that you have the ability to change someone's facial expression just by changing yours. Now that's pretty powerful.

The really neat thing about a smile is that it can change the way other people feel. Equally important is the fact that it can change the way you feel as well. Try it out and see for yourself. The next time you are feeling blue, smile really big and see if it doesn't change the way you feel. Try it on your spouse as well. Odds are pretty good that the first words that come out of his or her mouth will be "what are you smiling about?" Of course a great answer would be, "I'm smiling because I am so happy that I am with you." See if that doesn't bring a smile to your mate's face.

A smile can mean so many positive things. A smile can signify happiness, approval, pride, humor, excitement, etc. Don't just let it happen, but rather make it happen. Make it a point to smile at everyone that comes across your path. Smile just because you can. The next time you are at the grocery store, look at the person that you are approaching in the aisle until you make eye contact and then give him or her a smile and say hi. You may have just made someone's day, and it will definitely brighten up yours.

We tend to lose a little human kindness because of our busy, fast-paced, stressed-out lives. Our focus is mostly on ourselves or the task at hand. Our minds are so cluttered with "stuff" that we don't even give a second thought to the people around us. We walk by people without making eye contact. We know that they are there, but we act as though they are not important enough to us to slow down and acknowledge their existence. We appear as though we are self-absorbed and that time will be wasted if we break from our schedule or routine. We know that you don't really believe or think that way, however, your actions may make it appear as though you do.

Many of us escape into our homes, get nestled in, turn on the television and live our life within the confines of our four walls. The futurist Faith Popcorn calls this phenomenon *cocooning*. We think that the word *cocoon* is an excellent word picture for what many of us do, however, for some it is not much different than being in a coma and not being able to interact with the outside world.

As mentioned earlier, not reading is no different than not being able to read. We would like to expand that logic to include the following:

- Not smiling is no different than not being able to smile.
- Not being a friend is no different than not having friends.
- Not interacting with other people on a regular basis (outside of the work environment) is no different than not being able to interact.
- Not letting go, lightening up and enjoying life is no different than not being able to let go, lighten up or enjoy life.

Deep down, that is not who you are and it is not what you want to be. We were designed to have the desire to interact with other human beings, to smile, laugh and joke around. As a matter of fact, one of the most severe punishments one can be subjected to is solitary confinement. No one is an island, and we all need to feel that there are people out there that will accept us just as we are.

Everyone that you will come in contact with is a potential friend that you haven't met yet. And that friend may bless your life more than you could have ever imagined. We need human interaction. It is the way we are wired. When you develop a love for all humanity, you will feel an incredible sense of love being given back to you. When you learn to be less critical of yourself and others, life will in turn be less critical of you. When you smile, you are telling the world that you have something to be happy about. Be kind and smile at everyone, especially your spouse.

Smile as if each person you see is your friend,
And keep love in your heart for everyone.
Through a smile good thoughts you send,
Brightening their life like the morning sun.
Whatever you give will be given back in style,
So only give what you would like in return.
A kind hello, wave, nod or a smile,
Is one of life's simple yet fruitful habits to learn.
- Darren L. McNees -

The next time tensions grow strong between you and your mate, smile at him or her. We were once told that you could tell someone almost anything with a smile on your face. We have done just that on many occasions and it has definitely lightened up the mood. Don't worry about seeming fake. The more you smile the more it becomes part of you until you and your wonderful smile are inseparable. If the above statement regarding saying things with a smile on your face is true, then it would make sense to reason that laughter would have an even stronger impact.

"Once you get people laughing,
they're listening and you can tell them almost anything."
- Herbert Gardner -

When a smile explodes

We trust that you have heard that laughter is the best medicine. Laughter is a great medicine in that it can heal the body, mind and the soul. It is impossible to feel sad, angry, hurt, disappointed or bitter and laugh at the same time. One or the other must go. Either you hold on to your negative emotions and don't laugh, or you laugh and lose your negative emotions. We are not saying that these negative emotions won't come back again, because they will if you allow them to. However, if you fill your life with laughter, you won't have much room left for negative emotions. Your heart and mind cannot live in a vacuum. They must be filled up with something.

One of the first signs that a marriage is in trouble is when the laughter disappears. The laughter disappears because something negative has taken its place. It could be bitterness or unforgiveness, anger, hurt feelings, depression or stress. And like the cause and effect relationship discussed throughout this book, one can help elevate or minimize the effects of the other. Laughter is a great stress reliever, however, when you are under a lot of stress, you are not necessarily in a laughing mood. When you feel like laughing the least, that is the time that you need it the most. You need to take laughter more seriously. If you do, it will better enable you to take life less seriously. Laughter is an important ingredient in the Honeymoon Marriage.

We are not saying that laughter will save a failing marriage, however, it is without a doubt a very important aspect in a marriage and one that should not be overlooked. Laughter can play an important role in the "making up" process as well. When you are upset with your spouse because of something that he or she did or didn't do, nothing breaks the ice like laughter. In the words of Jay Leno, "You can't stay mad at somebody who makes you laugh."

A good sense of humor also makes you a more desirable person to be around. Fun-loving, happy people are a pleasure to spend time with. No one likes to be around a stick-in-the-mud. You will know when you have adequately lightened up when you start to see more humor in life. You will become a more healthy person when you can laugh at yourself instead of getting upset with yourself. Sometimes laughter is the only thing that keeps us sane.

> *"Among those whom I like or admire,*
> *I can find no common denominator,*
> *but among those whom I love, I can:*
> *all of them make me laugh."*
> - W. H. Auden -

Lighten up, smile, and laugh at yourself, at others, and at life. Don't be afraid to be a little goofy, childlike, or even vulnerable. This is your life, it isn't boot camp. Increase the fun factor in your relationship and you will never grow tired of each other, nor will your marriage grow stale. Have fun and enjoy life. Marriage is awesome!

CONCLUSION:
AND THEY LIVED
HAPPILY EVER AFTER

Congratulations! You have now finished what very few married couples will ever start. For that, you should be very proud of yourself. Make the finishing of this book a big deal. Celebrate, pamper yourself, do something this week that is a little out of the norm, something that is fun. You have earned it, so enjoy yourself.

You now know what we consider to be the secrets to achieving the relationship of your dreams. What you do from this point on will determine the quality of the rest of your life. As you know, knowledge is power; however, if you do not use this newly acquired power, it is of little use to you or anyone else for that matter. What you know will not get you results. It is what you do with what you know that will change your life forever.

Your next congratulations is due when you can take a look at yourself and your relationship and say that things have greatly improved.

We would love to hear of your progress and be able to personally congratulate you on your accomplishments. Please go to www.honeymoonmarriage.com and click on the keyword "success story" and tell us your story. With your permission, we may even use your story in our follow up book to Honeymoon Marriage entitled *Passionate Butterflies*™ *- Living the Honeymoon Marriage. Passionate Butterflies* will be an encouraging and inspiring collection of stories of couples just like you who have benefited by applying the principles taught in Honeymoon Marriage.

The final secret to achieving the relationship of your dreams

That's right, there is a final secret, which we have kept undisclosed until now. This secret is powerful and very rewarding. The final secret is taking part in something that is much bigger than yourself. It is contributing to a cause that will have a major impact on society as a whole. It is taking advantage of the *Law of the Harvest* in a major way. The final secret to achieving the relationship of your dreams is to teach others how they too can have the relationship of their dreams.

Something very powerful happens when you help others. Before starting our *Honeymoon Marriage* program we thought that we had a terrific marriage. Once we started helping and encouraging others in *their* marriages, *our* marriage started to improve as well. It makes perfect sense when you think about it. As mentioned throughout this book, we get back whatever we give out in life. Doesn't it make sense then that your marriage will improve when you help others improve their marriages? Some of the wealthiest people that we know are those who teach others how to become wealthy. Some of the happiest people that we know are those who share their happiness with others. Some of the most peaceful people on the planet are those who promote peace. And we believe that if you want to help others improve their marriage, you will experience improvement in your marriage in return.

We know that that may sound a little intimidating at first. We are not suggesting that you have to start marriage improvement seminars, write a book or have the perfect marriage. As you know, the perfect marriage doesn't exist. What we are suggesting is that you become more aware of the people who could benefit from the principles taught throughout this book, encourage them and tell them that you too are working on improving your marriage. When we decided to get out of debt, we told everybody. In doing so, several of these people decided to do the same. When we read a book that we think is good or had an impact on our lives, we suggest it to dozens of people. In doing so we are giving to others. We are giving them hope and a solution to their problems, and in return life takes on a greater meaning. Making a difference in people's lives is an extremely rewarding experience--an experience that money cannot buy.

You don't have to be an expert in order to achieve this kind of rewarding experience. If you have benefited or feel that you will benefit from this book, then suggest it to every couple that you know. Put your pride aside and let them know that you are excited about applying its principles and improving your own marriage. And when you start to see results, don't keep your new found knowledge and experiences to yourself, tell people what you have learned and give them the opportunity to benefit from your experience.

We need your help

It is our vision to save one million marriages within the next ten years. It is impossible for us to reach that goal on our own. We are only two people with a passion to save and improve marriages. If you have ever wanted to belong to something that was much bigger than yourself, then we would love for you to join our team. Only through the combined efforts of people like you, will we ever reach our goal.

Social scientists say that the average adult knows two thousand people by first name. We expect to reach our goal by initiating a grassroots effort, which will spread throughout America through word-of-mouth promotion. We would like to kick off this grassroots effort by teaming up with everyone who shares our vision and would like to contribute toward making this goal become a reality. They will be an encouragement to others and will enthusiastically suggest relationship improvement books like *Honeymoon Marriage* to their friends and family members. This group of people will become members of the *Honeymoon Marriage Encouragement Team*. If you would like to become a member of this team, please go to www.honeymoonmarriage.com and click on the keyword "Encouragement Team" for more information.

And they lived happily ever after

You have within you everything that it takes to have a Honeymoon Marriage. Apply everything that you have learned with passion, persistence and patience. Never give up, because the marriage of your dreams is closer than you think. We hope that we will be able to meet you in the not too distant future and wish you all the happiness that life has to offer.

God Bless,

Darren & Donna

Order Form

Website orders: www.honeymoonmarriage.com
Visa, MasterCard, Discover, American Express
and Checks accepted online.

Telephone orders: (800) 845-1545 toll free. 24-hour order
line. Please have your credit card or check
ready.

Fax orders: (775) 562-2683

Please provide the following information:

Name:_____

Address:_____

City:_____ State:_____ Zip:_____

Telephone:_____

Email address:_____

PRODUCT	QTY	US PRICE	TOTAL
Honeymoon Marriage 6x9 Hardcover Book		$24.95/ea +3.95 S&H*	
Honeymoon Marriage 6 cassette tape Audio Program		$69.95/ea +5.95 S&H	

*$1.95 S&H for each additional book

Payment:
❏ VISA   ❏ MasterCard   ❏ Discover   ❏ American Express

❏ Check

Card#:_____

Name on card:_____ Exp. Date:_____